P9-BXX-287

MUSIC, POETRY
& DANCING DIED.

THE FAMINE KILLED
EVERYTHING.

Published by
Quinnipiac University Press
275 Mount Carmel Ave.
Hamden, CT 06518-1908
www.quinnipiac.edu

Copyright © 2015 by
Christine Kinealy and John Walsh

All rights reserved.

www.badtimesgraphicnovel.com

Designed by Pentagram

ISBN 978-0-9909454-1-3.

The quote on the title page is from Recollections
of Máire Ní Grianna of Rannafast, Co. Donegal,
in Seamus Deane (ed.) *The Field Day Anthology*
(Derry, 1991), 203-4.

THE BAD TIMES

An Drochshaol

BY
CHRISTINE KINEALY
& JOHN WALSH

Letterer
Tommie Kelly

Color Production Assistant
Richie del Valle

Dedications

For Bernadette Barrington and Angela Farrell,
do mo chairde dílse
— CK

To Rachel: you still have my heart, don't ever let go.
Thanks for your bottomless well of patience
— JW

Acknowledgements

Many people, old friends, new friends and colleagues have helped to bring this project to fruition and our gratitude to them is enormous.

Our colleagues at Quinnipiac University have given us invaluable encouragement. Special thanks must go to Lynn Bushnell, vice president for public affairs, and Karla Natale, assistant vice president for public affairs, who have believed in this project from its vague beginnings, and who have supported us from concept to completion. We greatly appreciate the involvement of Keith Rhodes, vice president of brand strategy and integrated communications, whose enthusiasm and vision have kept us energized during the final stages of production. The librarians of the Arnold Bernhard Library, which is the beating heart of Quinnipiac University, have lent their wisdom to this project, in particular Robert Joven, Robert Young, Sandy O'Hare and June DeGennaro. Dean Robert Smart, Dr. Nicholas Robinette and Grace Brady are also thanked for their ongoing interest, and Donna Pintek for her copy editing expertise. Of course, none of this work would have been possible without the continuing commitment of President John Lahey to educate people about the Great Hunger.

Practical assistance has been provided by Dr. Anne Dichele, professor of education at Quinnipiac University, who has advised on curriculum matters and contributed her expertise to the website materials. We are also indebted to Dr. Greg Garvey, for working with students in digital design in order to bring the story of Brigit, Dan, Liam and Cú to a different audience. We thank Anne and Greg for taking time to discuss these projects despite their heavy teaching schedule—and for making the multiple meetings such pleasant experiences.

A number of students have acted as focus groups as this book developed. The enthusiastic reception to the early stages of this story by young people (aged 4–17) who attend the annual Gael Scoil at the Notre Dame High School in Lawrenceville, New Jersey, under the gentle guidance of Jim MacFarland, Tom Slattery and other members of AOH Division 10 in Trenton, was much appreciated.

Dr. Maureen Murphy of Hofstra University, Máirtín Ó Muilleoir of the Irish Echo, the Kenny brothers in Galway, the Callery family and their colleagues in Strokestown House, Dr. Alan Delozier in Seton Hall University, Matthew Skwiat of Rochester University, and John Foley Esq. in Boston, are warmly thanked for the various ways in which they have provided assistance to this project. Special gratitude is owed to Jonathan O'Neill, a Clare man and a former Fulbright scholar. He kindly acted as consultant on the use of the Irish language. Thanks also are extended to Rich Gribaudo, Suzanne Bacon and, most especially, Father Jack Ahern.

We are particularly grateful for the support of the Irish government, in particular, the Minister for Diaspora Affairs, Mr. Jimmy Deenihan, T.D., and Ms. Barbara Jones, Consul General of Ireland in New York. As a result of their generosity, an Irish language version of The Bad Times will be published. An Taoiseach, Enda Kenny T.D., whose home county of Mayo suffered so acutely both during the Great Hunger and in the decades that followed, has made fighting global poverty a goal of his time in office. President Michael D. Higgins is also warmly thanked for all that he has done to help disseminate the story of the Great Hunger worldwide, and to champion the rights of all those who suffer from hunger today.

Finally, and most importantly, we want to thank our families who have encouraged us throughout this project, with good humor and love. A massive go raibh míle maith agaibh to them all. In particular, Rachel and Fiona Walsh, and parents, Joe and Mary Ann Walsh, for a lifetime of support. Much appreciation is also due to Mike, Bill, Den and Joe Walsh and their families, as well as to the Smith and Marchese families. Eternal gratitude is owed to Siobhán and Ciarán Kinealy, for their constant patience and counsel. And—of course—thanks is due to Cú, our canine inspiration, for a judicious combination of love and licks.

Christine Kinealy
John Walsh

Prologue

The Bad Times is set during the Irish Famine (or, the Great Hunger)—a disaster precipitated by the failure of the potato crop—and takes place between 1846 and 1849. It is based on three young adults, Dan, Brigit and Liam, who are close friends. When it commences, in late summer 1846, the potato crop is about to fail for a second time.

Location

Kilkee, County Clare, the west of Ireland. Kilkee is approximately 8 miles from Kilrush, the location of the Kilrush workhouse. Irish would have been widely spoken, so Irish phrases have been included to reflect this. These phrases are included in the Glossary.

The Main Characters

Liam Hayes – Liam lives with his father, William Hayes, a shopkeeper and pawnbroker. His mother is dead.

Dan O'Brien – Dan is named after the Irish nationalist leader, Daniel O'Connell. He lives with his father, Patrick (Pat) O'Brien, and his mother, Biddy O'Brien. Dan is the youngest child; his brother, Séamus, emigrated from Kilkee, settling in Boston in the U.S. some years earlier; his older sister, Honora, is a maid in the "Big House" owned by Colonel Vandeleur. Vandeleur also owns the land on which Dan and Brigit's families live. The O'Briens occupy (rent) a quarter of an acre of land. Brigit's family occupies two acres. Dan is always accompanied by his beloved dog, Cú (pronounced Coo).

Brigit O'Dea – Brigit lives with her father, John O'Dea, her mother, Mary O'Dea, and her twin siblings, who are younger than she is, Marie and Michael. Her grandmother (Mamó) is named Peggy and lives with the family.

Cú – Cú is a border collie. He is 4 years old. Dan found him when he was a puppy, and they have been inseparable ever since.

Liam and Dan are aged 14 and Brigit is 13 in 1846.

The opening scene takes place on 26 July 1846, the festival of Lughnasa, which marks the start of the harvest season.

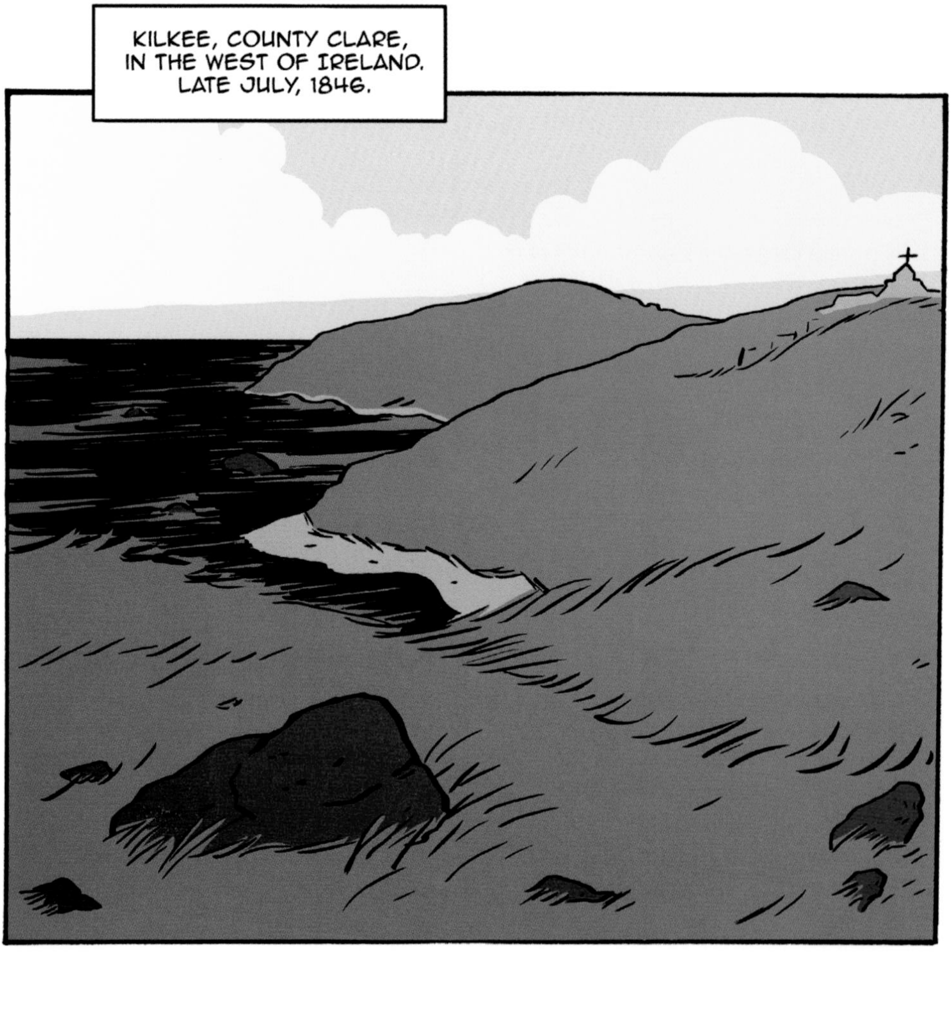
KILKEE, COUNTY CLARE, IN THE WEST OF IRELAND. LATE JULY, 1846.

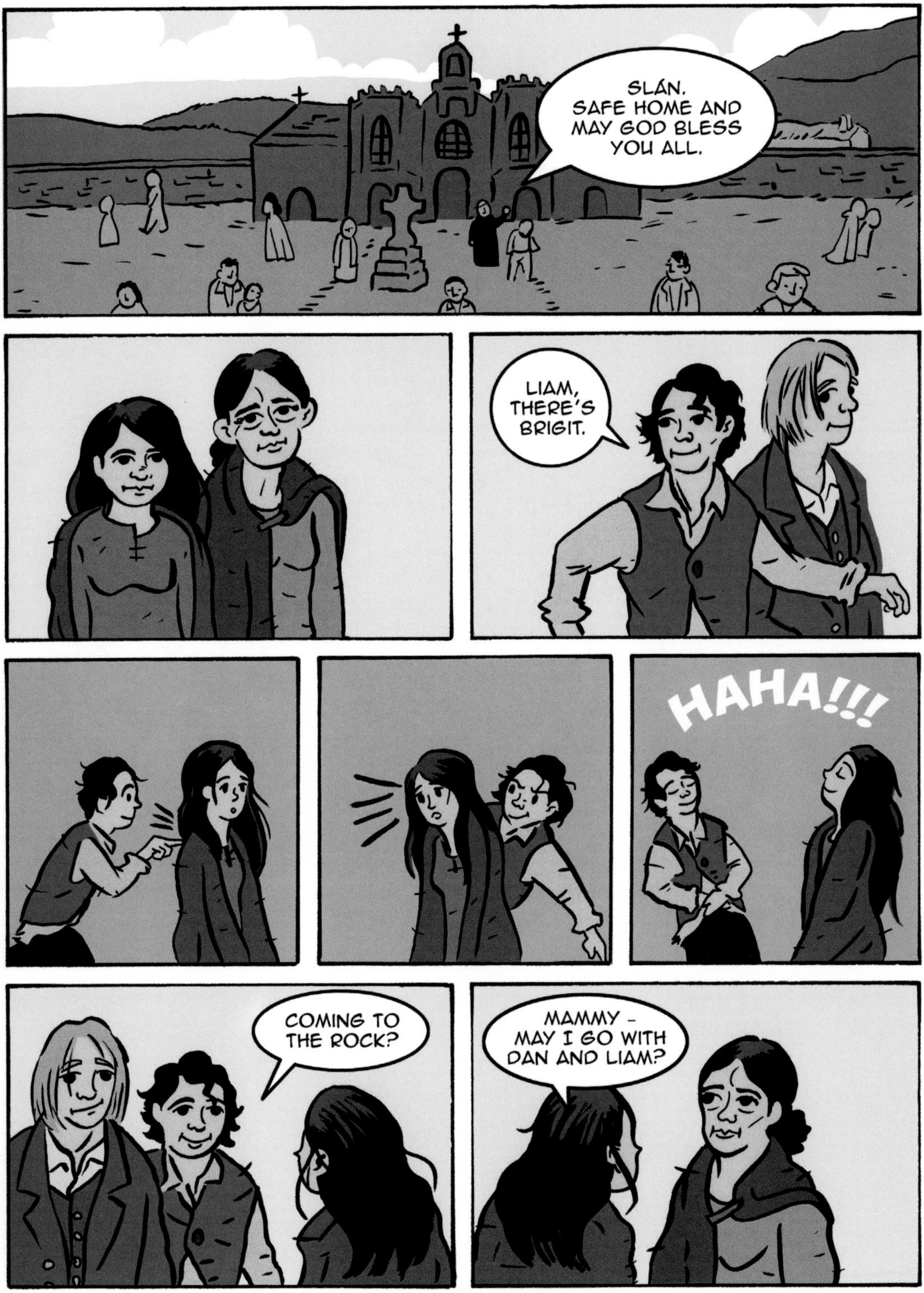
SLÁN.
SAFE HOME AND MAY GOD BLESS YOU ALL.
LIAM, THERE'S BRIGIT.
HAHA!!!
COMING TO THE ROCK?
MAMMY – MAY I GO WITH DAN AND LIAM?

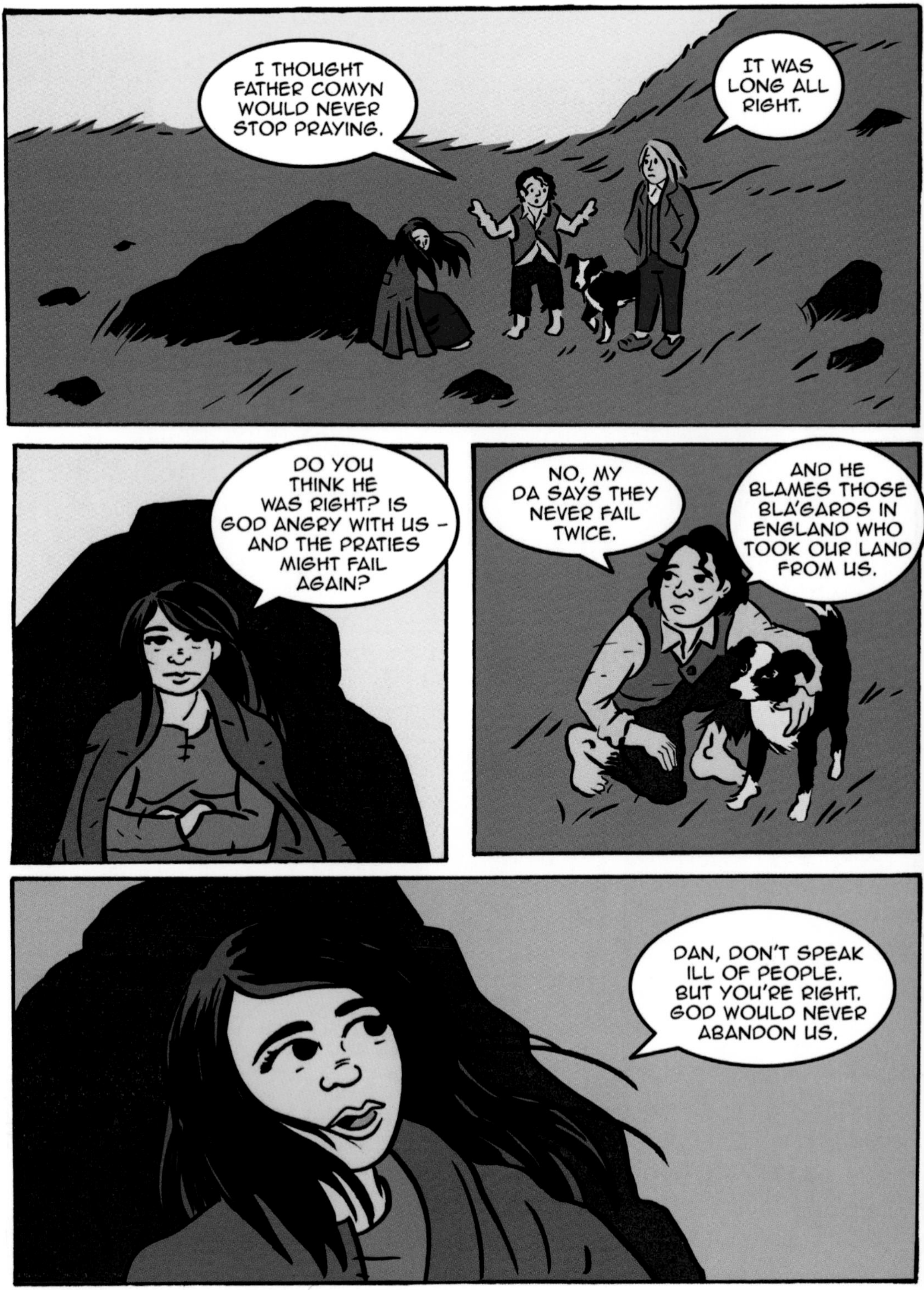
I THOUGHT FATHER COMYN WOULD NEVER STOP PRAYING.
IT WAS LONG ALL RIGHT.
DO YOU THINK HE WAS RIGHT? IS GOD ANGRY WITH US – AND THE PRATIES MIGHT FAIL AGAIN?
NO, MY DA SAYS THEY NEVER FAIL TWICE.
AND HE BLAMES THOSE BLA'GARDS IN ENGLAND WHO TOOK OUR LAND FROM US.
DAN, DON'T SPEAK ILL OF PEOPLE. BUT YOU'RE RIGHT. GOD WOULD NEVER ABANDON US.

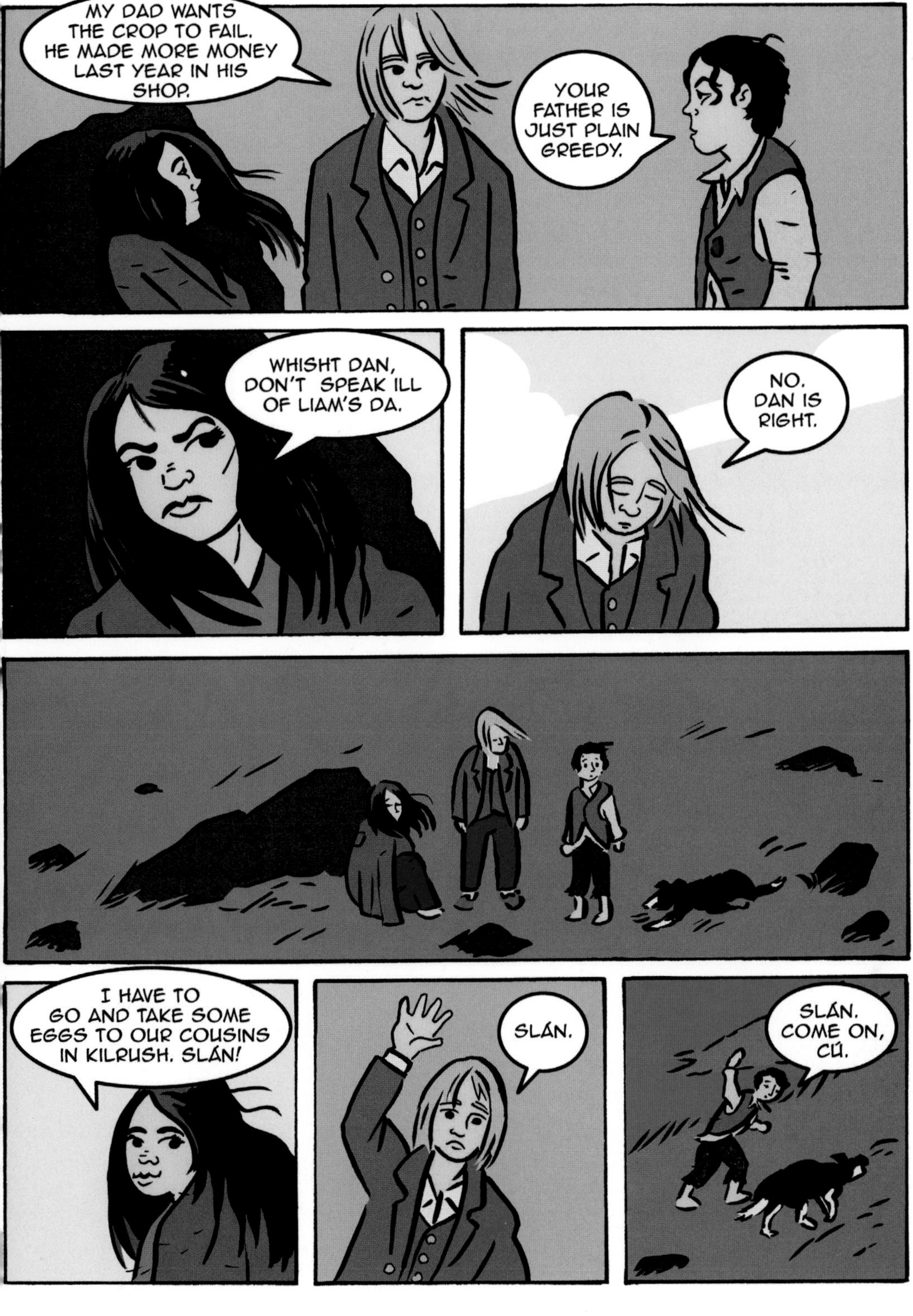
MY DAD WANTS THE CROP TO FAIL. HE MADE MORE MONEY LAST YEAR IN HIS SHOP.
YOUR FATHER IS JUST PLAIN GREEDY.
WHISHT DAN, DON'T SPEAK ILL OF LIAM'S DA.
NO. DAN IS RIGHT.
I HAVE TO GO AND TAKE SOME EGGS TO OUR COUSINS IN KILRUSH. SLÁN!
SLÁN.
SLÁN. COME ON, CÚ.

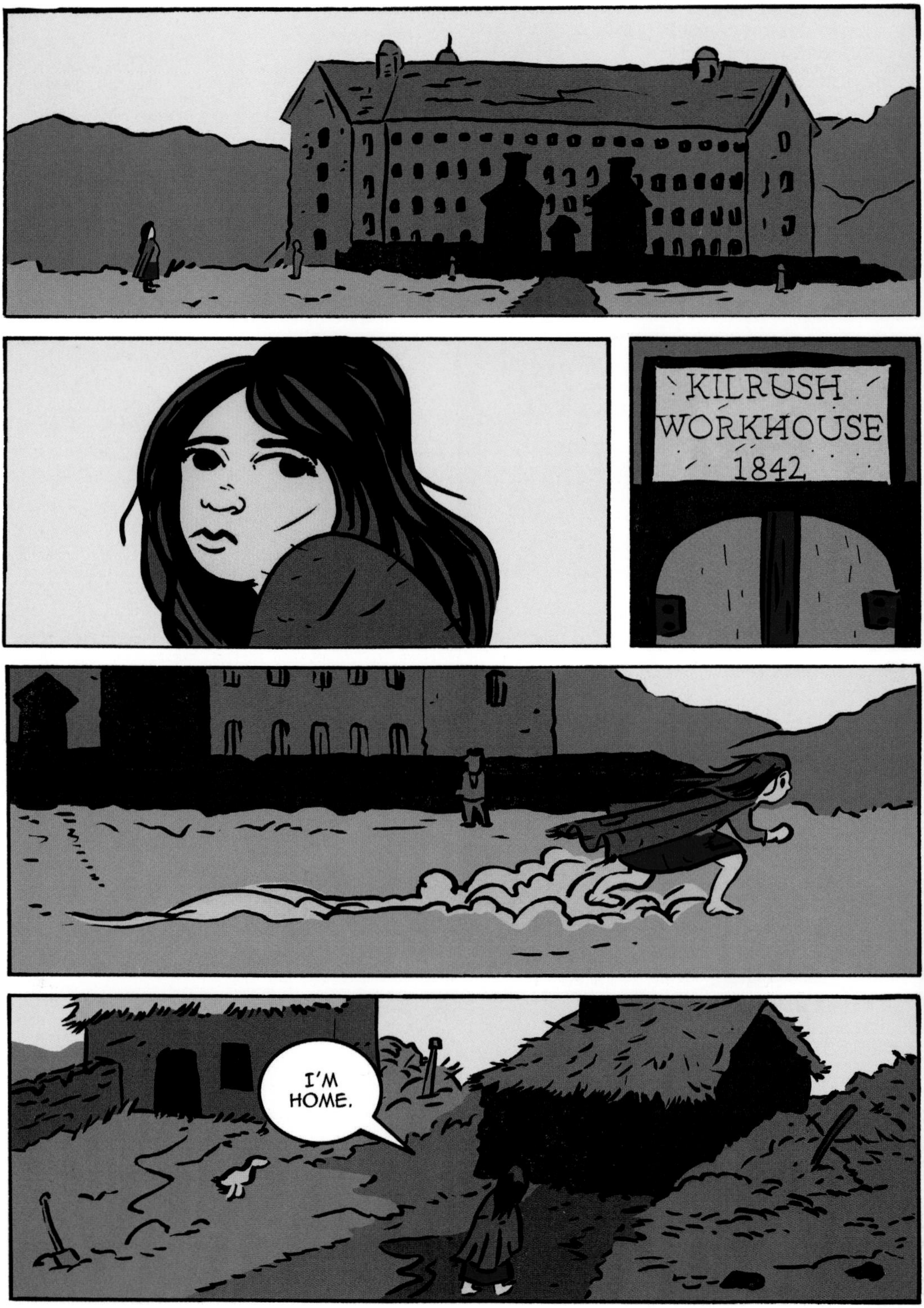
KILRUSH
WORKHOUSE
1842
I'M HOME.

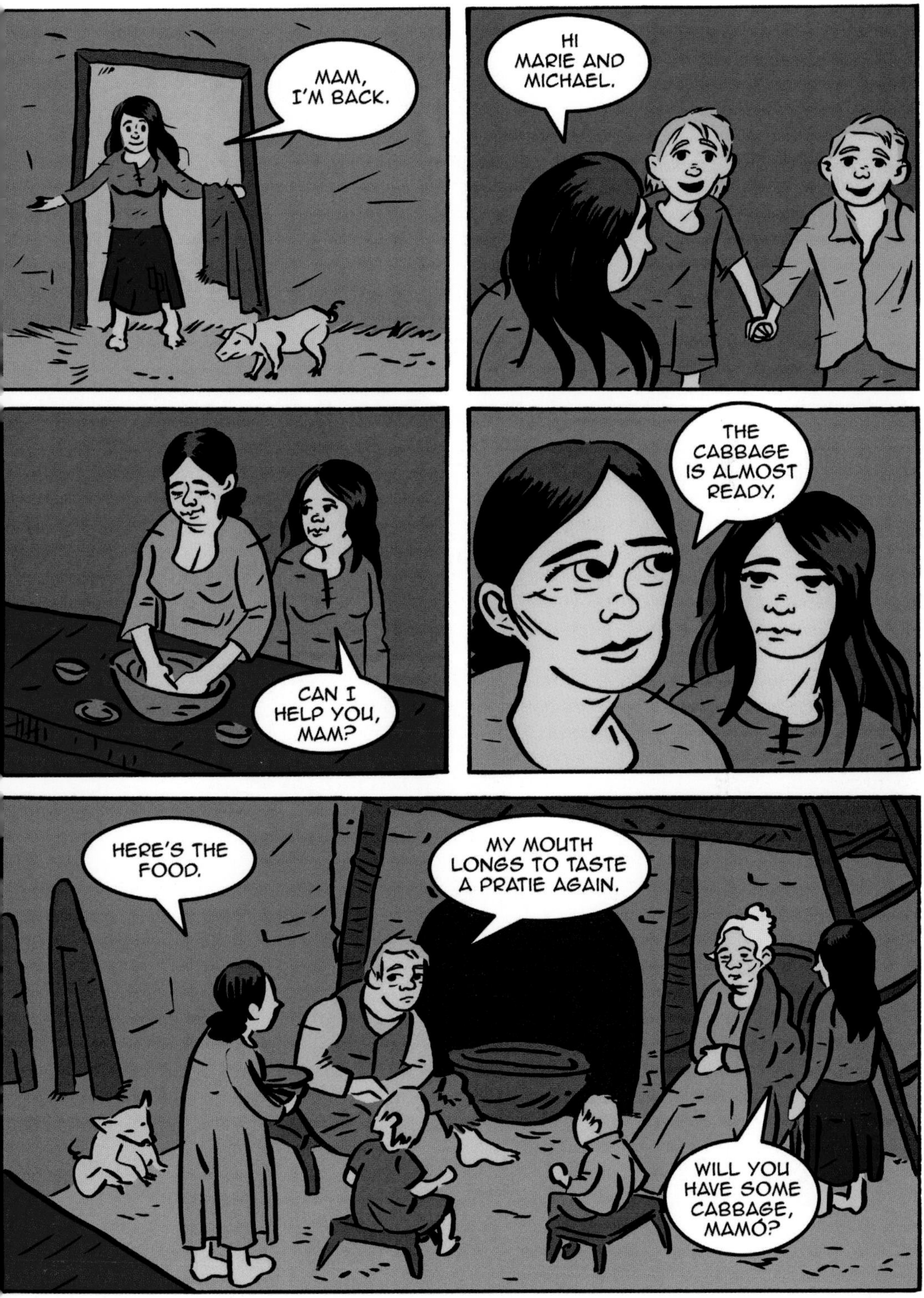
MAM, I'M BACK.
HI MARIE AND MICHAEL.
CAN I HELP YOU, MAM?
THE CABBAGE IS ALMOST READY.
HERE'S THE FOOD.
MY MOUTH LONGS TO TASTE A PRATIE AGAIN.
WILL YOU HAVE SOME CABBAGE, MAMÓ?

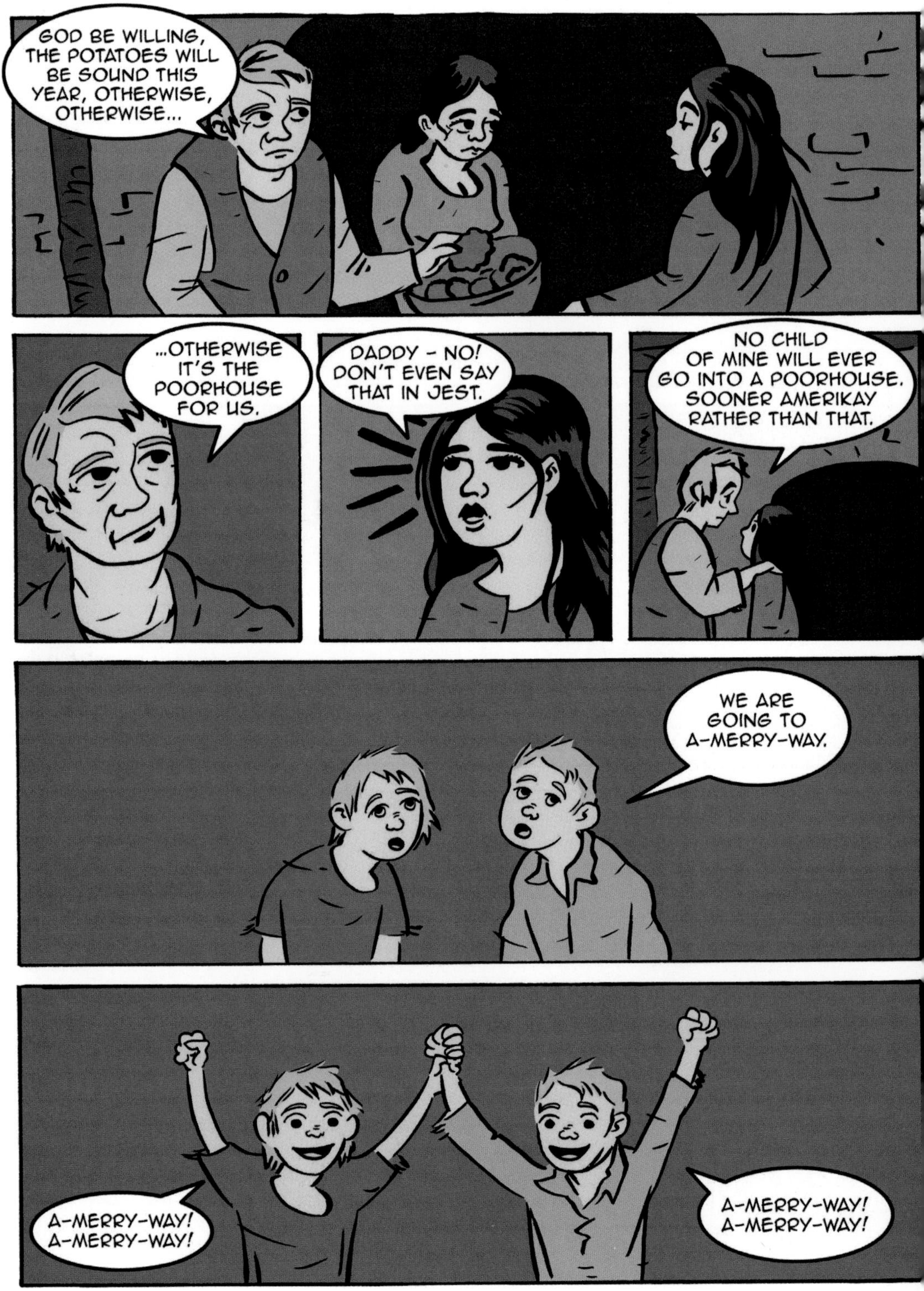
GOD BE WILLING, THE POTATOES WILL BE SOUND THIS YEAR, OTHERWISE, OTHERWISE...
...OTHERWISE IT'S THE POORHOUSE FOR US.
DADDY - NO! DON'T EVEN SAY THAT IN JEST.
NO CHILD OF MINE WILL EVER GO INTO A POORHOUSE. SOONER AMERIKAY RATHER THAN THAT.
WE ARE GOING TO A-MERRY-WAY.
A-MERRY-WAY! A-MERRY-WAY!
A-MERRY-WAY! A-MERRY-WAY!

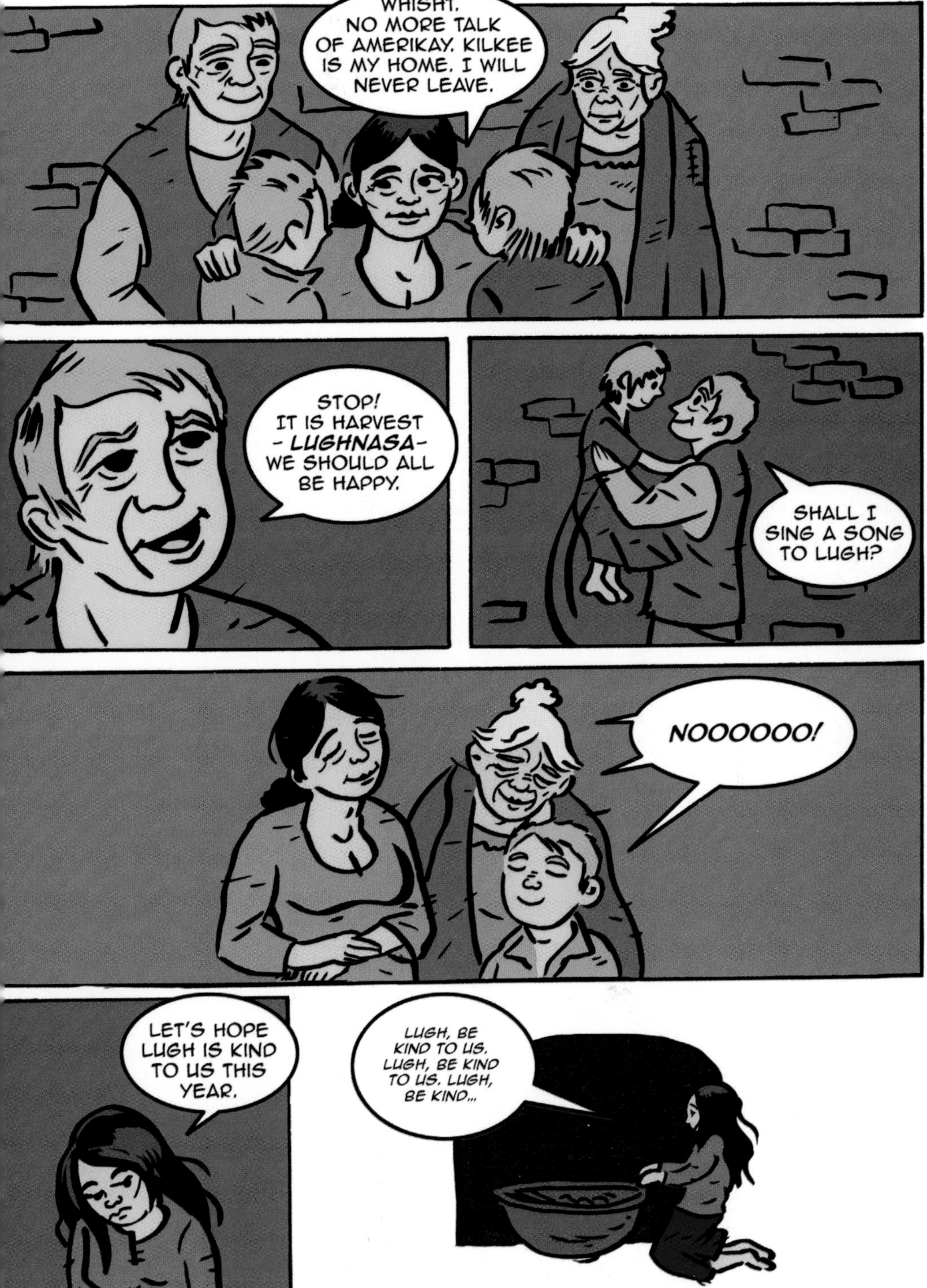
WHISHT. NO MORE TALK OF AMERIKAY. KILKEE IS MY HOME. I WILL NEVER LEAVE.
STOP! IT IS HARVEST -LUGHNASA- WE SHOULD ALL BE HAPPY.
SHALL I SING A SONG TO LUGH?
NOOOOOO!
LET'S HOPE LUGH IS KIND TO US THIS YEAR.
LUGH, BE KIND TO US. LUGH, BE KIND TO US. LUGH, BE KIND...

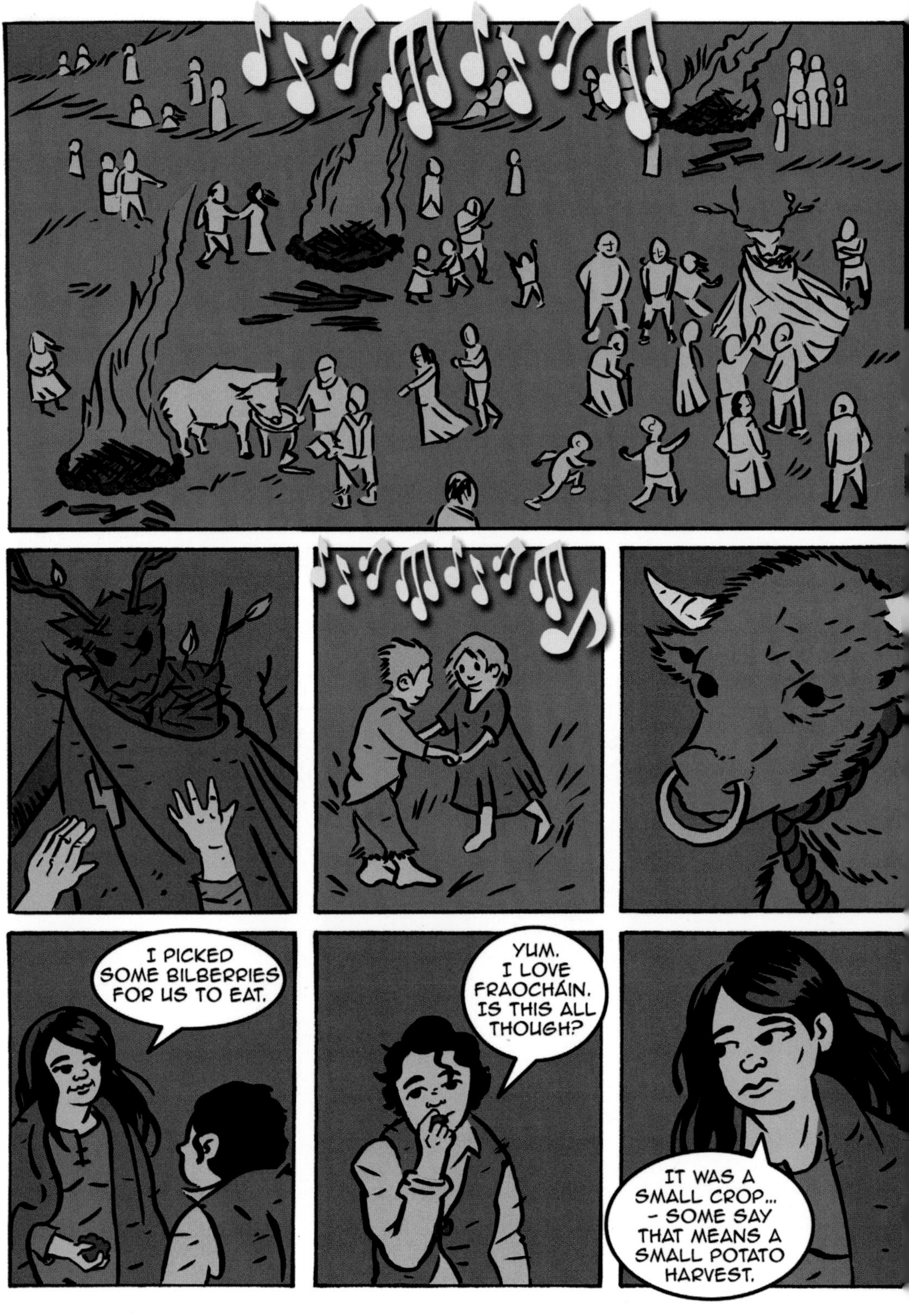
I PICKED SOME BILBERRIES FOR US TO EAT.
YUM. I LOVE FRAOCHÁIN. IS THIS ALL THOUGH?
IT WAS A SMALL CROP... - SOME SAY THAT MEANS A SMALL POTATO HARVEST.

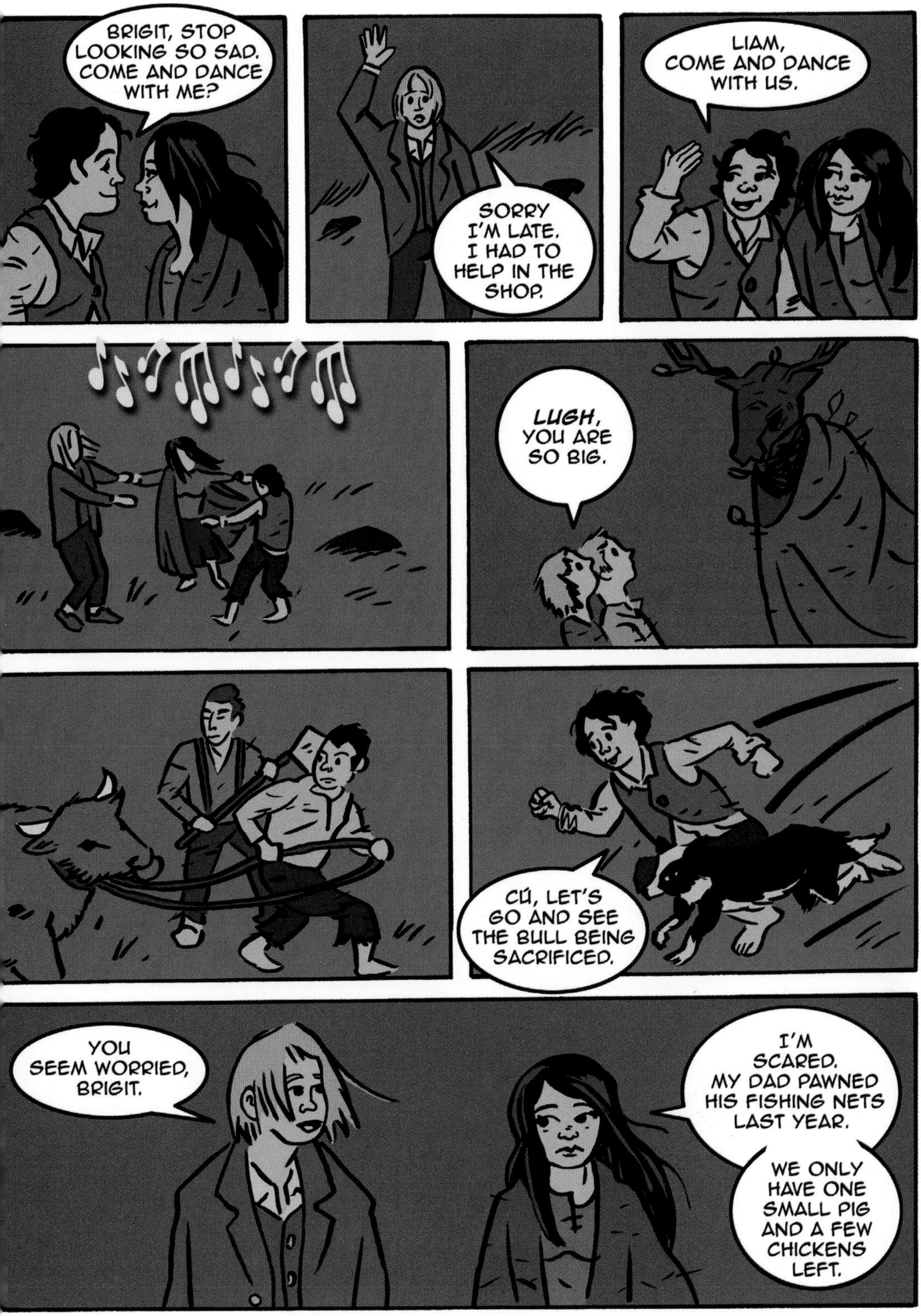
BRIGIT, STOP LOOKING SO SAD. COME AND DANCE WITH ME?
SORRY I'M LATE. I HAD TO HELP IN THE SHOP.
LIAM, COME AND DANCE WITH US.
LUGH, YOU ARE SO BIG.
CÚ, LET'S GO AND SEE THE BULL BEING SACRIFICED.
YOU SEEM WORRIED, BRIGIT.
I'M SCARED. MY DAD PAWNED HIS FISHING NETS LAST YEAR.
WE ONLY HAVE ONE SMALL PIG AND A FEW CHICKENS LEFT.

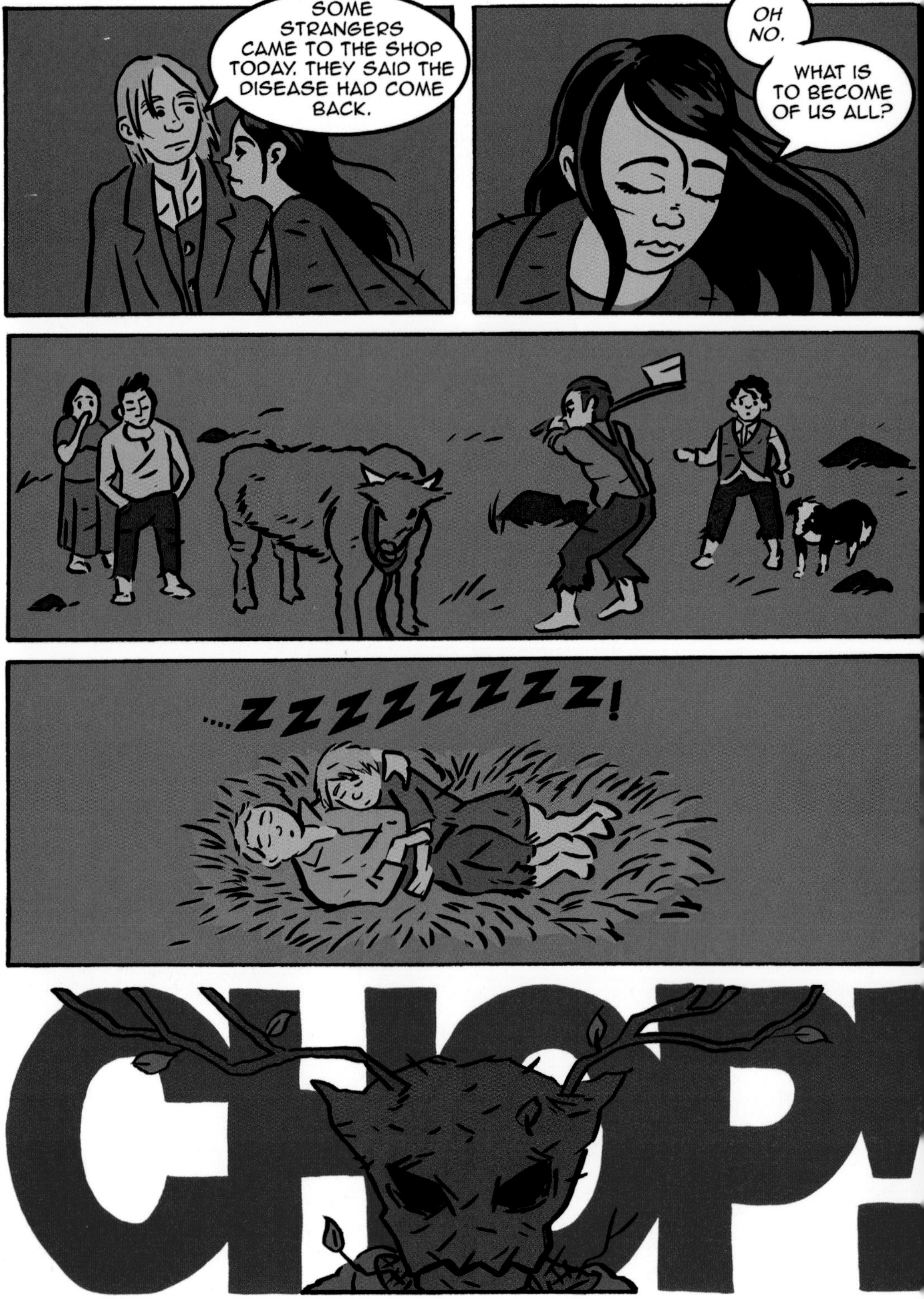
SOME STRANGERS CAME TO THE SHOP TODAY. THEY SAID THE DISEASE HAD COME BACK.
OH NO.
WHAT IS TO BECOME OF US ALL?
....ZZZZZZZZZ!
CHOP!

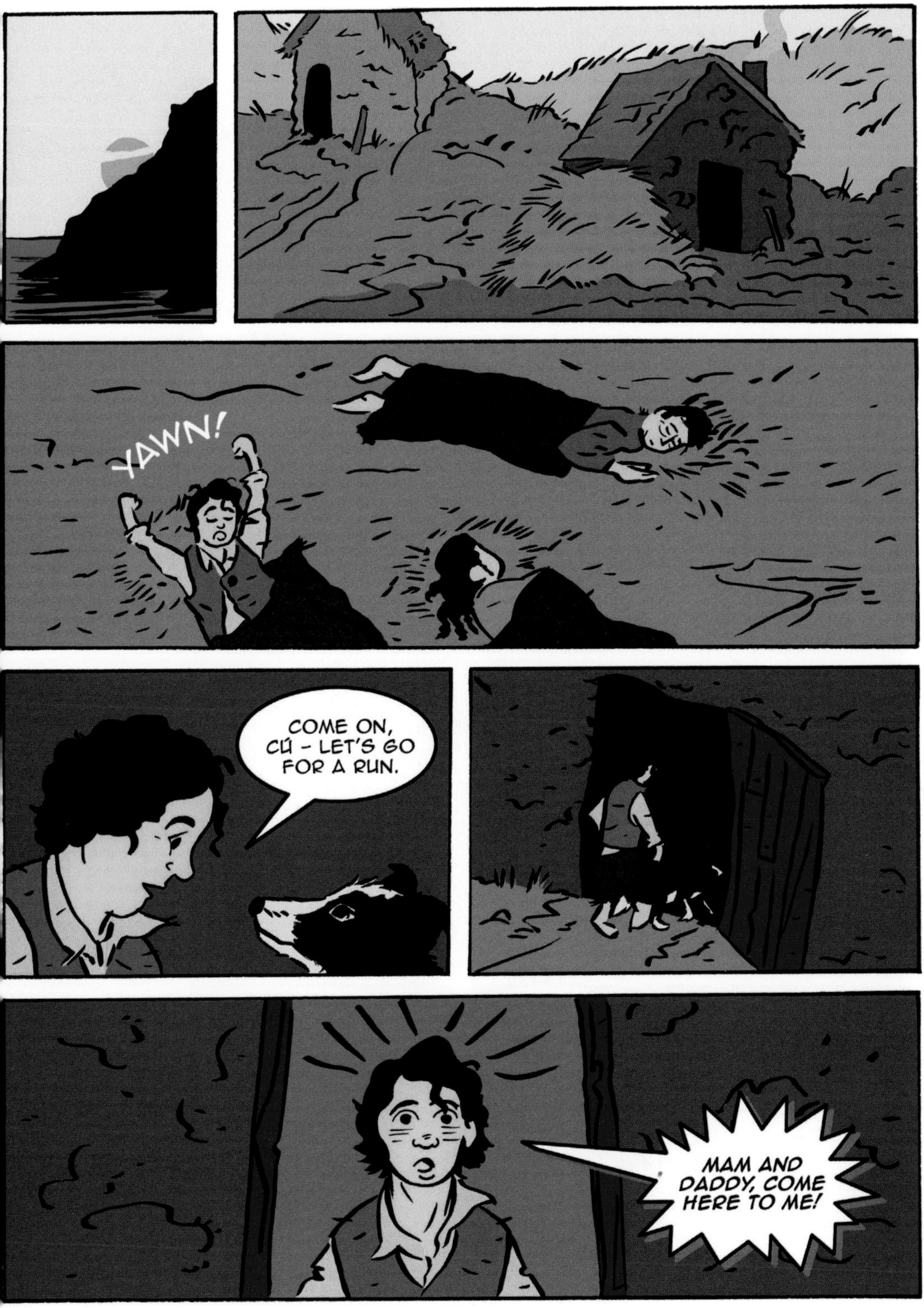
YAWN!
COME ON, CÚ - LET'S GO FOR A RUN.
MAM AND DADDY, COME HERE TO ME!

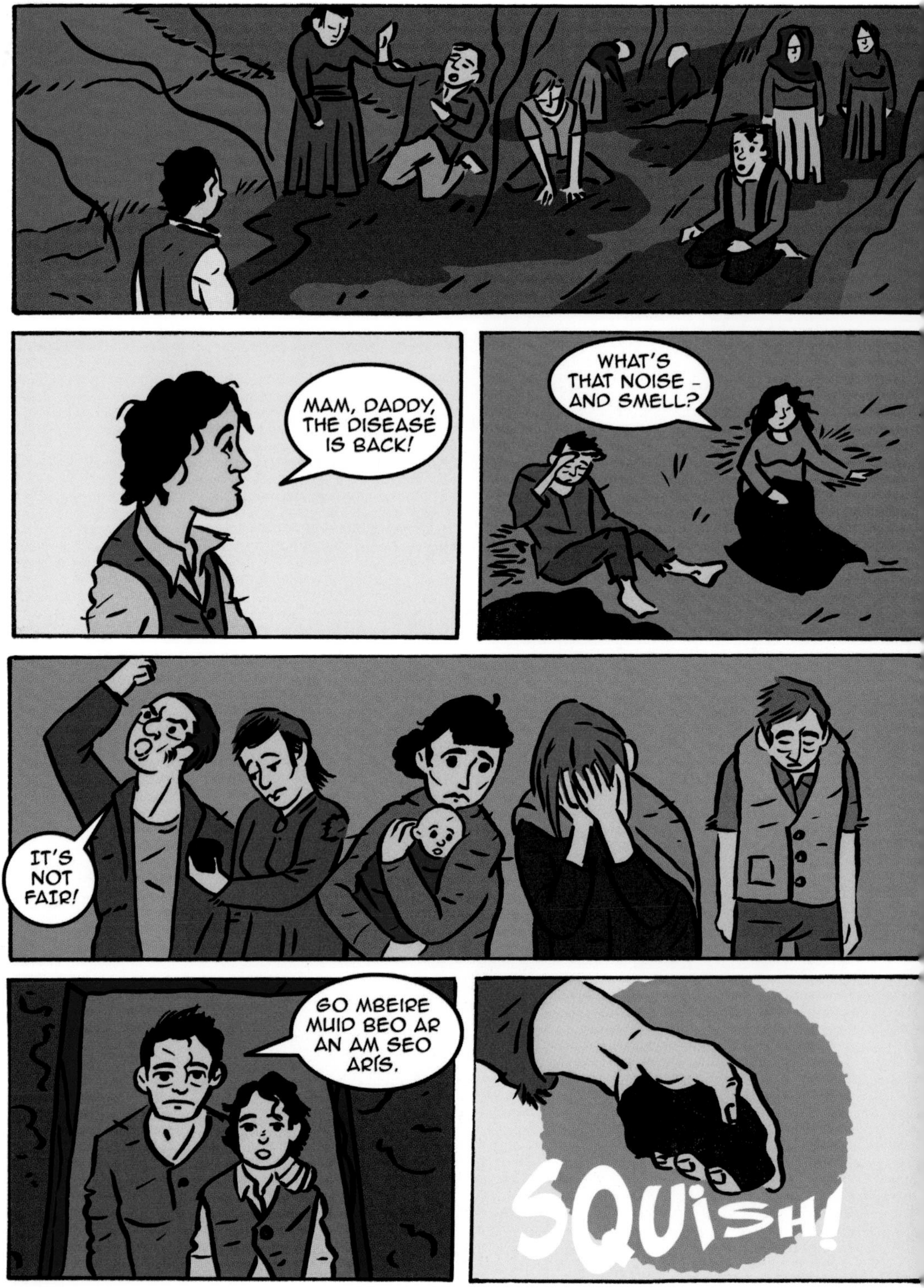
MAM, DADDY, THE DISEASE IS BACK!
WHAT'S THAT NOISE - AND SMELL?
IT'S NOT FAIR!
GO MBEIRE MUID BEO AR AN AM SEO ARÍS.
SQUISH!

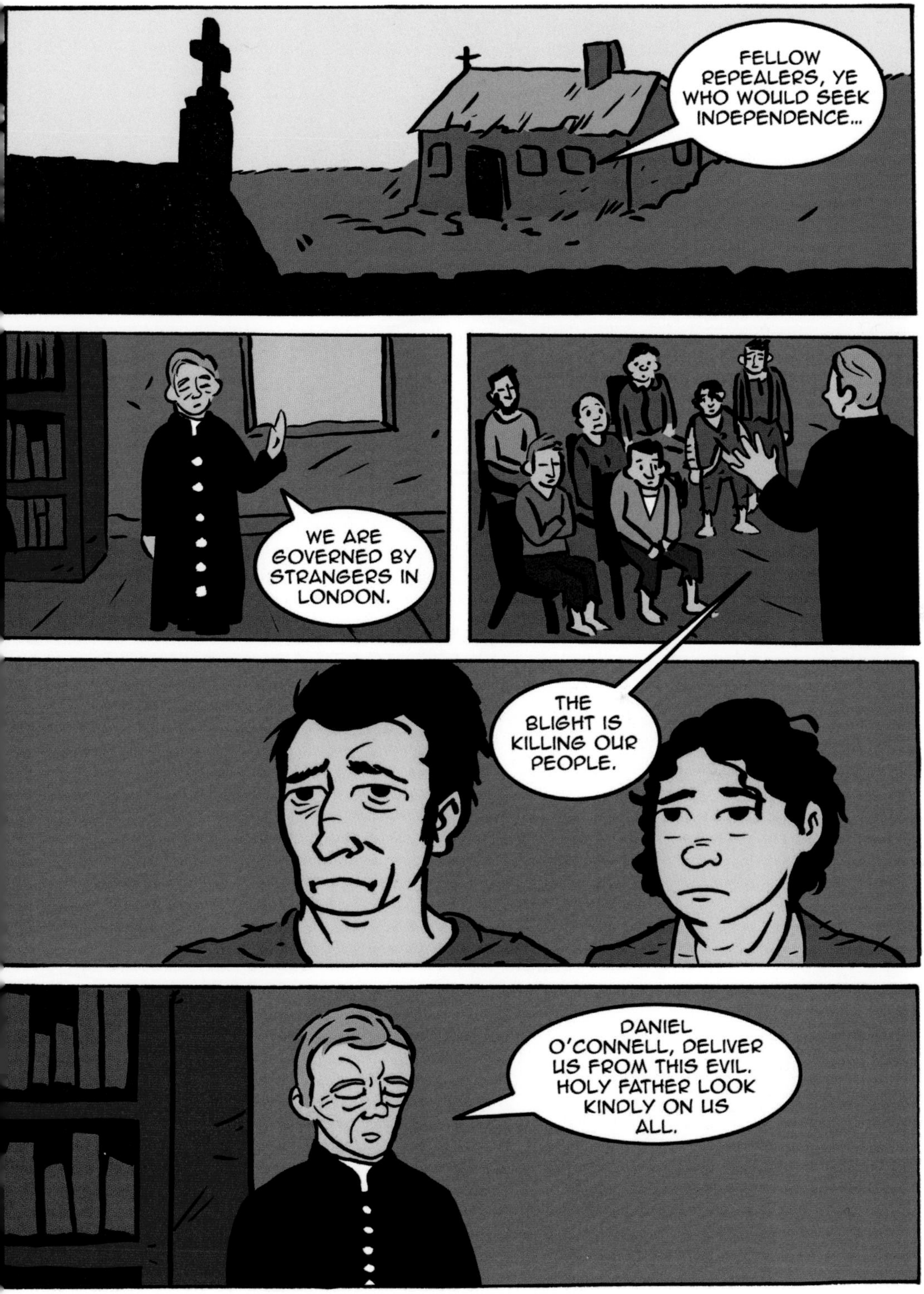
FELLOW REPEALERS, YE WHO WOULD SEEK INDEPENDENCE...
WE ARE GOVERNED BY STRANGERS IN LONDON.
THE BLIGHT IS KILLING OUR PEOPLE.
DANIEL O'CONNELL, DELIVER US FROM THIS EVIL. HOLY FATHER LOOK KINDLY ON US ALL.

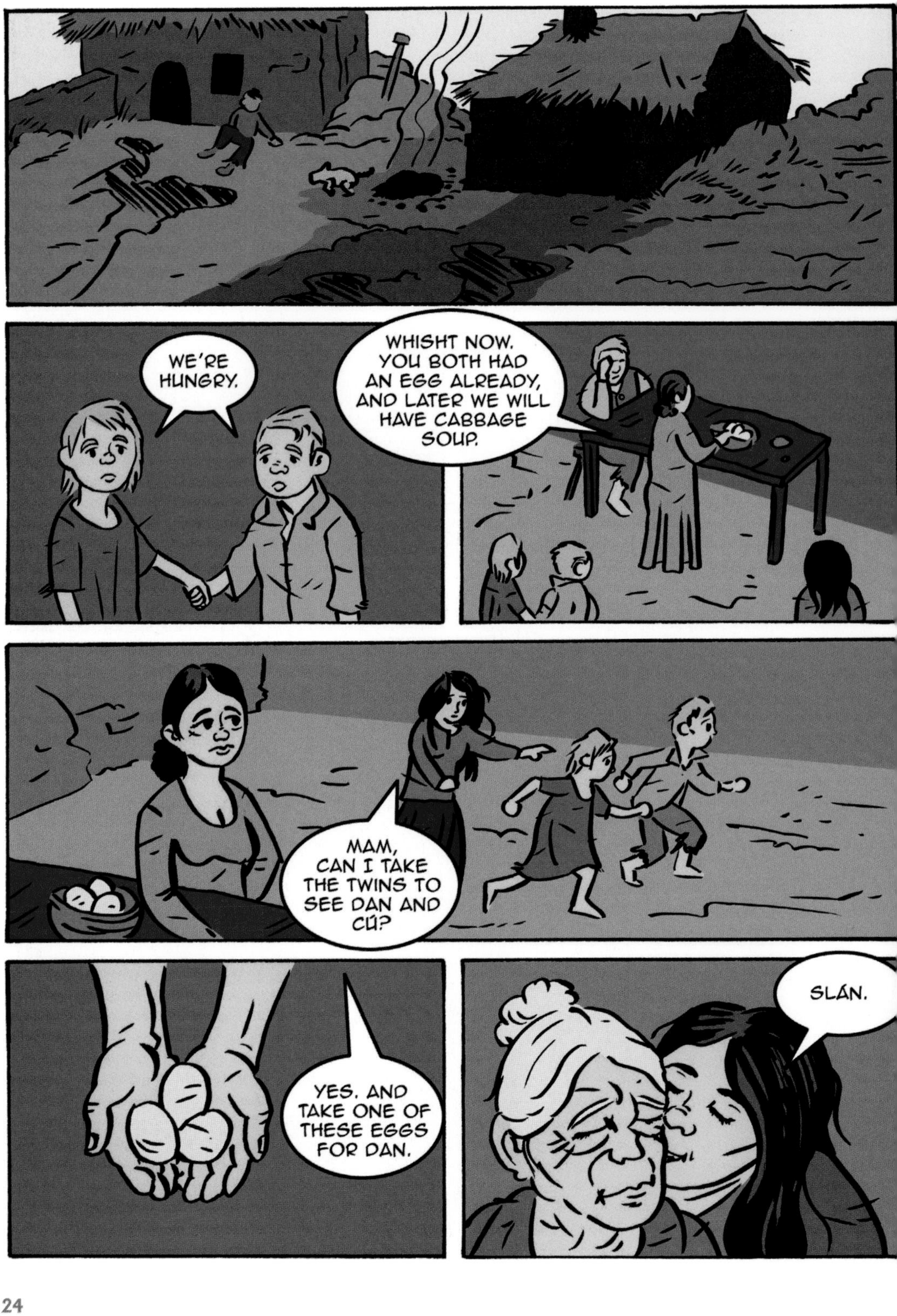
WE'RE HUNGRY.
WHISHT NOW. YOU BOTH HAD AN EGG ALREADY, AND LATER WE WILL HAVE CABBAGE SOUP.
MAM, CAN I TAKE THE TWINS TO SEE DAN AND CÚ?
YES. AND TAKE ONE OF THESE EGGS FOR DAN.
SLÁN.

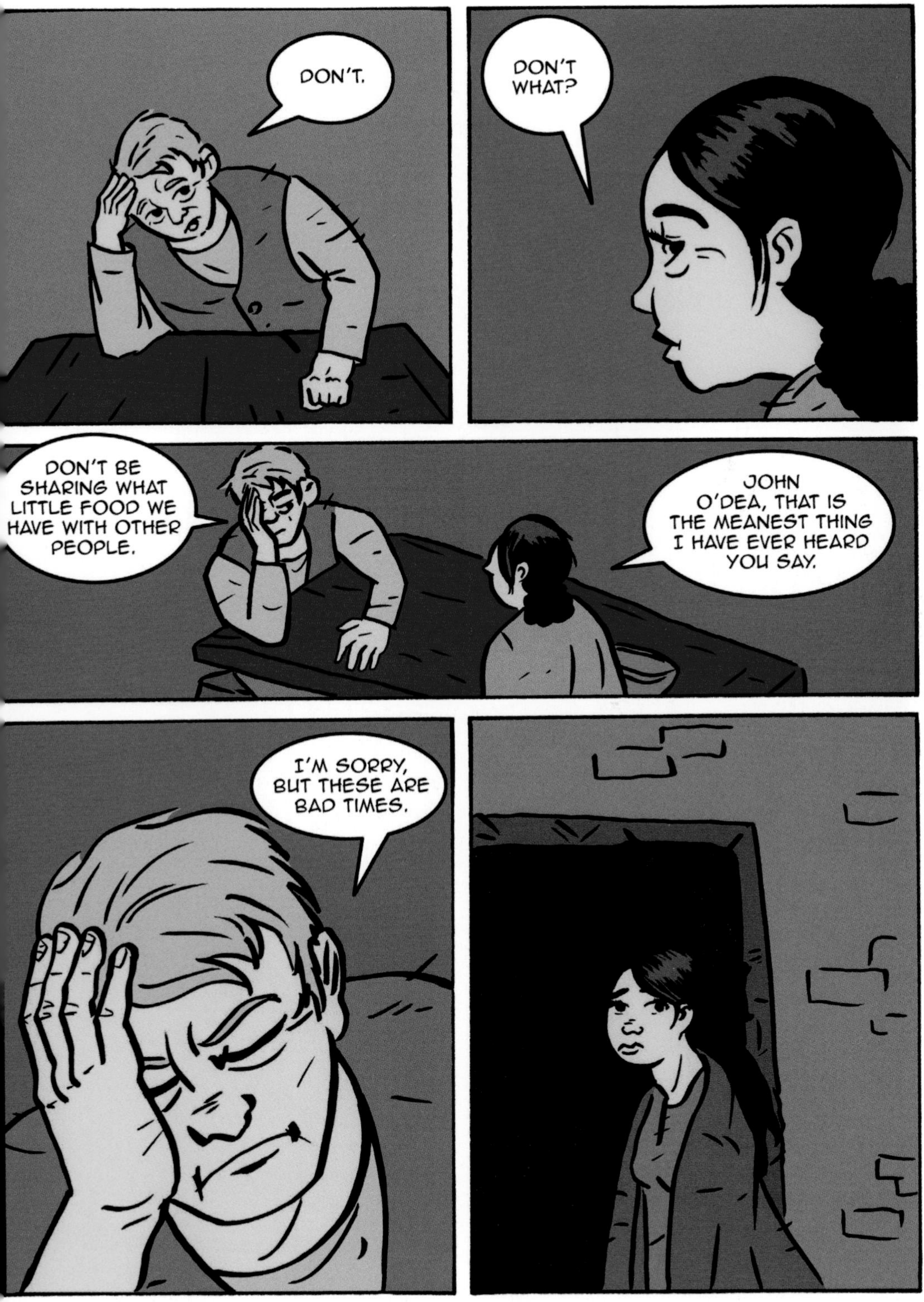
DON'T.
DON'T WHAT?
DON'T BE SHARING WHAT LITTLE FOOD WE HAVE WITH OTHER PEOPLE.
JOHN O'DEA, THAT IS THE MEANEST THING I HAVE EVER HEARD YOU SAY.
I'M SORRY, BUT THESE ARE BAD TIMES.

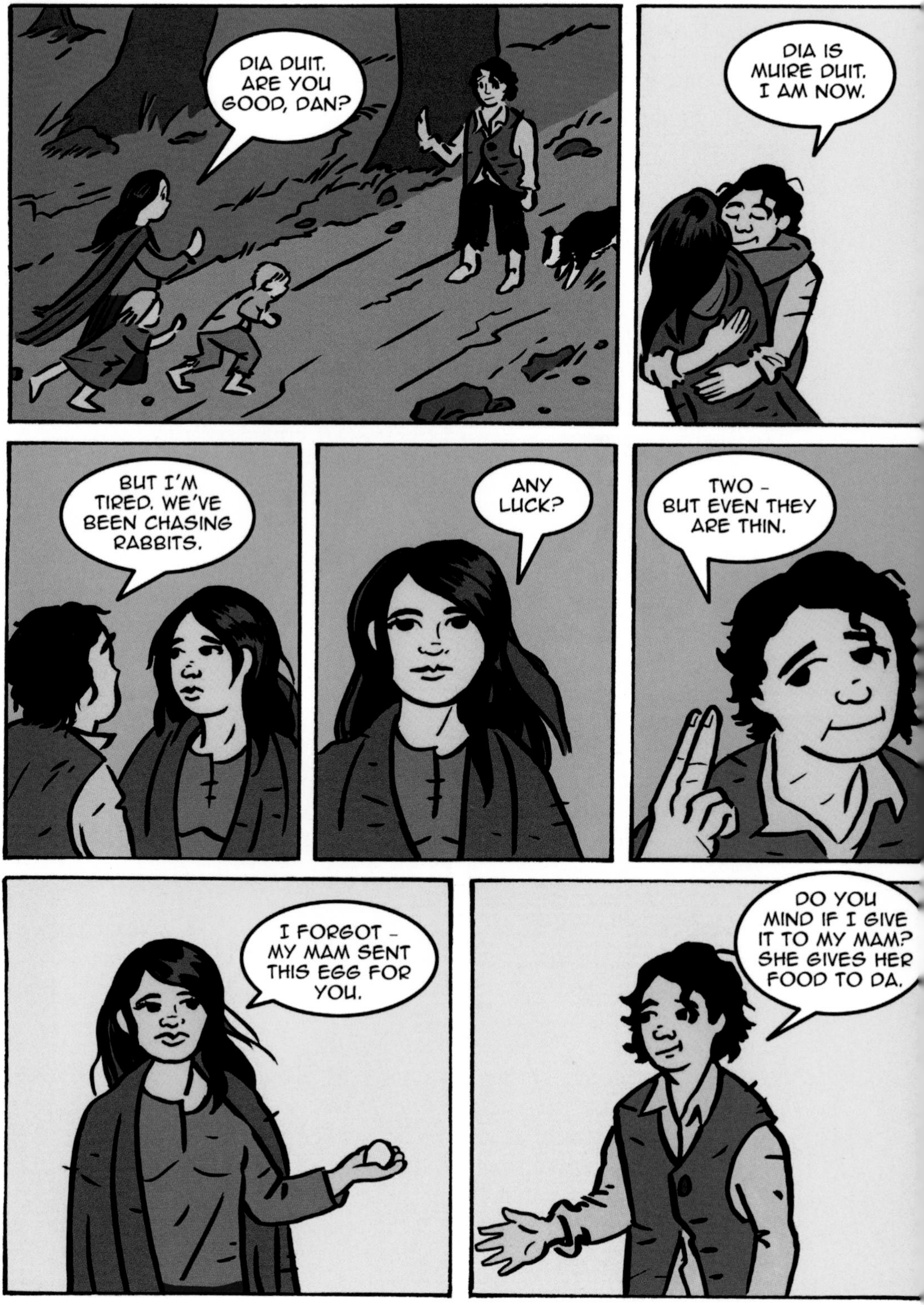
DIA DUIT. ARE YOU GOOD, DAN?
DIA IS MUIRE DUIT. I AM NOW.
BUT I'M TIRED. WE'VE BEEN CHASING RABBITS.
ANY LUCK?
TWO - BUT EVEN THEY ARE THIN.
I FORGOT - MY MAM SENT THIS EGG FOR YOU.
DO YOU MIND IF I GIVE IT TO MY MAM? SHE GIVES HER FOOD TO DA.

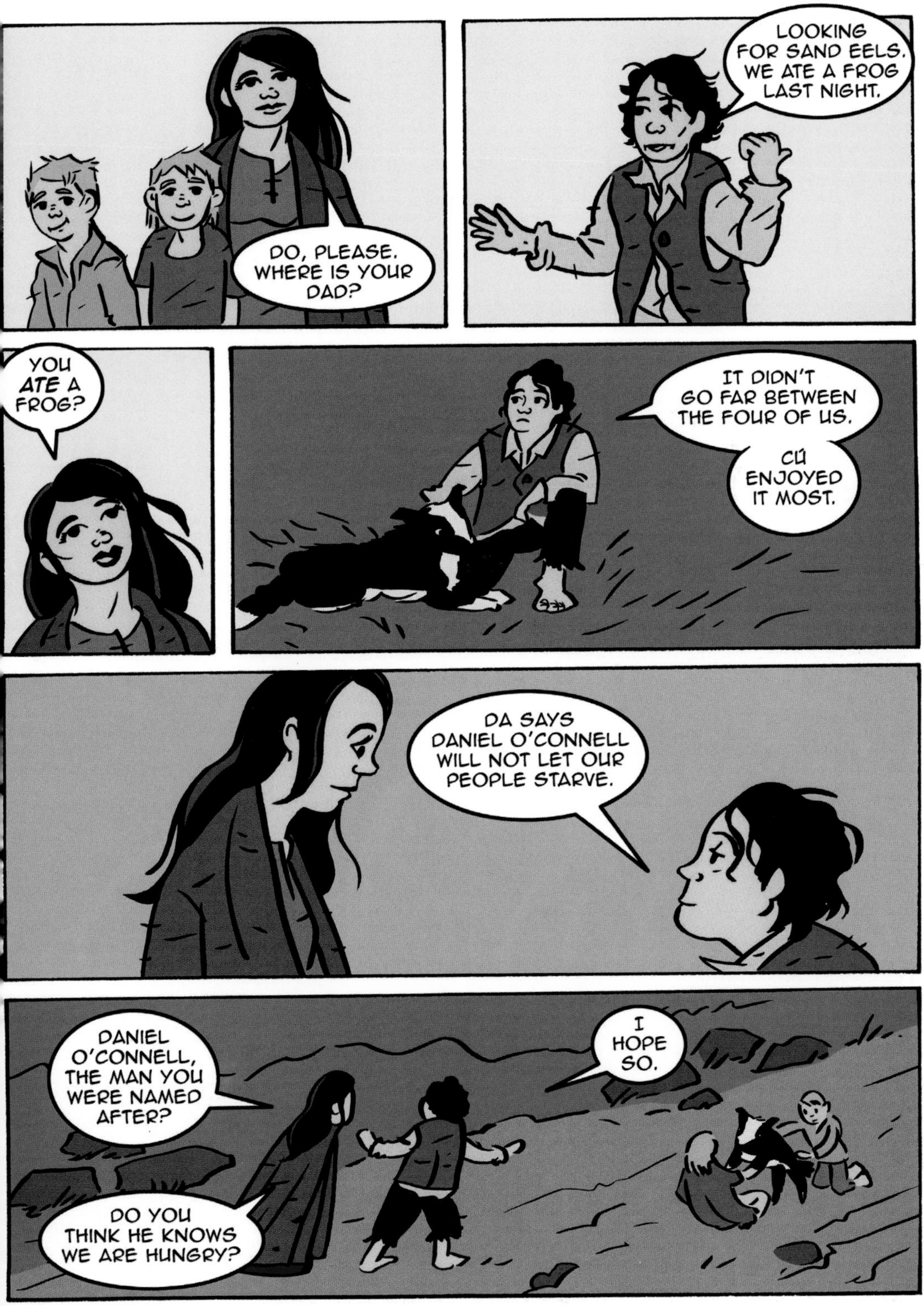
DO, PLEASE. WHERE IS YOUR DAD?
LOOKING FOR SAND EELS. WE ATE A FROG LAST NIGHT.
YOU *ATE* A FROG?
IT DIDN'T GO FAR BETWEEN THE FOUR OF US.
CÚ ENJOYED IT MOST.
DA SAYS DANIEL O'CONNELL WILL NOT LET OUR PEOPLE STARVE.
DANIEL O'CONNELL, THE MAN YOU WERE NAMED AFTER?
I HOPE SO.
DO YOU THINK HE KNOWS WE ARE HUNGRY?

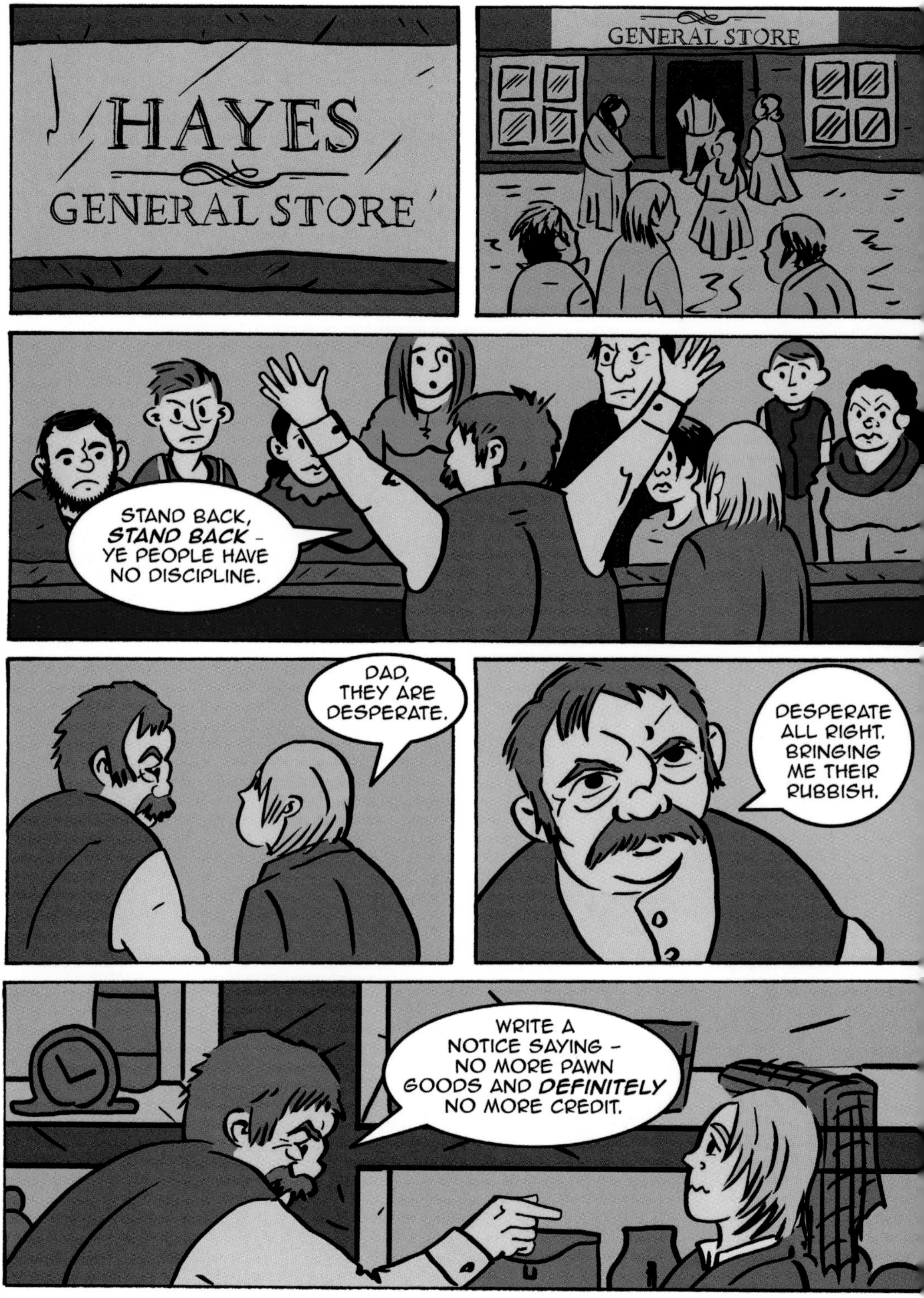
HAYES
GENERAL STORE
GENERAL STORE
STAND BACK, STAND BACK - YE PEOPLE HAVE NO DISCIPLINE.
DAD, THEY ARE DESPERATE.
DESPERATE ALL RIGHT. BRINGING ME THEIR RUBBISH.
WRITE A NOTICE SAYING - NO MORE PAWN GOODS AND DEFINITELY NO MORE CREDIT.

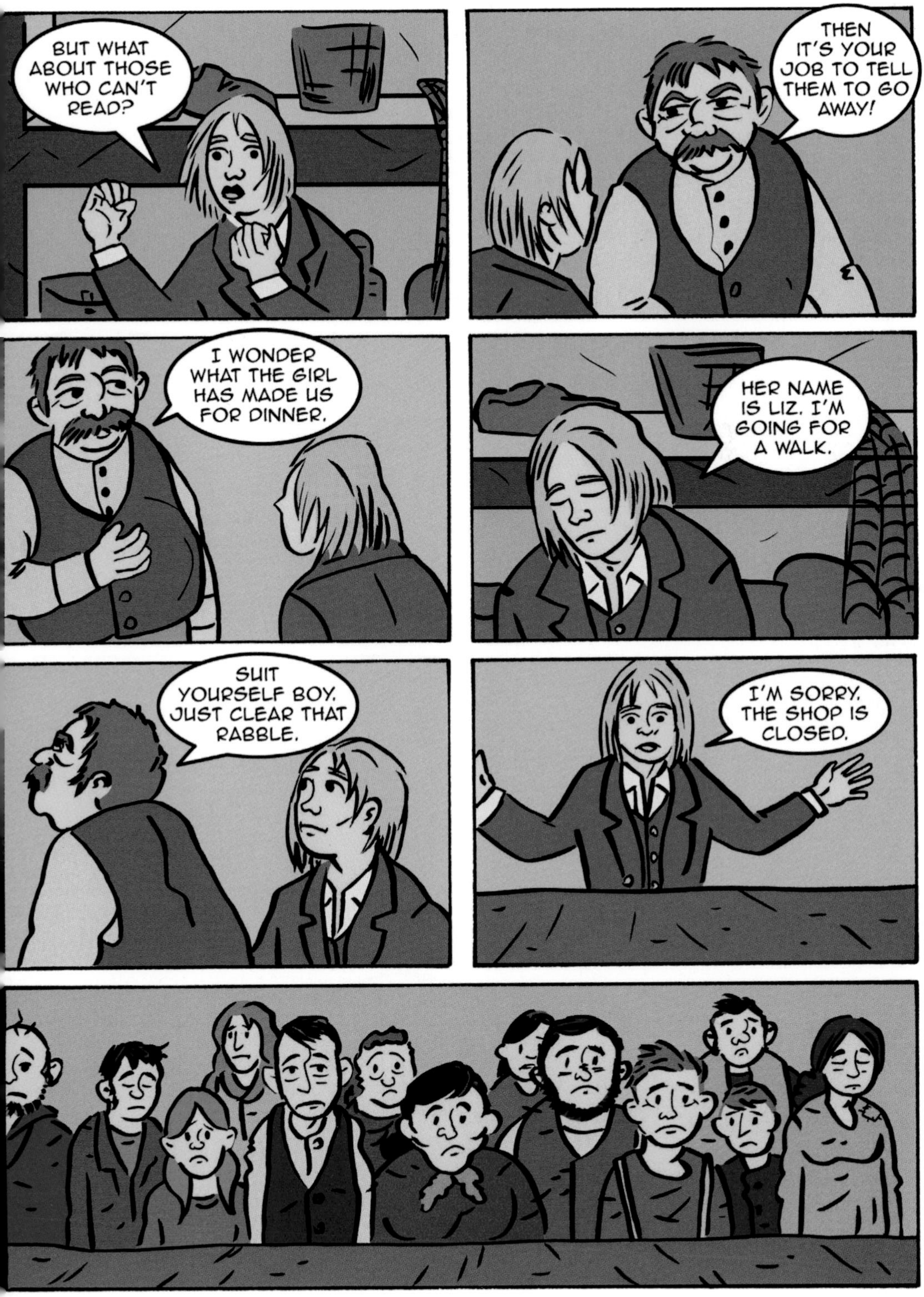
BUT WHAT ABOUT THOSE WHO CAN'T READ?
THEN IT'S YOUR JOB TO TELL THEM TO GO AWAY!
I WONDER WHAT THE GIRL HAS MADE US FOR DINNER.
HER NAME IS LIZ. I'M GOING FOR A WALK.
SUIT YOURSELF BOY. JUST CLEAR THAT RABBLE.
I'M SORRY. THE SHOP IS CLOSED.

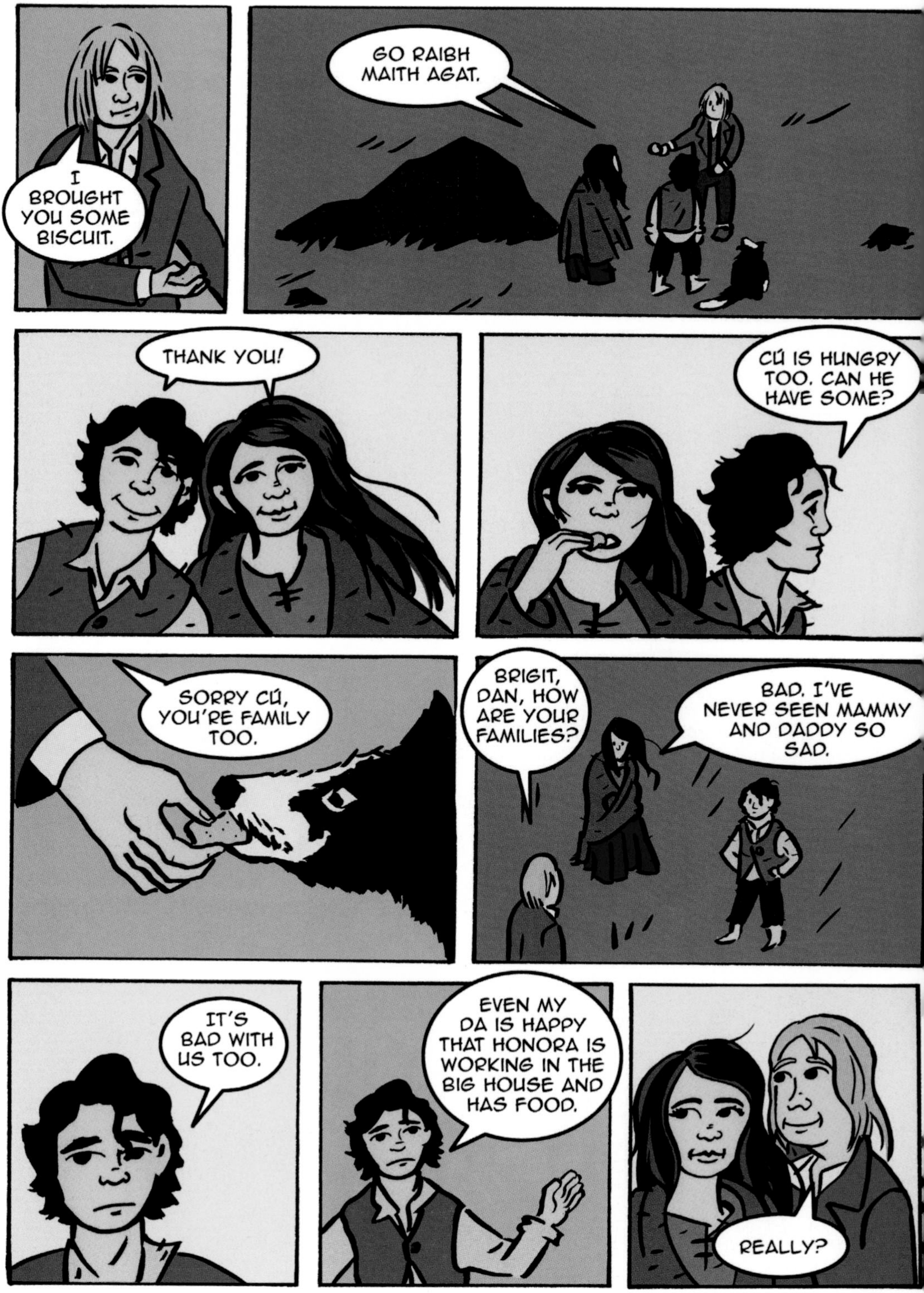
I BROUGHT YOU SOME BISCUIT.
GO RAIBH MAITH AGAT.
THANK YOU!
CÚ IS HUNGRY TOO. CAN HE HAVE SOME?
SORRY CÚ, YOU'RE FAMILY TOO.
BRIGIT, DAN, HOW ARE YOUR FAMILIES?
BAD. I'VE NEVER SEEN MAMMY AND DADDY SO SAD.
IT'S BAD WITH US TOO.
EVEN MY DA IS HAPPY THAT HONORA IS WORKING IN THE BIG HOUSE AND HAS FOOD.
REALLY?

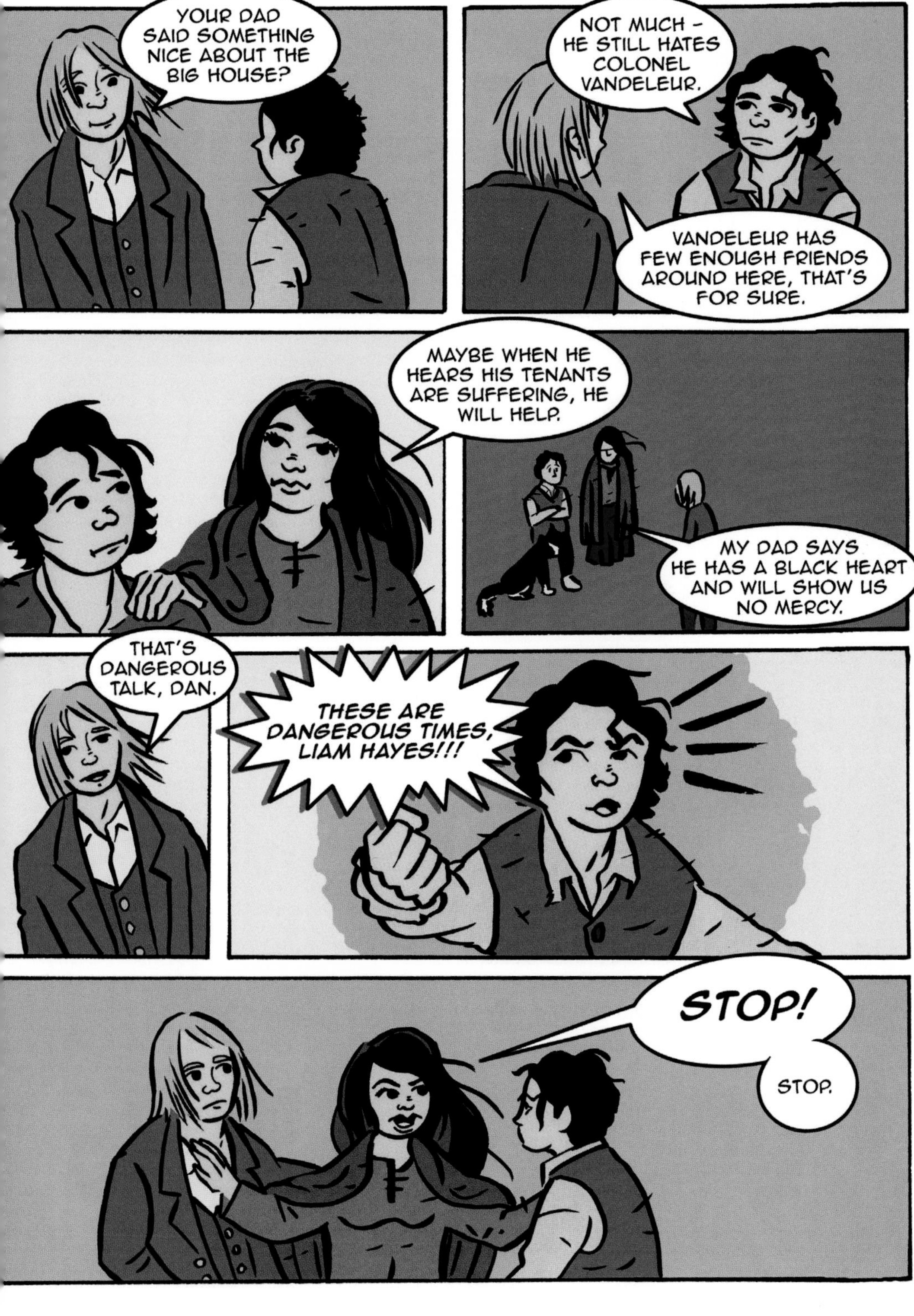
YOUR DAD SAID SOMETHING NICE ABOUT THE BIG HOUSE?
NOT MUCH - HE STILL HATES COLONEL VANDELEUR.
VANDELEUR HAS FEW ENOUGH FRIENDS AROUND HERE, THAT'S FOR SURE.
MAYBE WHEN HE HEARS HIS TENANTS ARE SUFFERING, HE WILL HELP.
MY DAD SAYS HE HAS A BLACK HEART AND WILL SHOW US NO MERCY.
THAT'S DANGEROUS TALK, DAN.
THESE ARE DANGEROUS TIMES, LIAM HAYES!!!
STOP!
STOP.

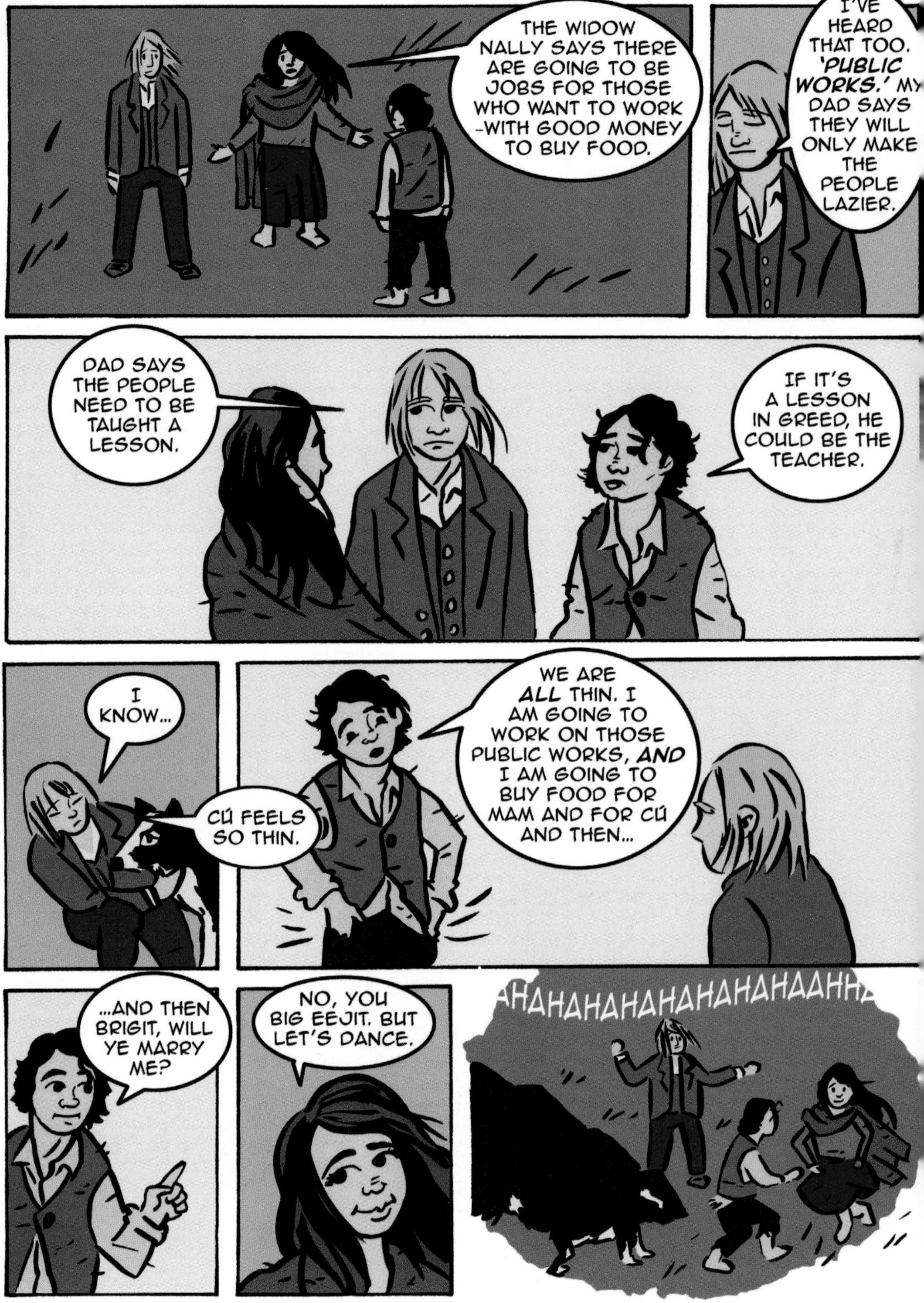
THE WIDOW NALLY SAYS THERE ARE GOING TO BE JOBS FOR THOSE WHO WANT TO WORK -WITH GOOD MONEY TO BUY FOOD.
I'VE HEARD THAT TOO. '**PUBLIC WORKS.**' MY DAD SAYS THEY WILL ONLY MAKE THE PEOPLE LAZIER.
DAD SAYS THE PEOPLE NEED TO BE TAUGHT A LESSON.
IF IT'S A LESSON IN GREED, HE COULD BE THE TEACHER.
I KNOW...
CÚ FEELS SO THIN.
WE ARE ***ALL*** THIN. I AM GOING TO WORK ON THOSE PUBLIC WORKS, ***AND*** I AM GOING TO BUY FOOD FOR MAM AND FOR CÚ AND THEN...
...AND THEN BRIGIT, WILL YE MARRY ME?
NO, YOU BIG EEJIT. BUT LET'S DANCE.
AHAHAHAHAHAHAHAHAHAAHHA

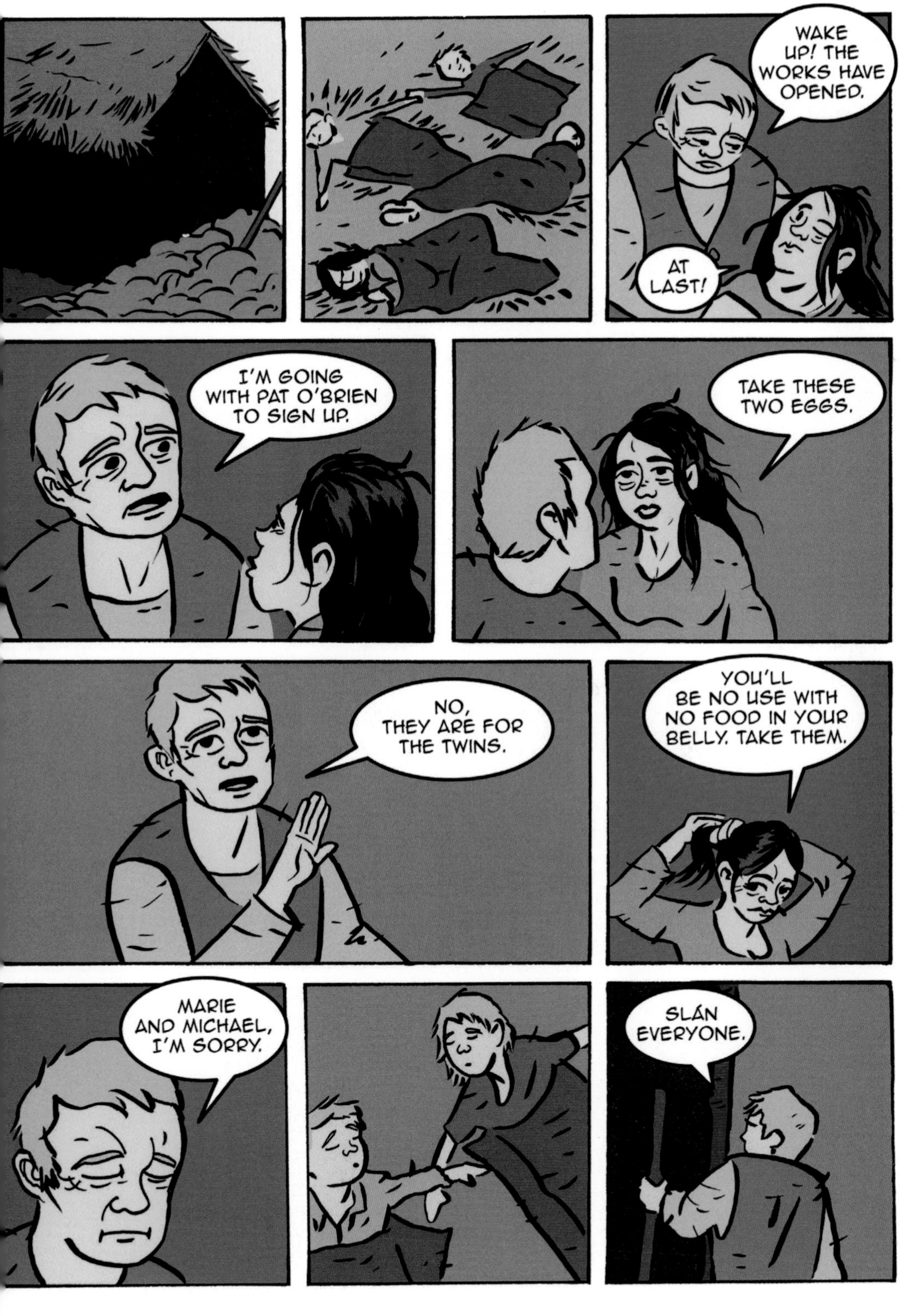
WAKE UP! THE WORKS HAVE OPENED.
AT LAST!
I'M GOING WITH PAT O'BRIEN TO SIGN UP.
TAKE THESE TWO EGGS.
NO, THEY ARE FOR THE TWINS.
YOU'LL BE NO USE WITH NO FOOD IN YOUR BELLY. TAKE THEM.
MARIE AND MICHAEL, I'M SORRY.
SLÁN EVERYONE.

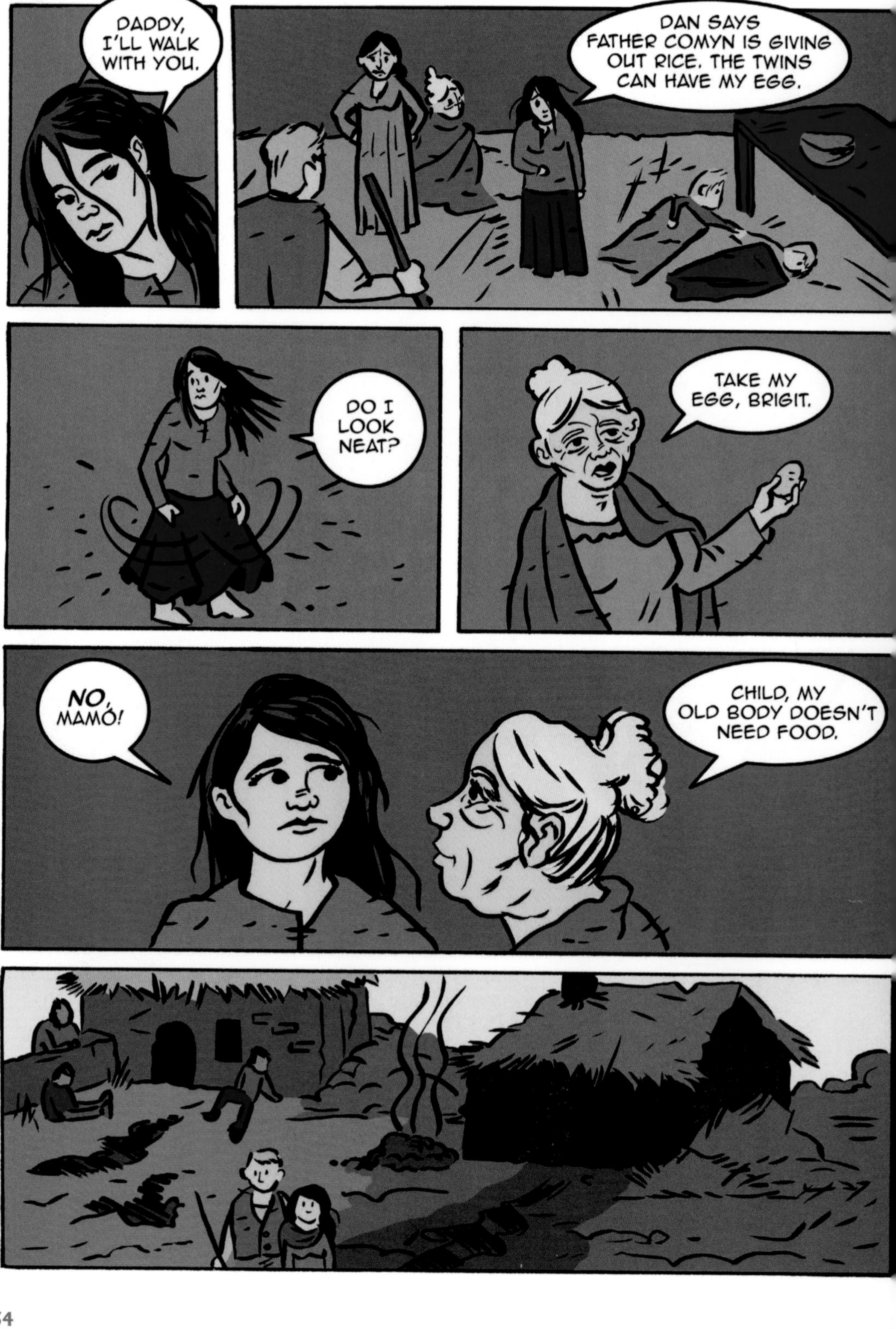
DADDY, I'LL WALK WITH YOU.
DAN SAYS FATHER COMYN IS GIVING OUT RICE. THE TWINS CAN HAVE MY EGG.
DO I LOOK NEAT?
TAKE MY EGG, BRIGIT.
NO, MAMÓ!
CHILD, MY OLD BODY DOESN'T NEED FOOD.

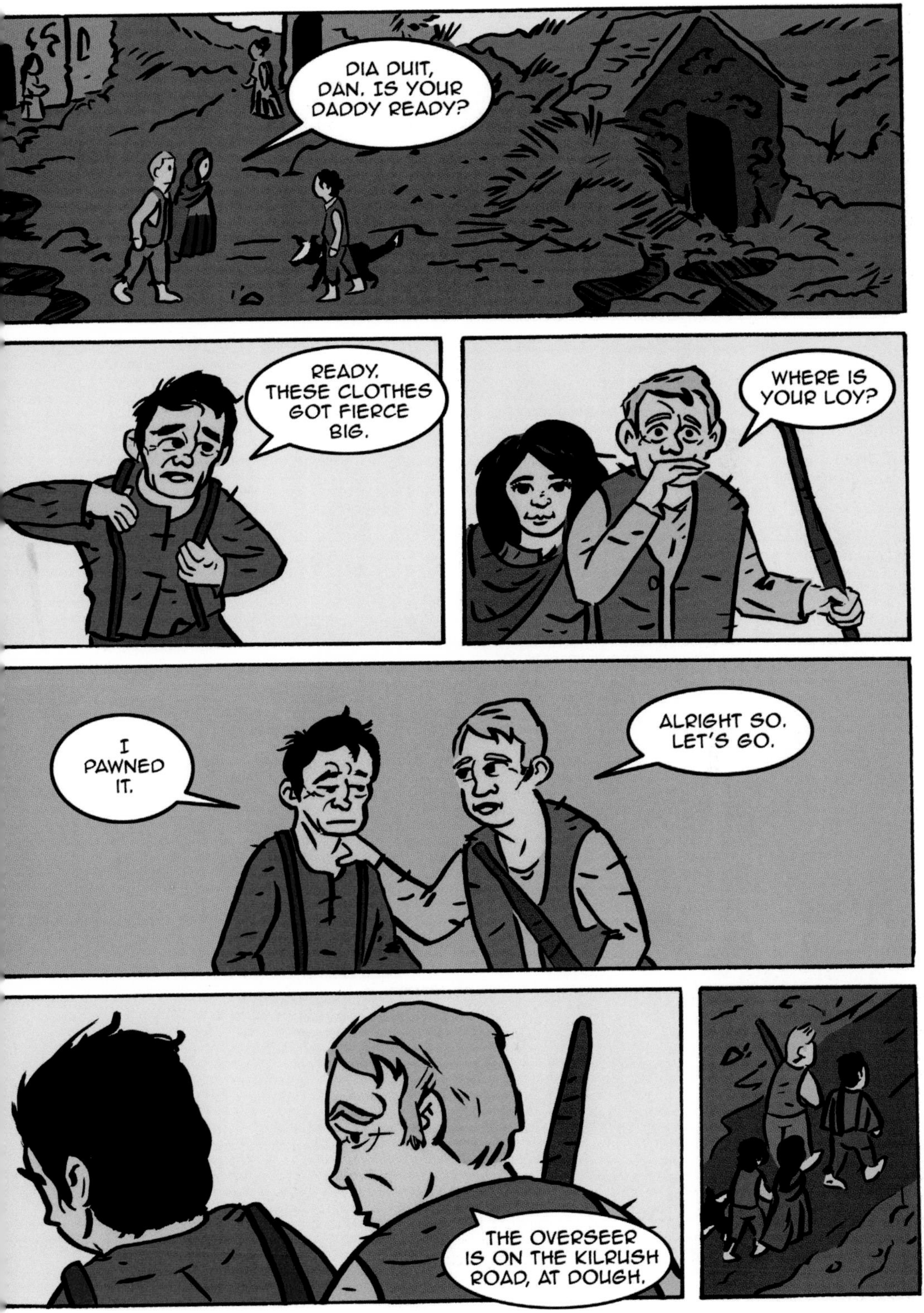
DIA DUIT, DAN. IS YOUR DADDY READY?
READY. THESE CLOTHES GOT FIERCE BIG.
WHERE IS YOUR LOY?
I PAWNED IT.
ALRIGHT SO. LET'S GO.
THE OVERSEER IS ON THE KILRUSH ROAD, AT DOUGH.

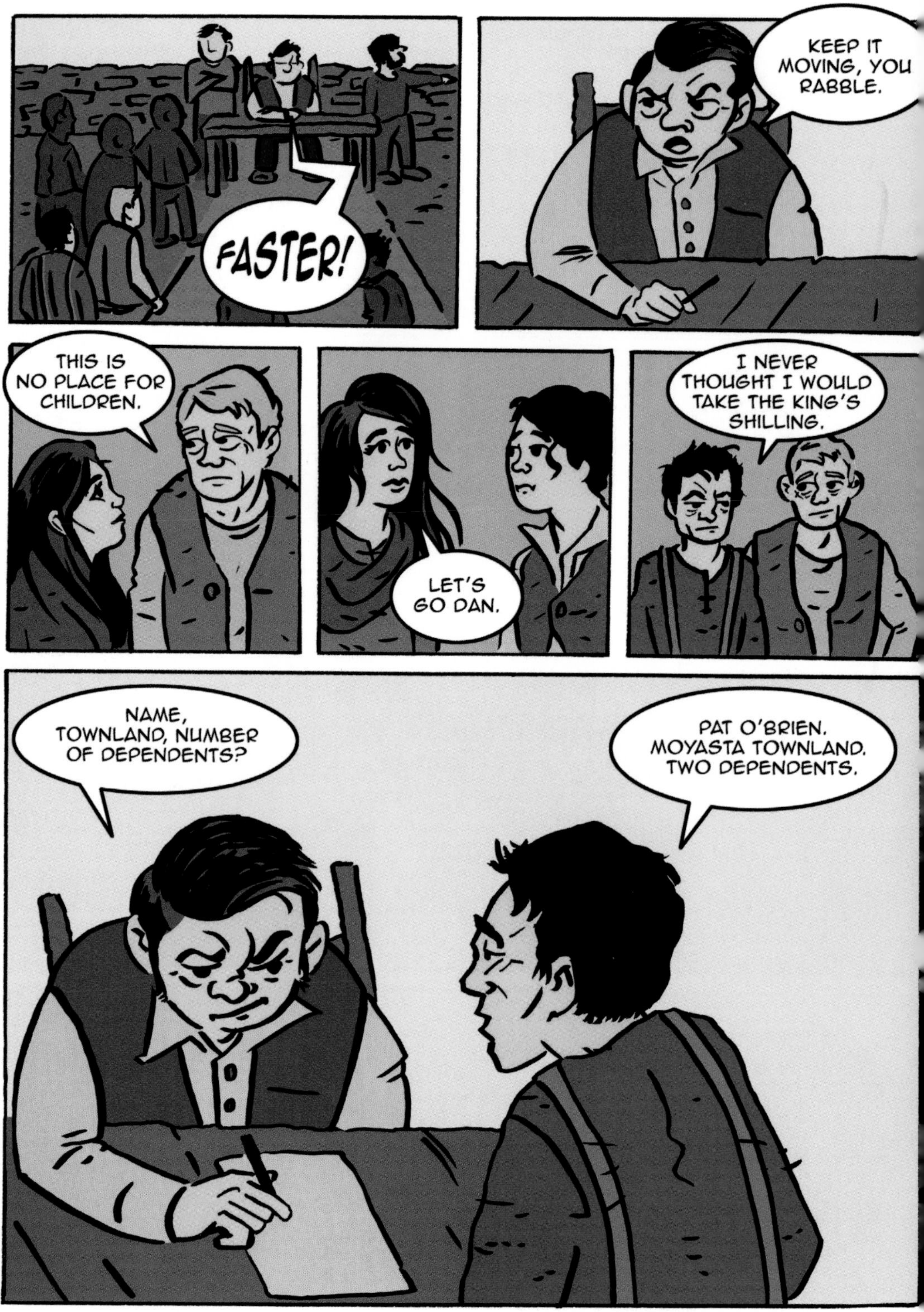
FASTER!
KEEP IT MOVING, YOU RABBLE.
THIS IS NO PLACE FOR CHILDREN.
LET'S GO DAN.
I NEVER THOUGHT I WOULD TAKE THE KING'S SHILLING.
NAME, TOWNLAND, NUMBER OF DEPENDENTS?
PAT O'BRIEN. MOYASTA TOWNLAND. TWO DEPENDENTS.

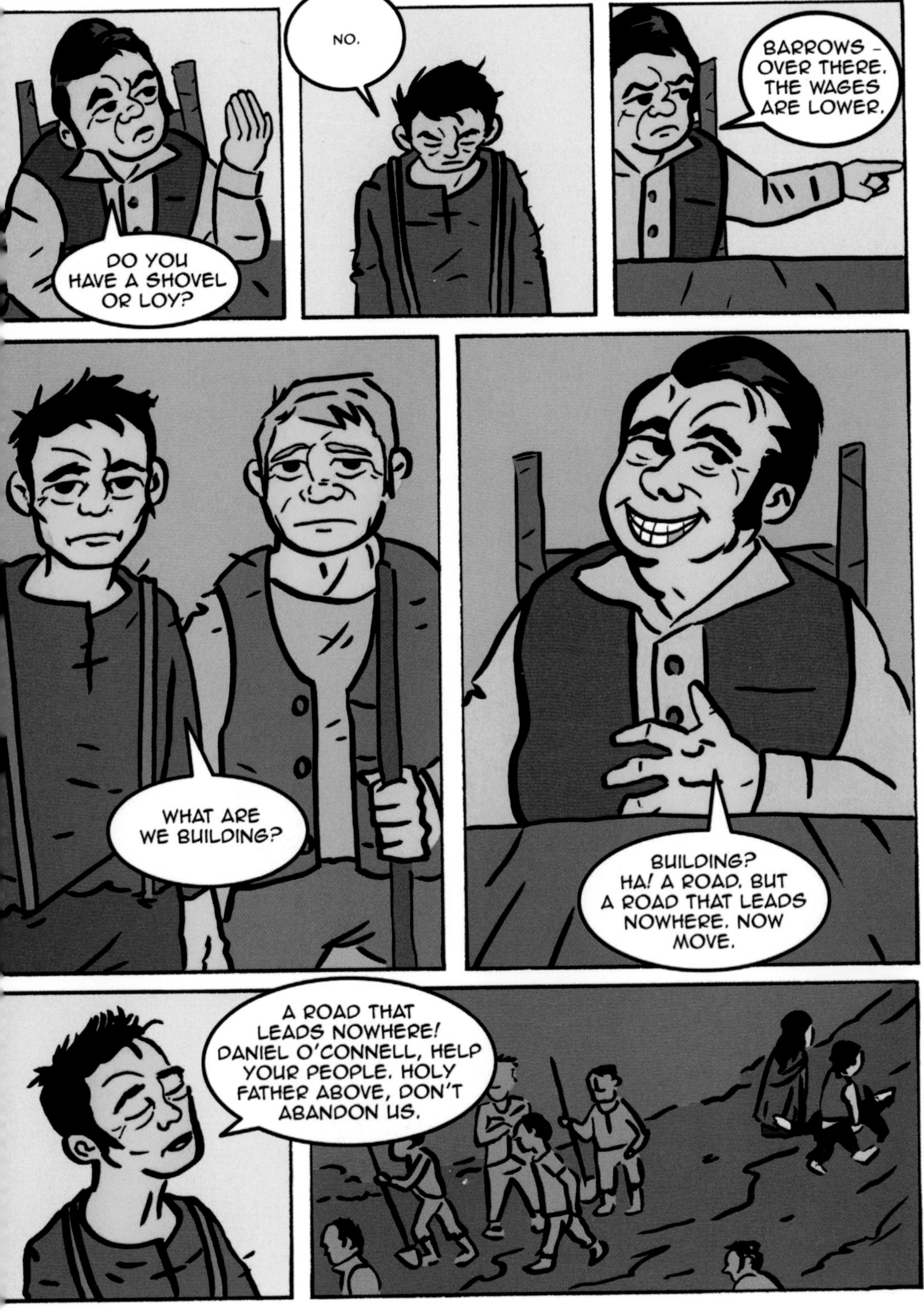
DO YOU HAVE A SHOVEL OR LOY?
NO.
BARROWS - OVER THERE. THE WAGES ARE LOWER.
WHAT ARE WE BUILDING?
BUILDING? HA! A ROAD, BUT A ROAD THAT LEADS NOWHERE. NOW MOVE.
A ROAD THAT LEADS NOWHERE! DANIEL O'CONNELL, HELP YOUR PEOPLE. HOLY FATHER ABOVE, DON'T ABANDON US.

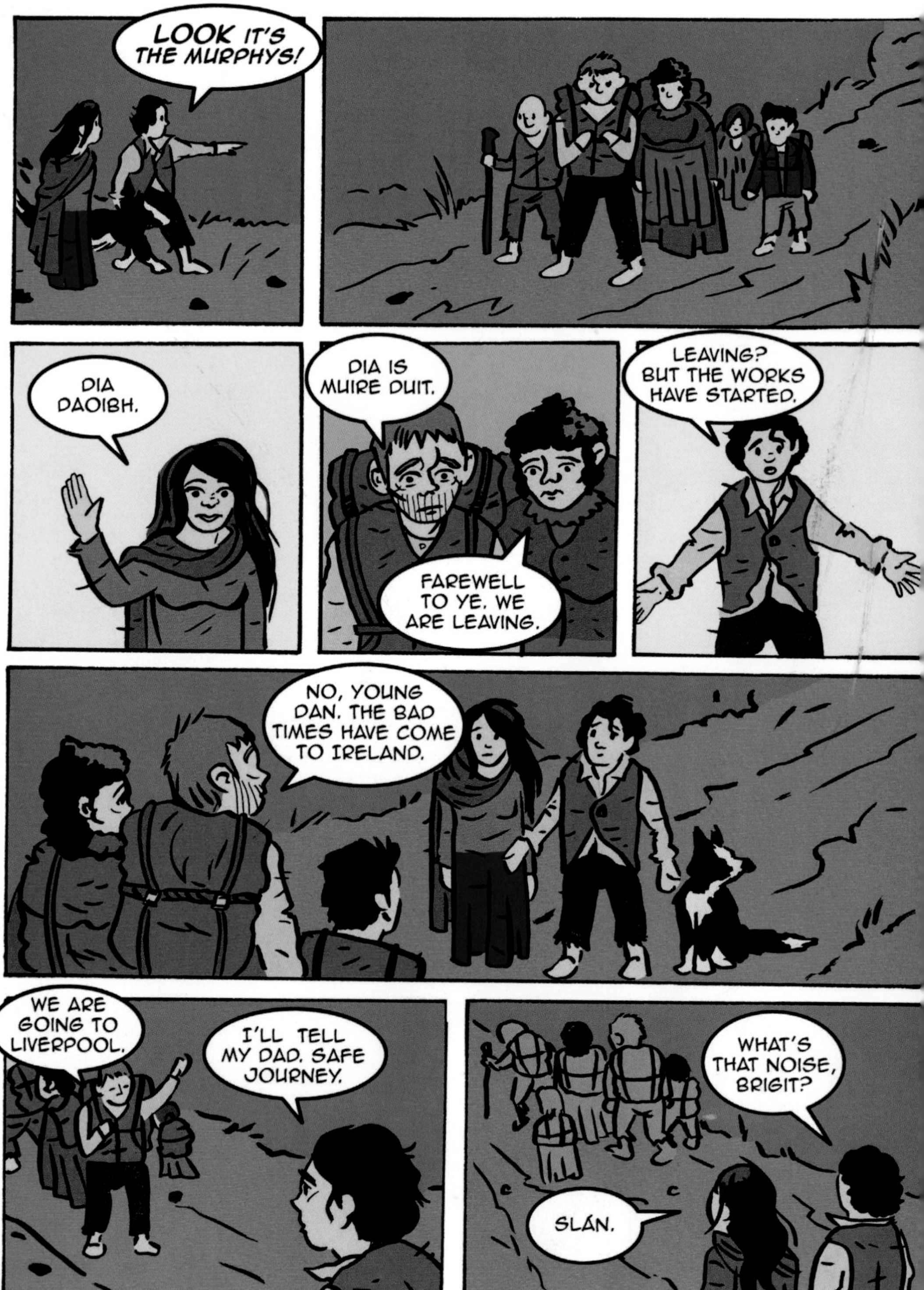
LOOK IT'S THE MURPHYS!
DIA DAOIBH.
DIA IS MUIRE DUIT.
FAREWELL TO YE. WE ARE LEAVING.
LEAVING? BUT THE WORKS HAVE STARTED.
NO, YOUNG DAN. THE BAD TIMES HAVE COME TO IRELAND.
WE ARE GOING TO LIVERPOOL.
I'LL TELL MY DAD. SAFE JOURNEY.
SLÁN.
WHAT'S THAT NOISE, BRIGIT?

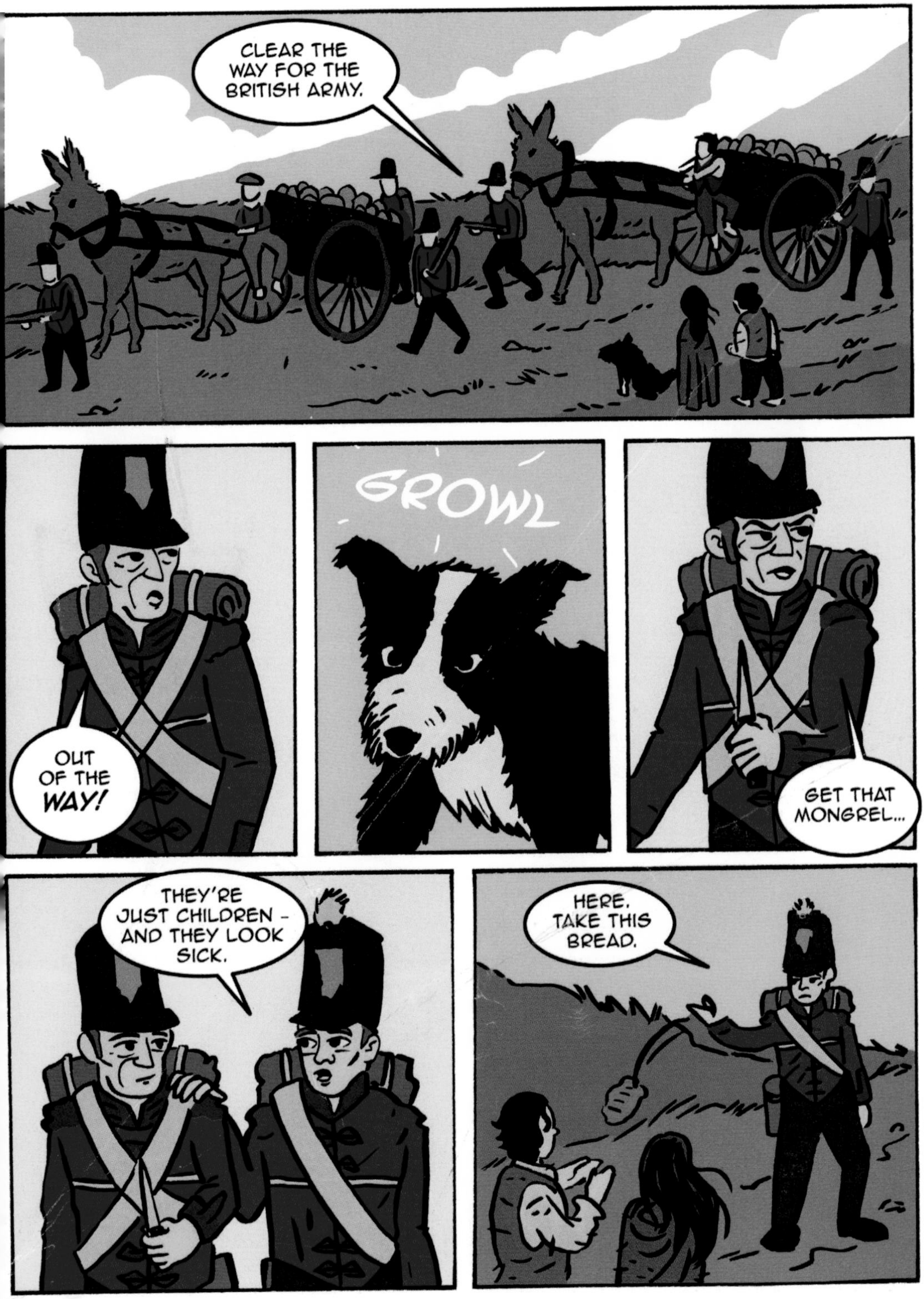
CLEAR THE WAY FOR THE BRITISH ARMY.
OUT OF THE WAY!
GROWL
GET THAT MONGREL...
THEY'RE JUST CHILDREN - AND THEY LOOK SICK.
HERE. TAKE THIS BREAD.

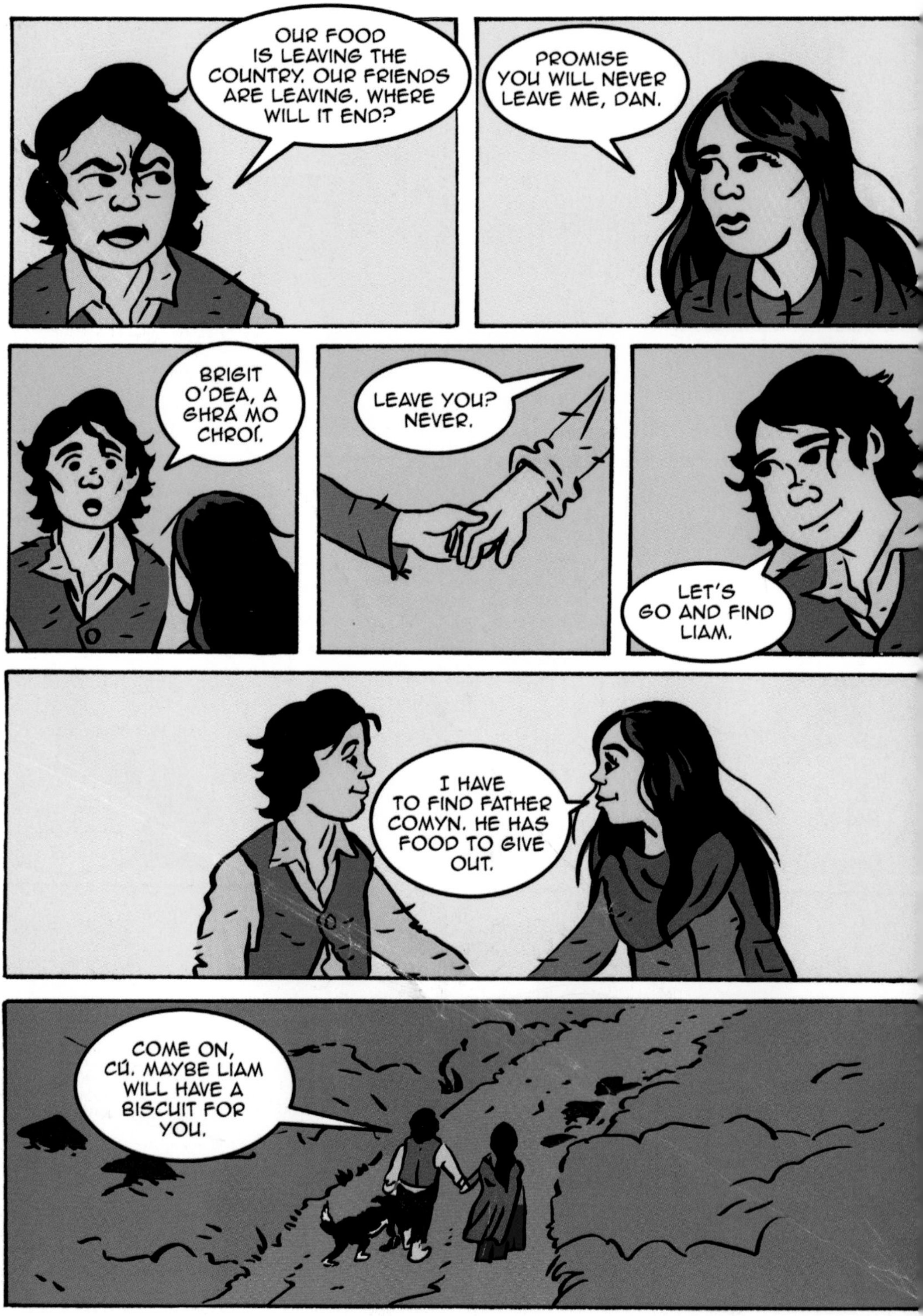
OUR FOOD IS LEAVING THE COUNTRY. OUR FRIENDS ARE LEAVING. WHERE WILL IT END?
PROMISE YOU WILL NEVER LEAVE ME, DAN.
BRIGIT O'DEA, A GHRÁ MO CHROÍ.
LEAVE YOU? NEVER.
LET'S GO AND FIND LIAM.
I HAVE TO FIND FATHER COMYN. HE HAS FOOD TO GIVE OUT.
COME ON, CÚ. MAYBE LIAM WILL HAVE A BISCUIT FOR YOU.

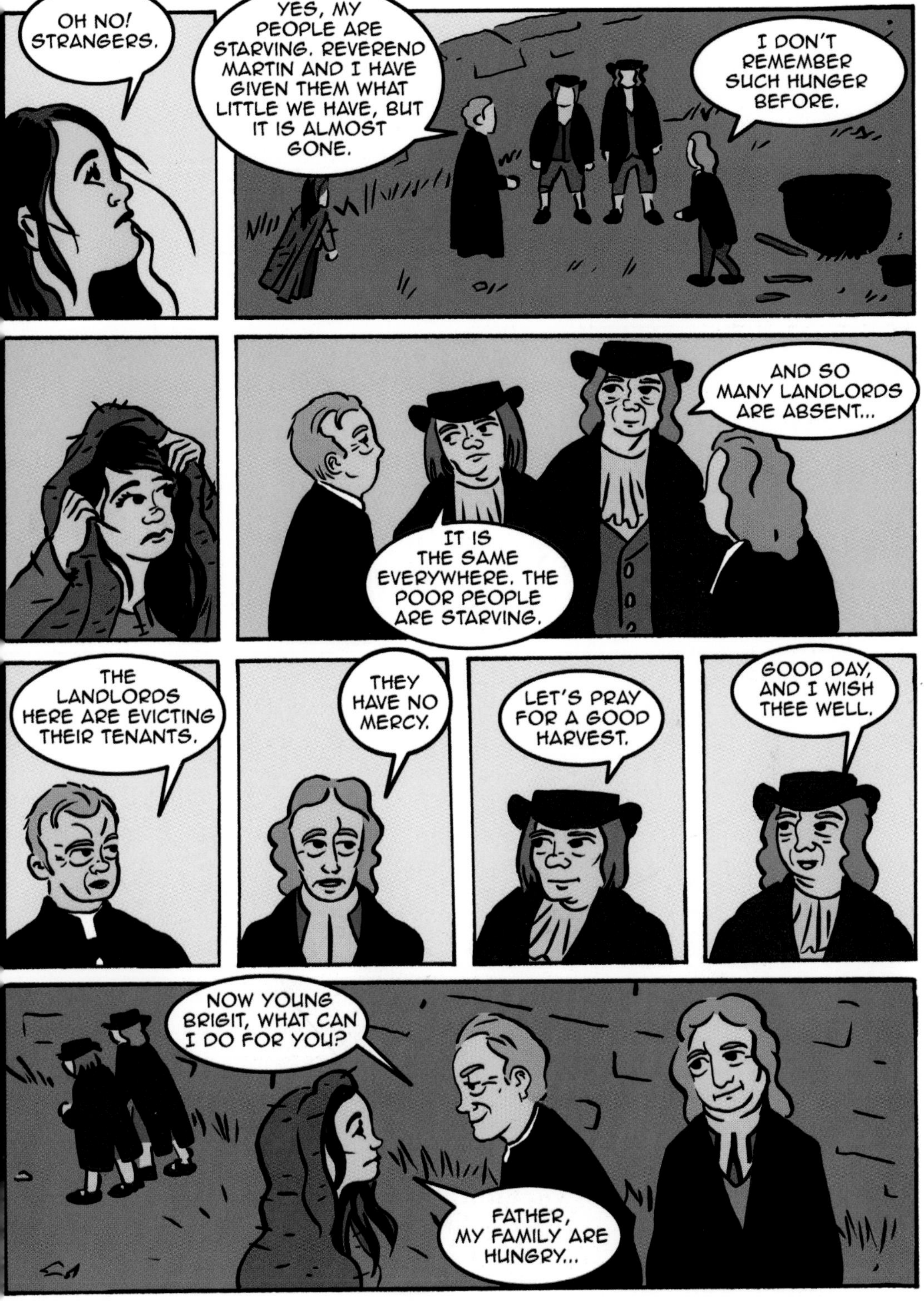
OH NO! STRANGERS.
YES, MY PEOPLE ARE STARVING. REVEREND MARTIN AND I HAVE GIVEN THEM WHAT LITTLE WE HAVE, BUT IT IS ALMOST GONE.
I DON'T REMEMBER SUCH HUNGER BEFORE.
AND SO MANY LANDLORDS ARE ABSENT...
IT IS THE SAME EVERYWHERE. THE POOR PEOPLE ARE STARVING.
THE LANDLORDS HERE ARE EVICTING THEIR TENANTS.
THEY HAVE NO MERCY.
LET'S PRAY FOR A GOOD HARVEST.
GOOD DAY, AND I WISH THEE WELL.
NOW YOUNG BRIGIT, WHAT CAN I DO FOR YOU?
FATHER, MY FAMILY ARE HUNGRY...

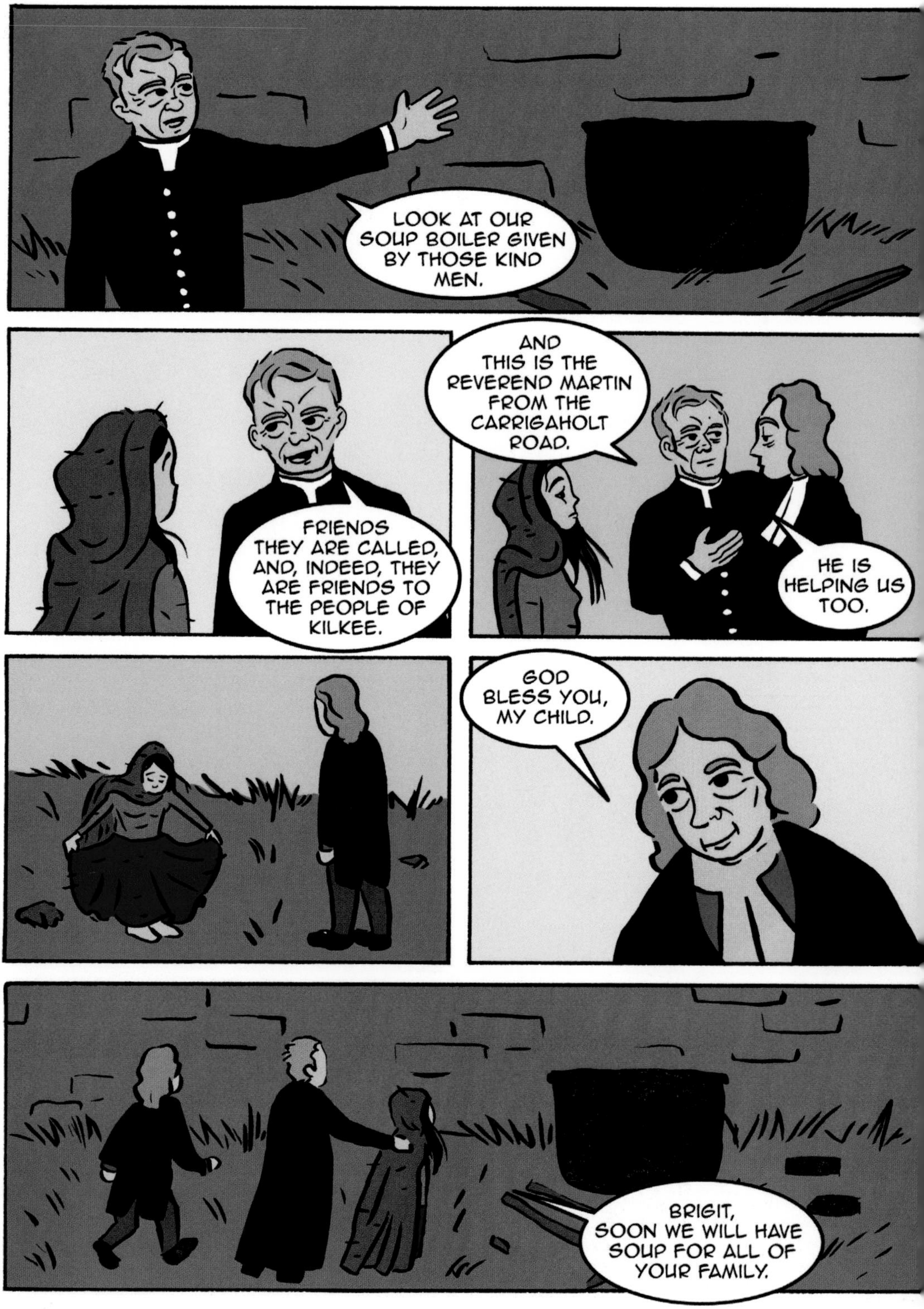
LOOK AT OUR SOUP BOILER GIVEN BY THOSE KIND MEN.
FRIENDS THEY ARE CALLED, AND, INDEED, THEY ARE FRIENDS TO THE PEOPLE OF KILKEE.
AND THIS IS THE REVEREND MARTIN FROM THE CARRIGAHOLT ROAD.
HE IS HELPING US TOO.
GOD BLESS YOU, MY CHILD.
BRIGIT, SOON WE WILL HAVE SOUP FOR ALL OF YOUR FAMILY.

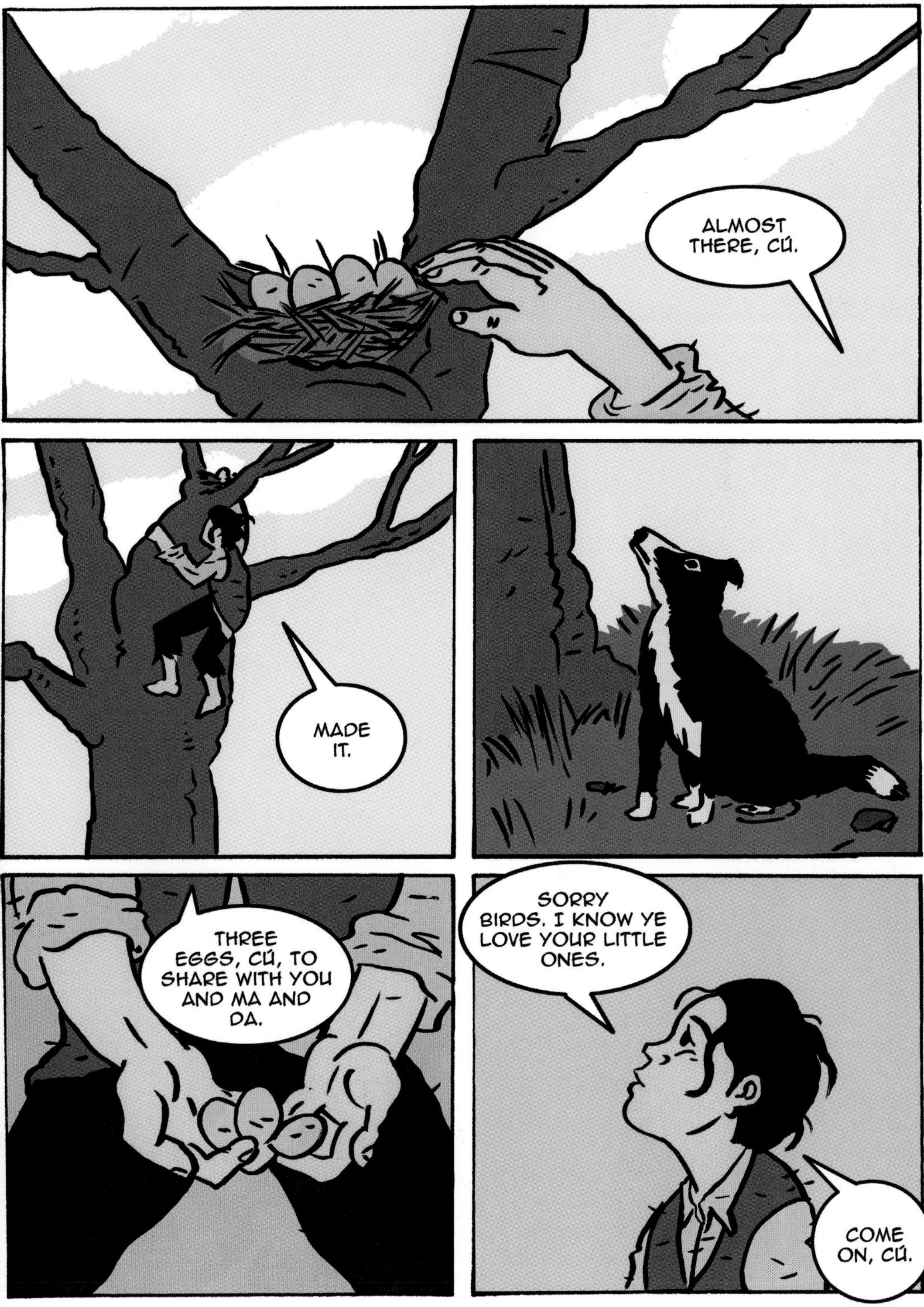
ALMOST THERE, CÚ.
MADE IT.
THREE EGGS, CÚ, TO SHARE WITH YOU AND MA AND DA.
SORRY BIRDS. I KNOW YE LOVE YOUR LITTLE ONES.
COME ON, CÚ.

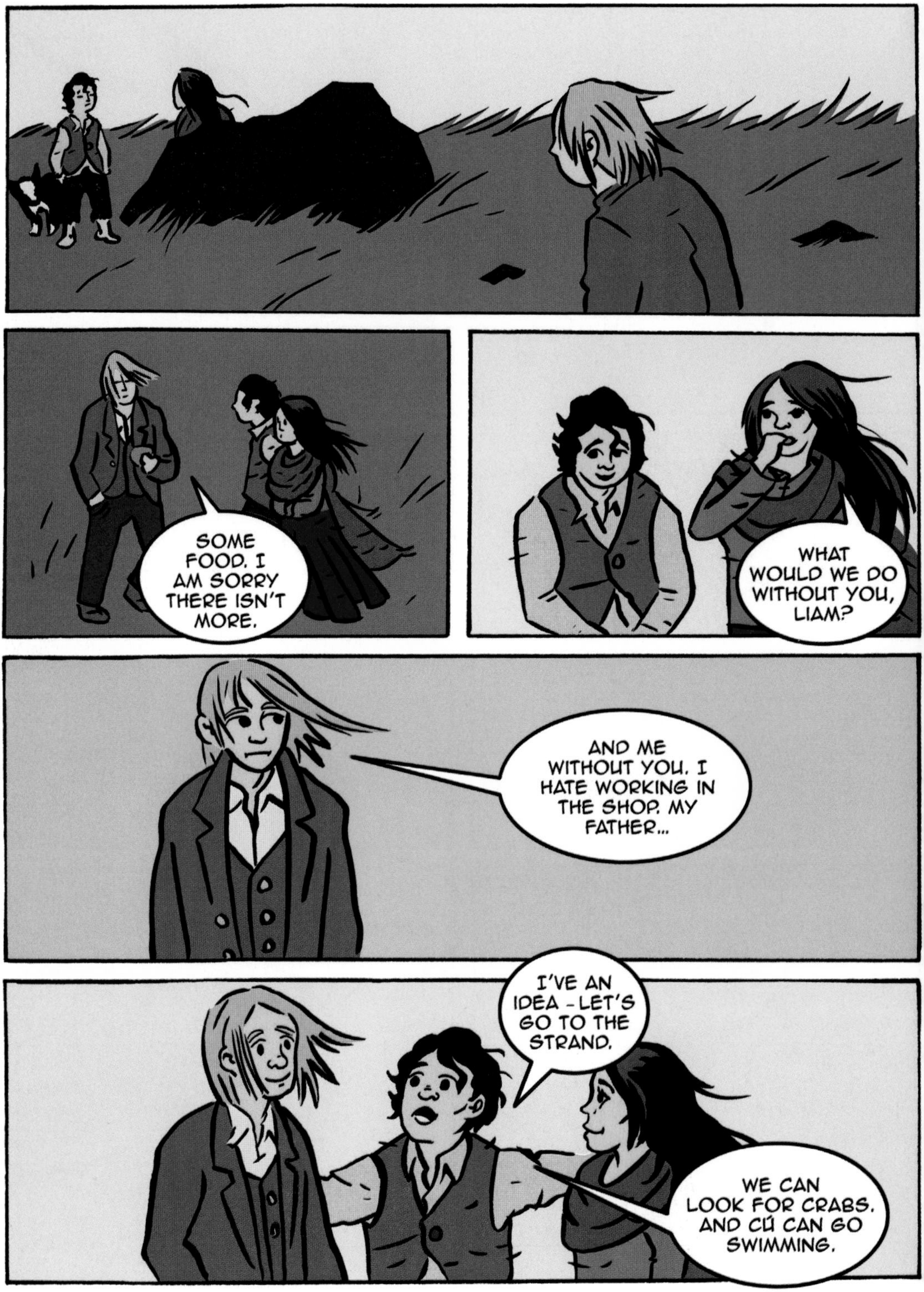
SOME FOOD. I AM SORRY THERE ISN'T MORE.
WHAT WOULD WE DO WITHOUT YOU, LIAM?
AND ME WITHOUT YOU. I HATE WORKING IN THE SHOP. MY FATHER...
I'VE AN IDEA - LET'S GO TO THE STRAND.
WE CAN LOOK FOR CRABS. AND CÚ CAN GO SWIMMING.

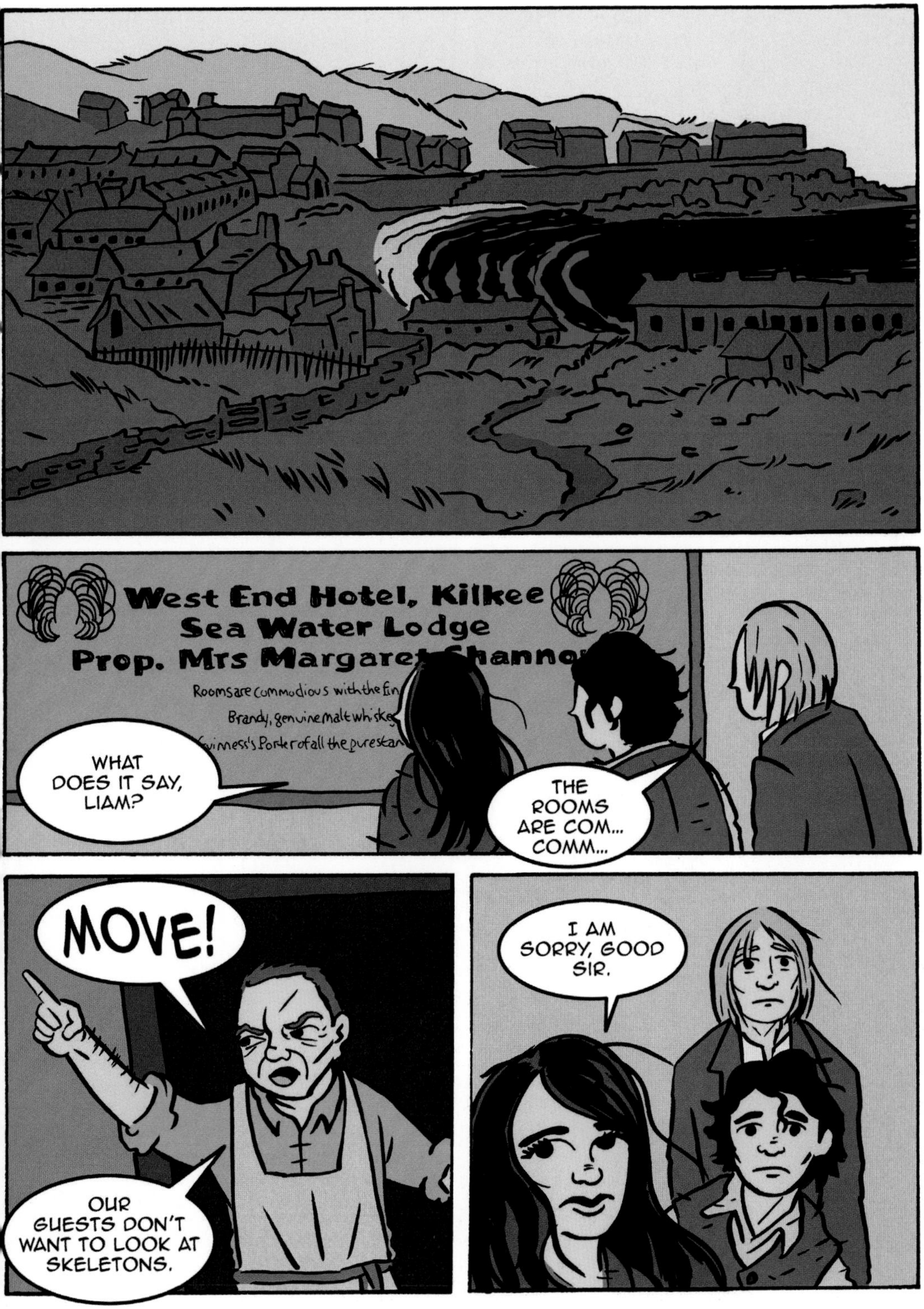
West End Hotel, Kilkee
Sea Water Lodge
Prop. Mrs Margaret
Roomsare commodious with the
Brandy, genuine malt
Guiness's Porter of all the pure
WHAT DOES IT SAY, LIAM?
THE ROOMS ARE COM... COMM...
MOVE!
OUR GUESTS DON'T WANT TO LOOK AT SKELETONS.
I AM SORRY, GOOD SIR.

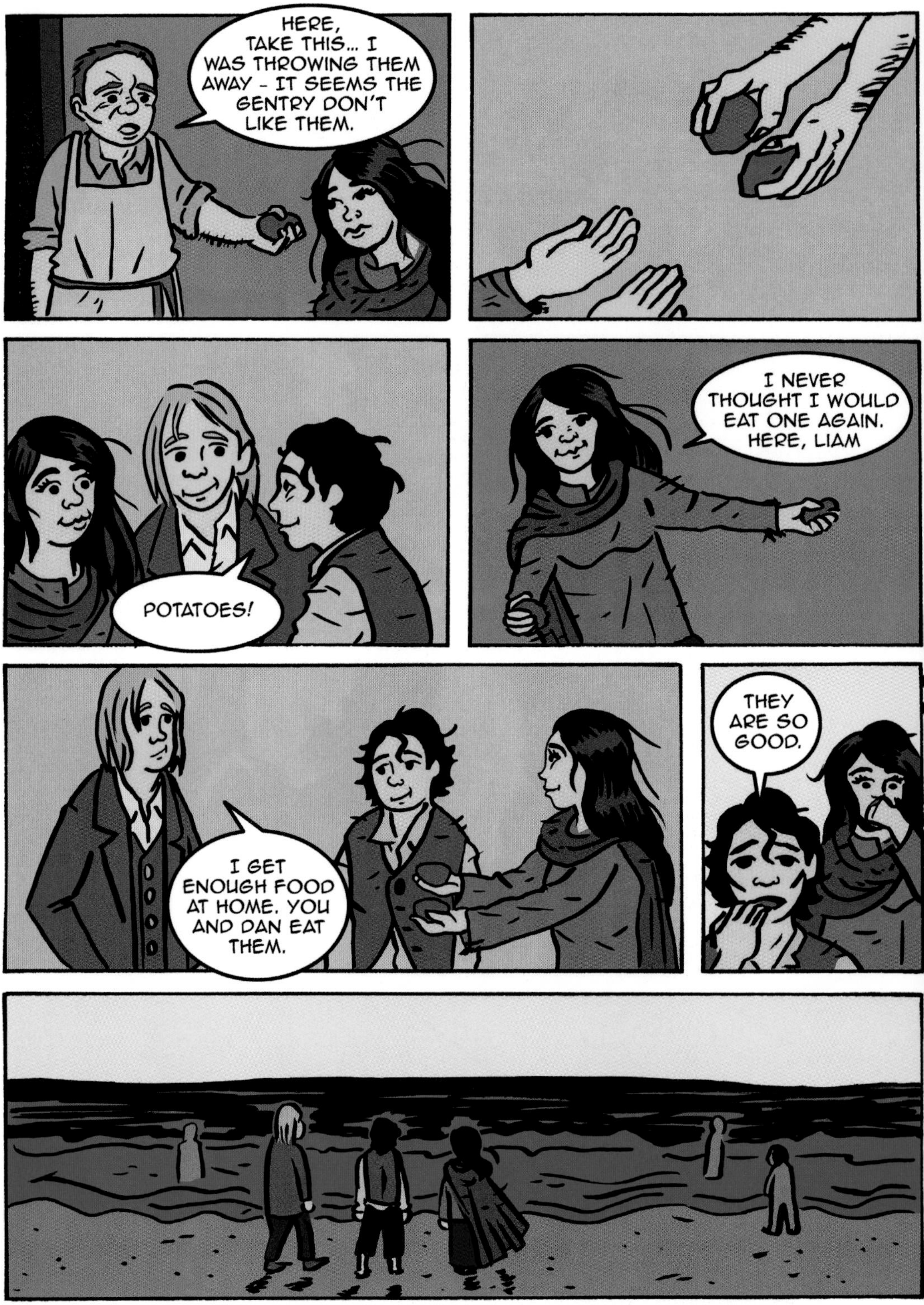

HERE, TAKE THIS... I WAS THROWING THEM AWAY - IT SEEMS THE GENTRY DON'T LIKE THEM.
POTATOES!
I NEVER THOUGHT I WOULD EAT ONE AGAIN. HERE, LIAM
I GET ENOUGH FOOD AT HOME. YOU AND DAN EAT THEM.
THEY ARE SO GOOD.

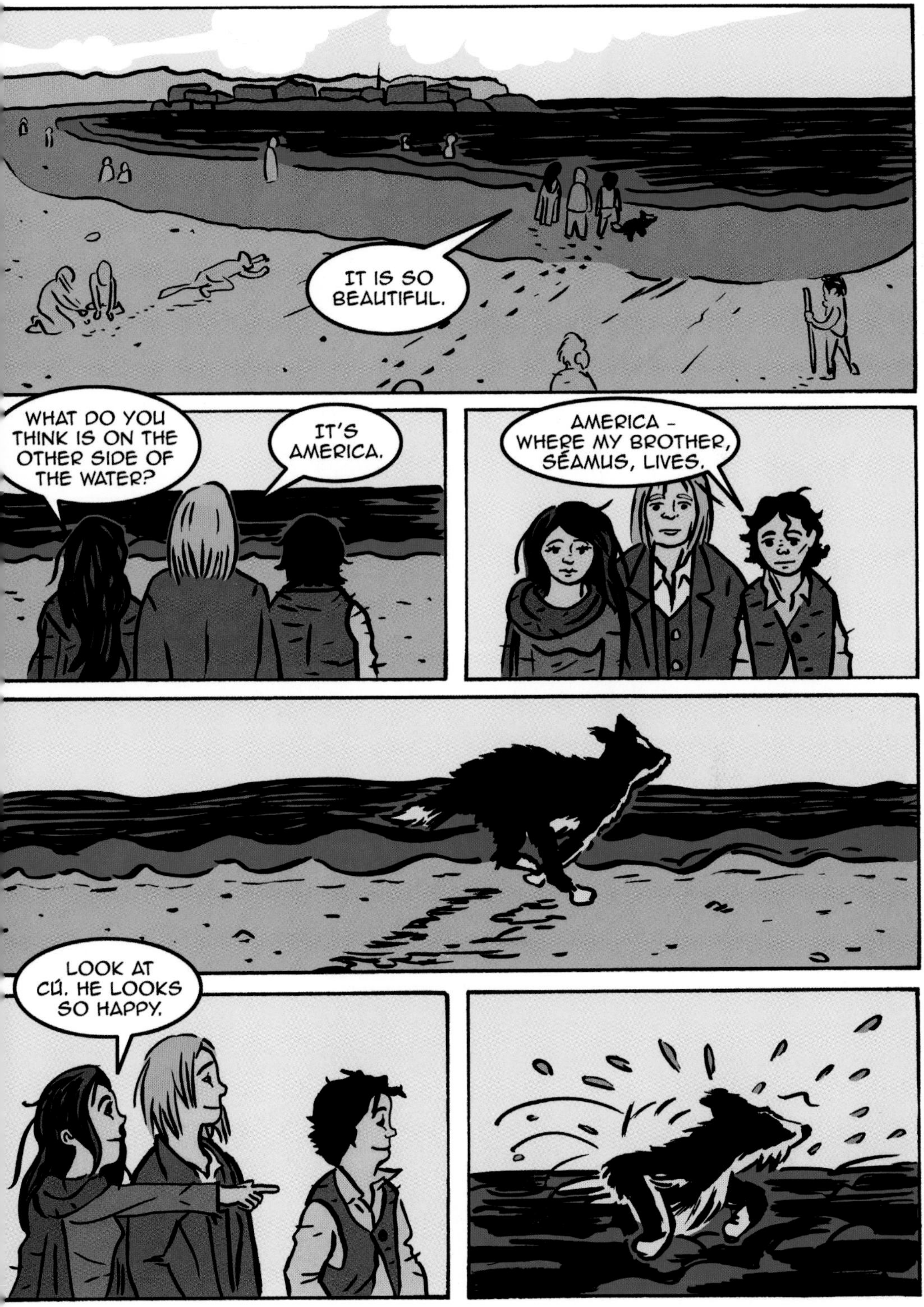
IT IS SO BEAUTIFUL.
WHAT DO YOU THINK IS ON THE OTHER SIDE OF THE WATER?
IT'S AMERICA.
AMERICA - WHERE MY BROTHER, SÉAMUS, LIVES.
LOOK AT CÚ. HE LOOKS SO HAPPY.

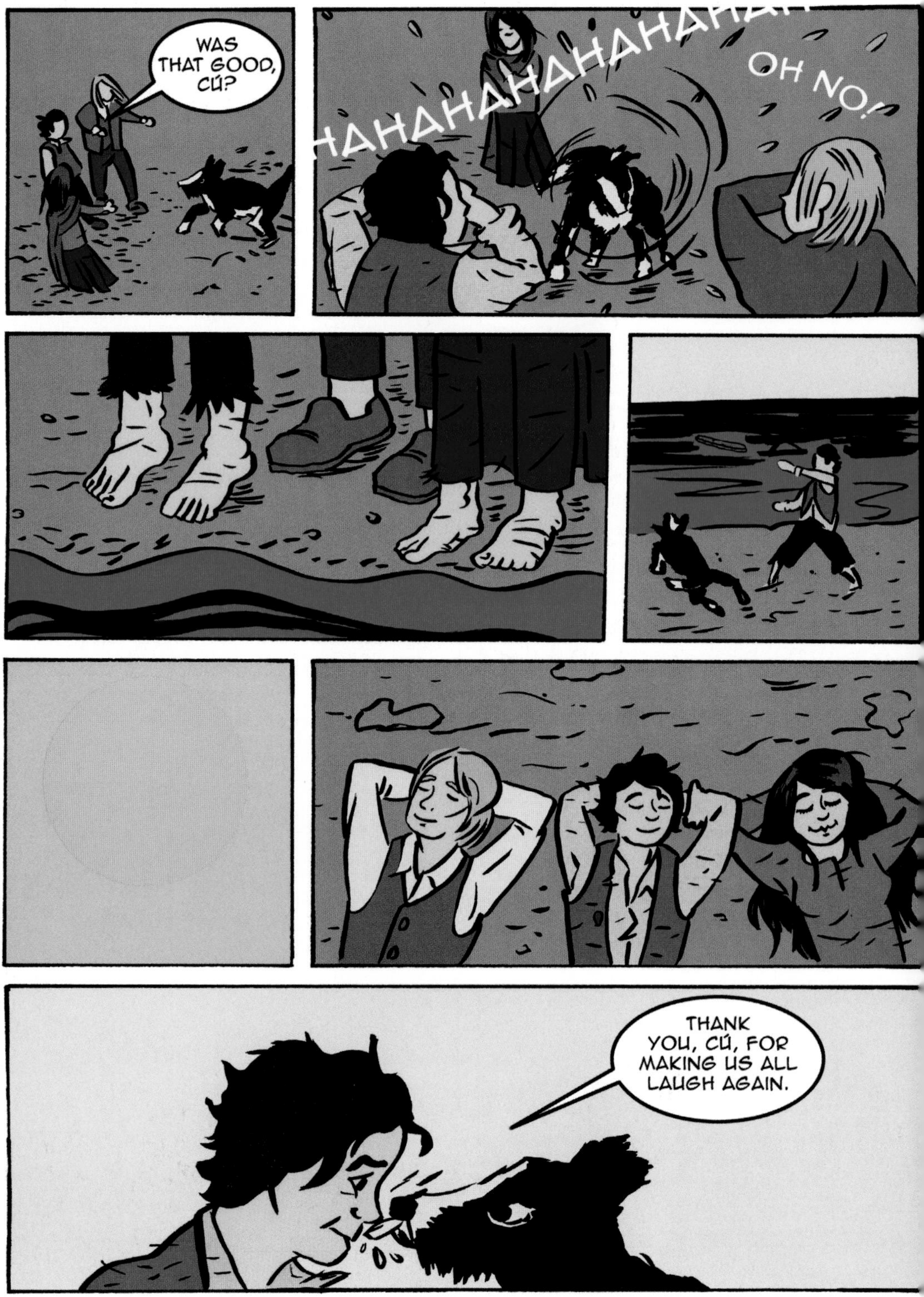
WAS THAT GOOD, CÚ?
HAHAHAHAHAHAHAHA
OH NO!
THANK YOU, CÚ, FOR MAKING US ALL LAUGH AGAIN.

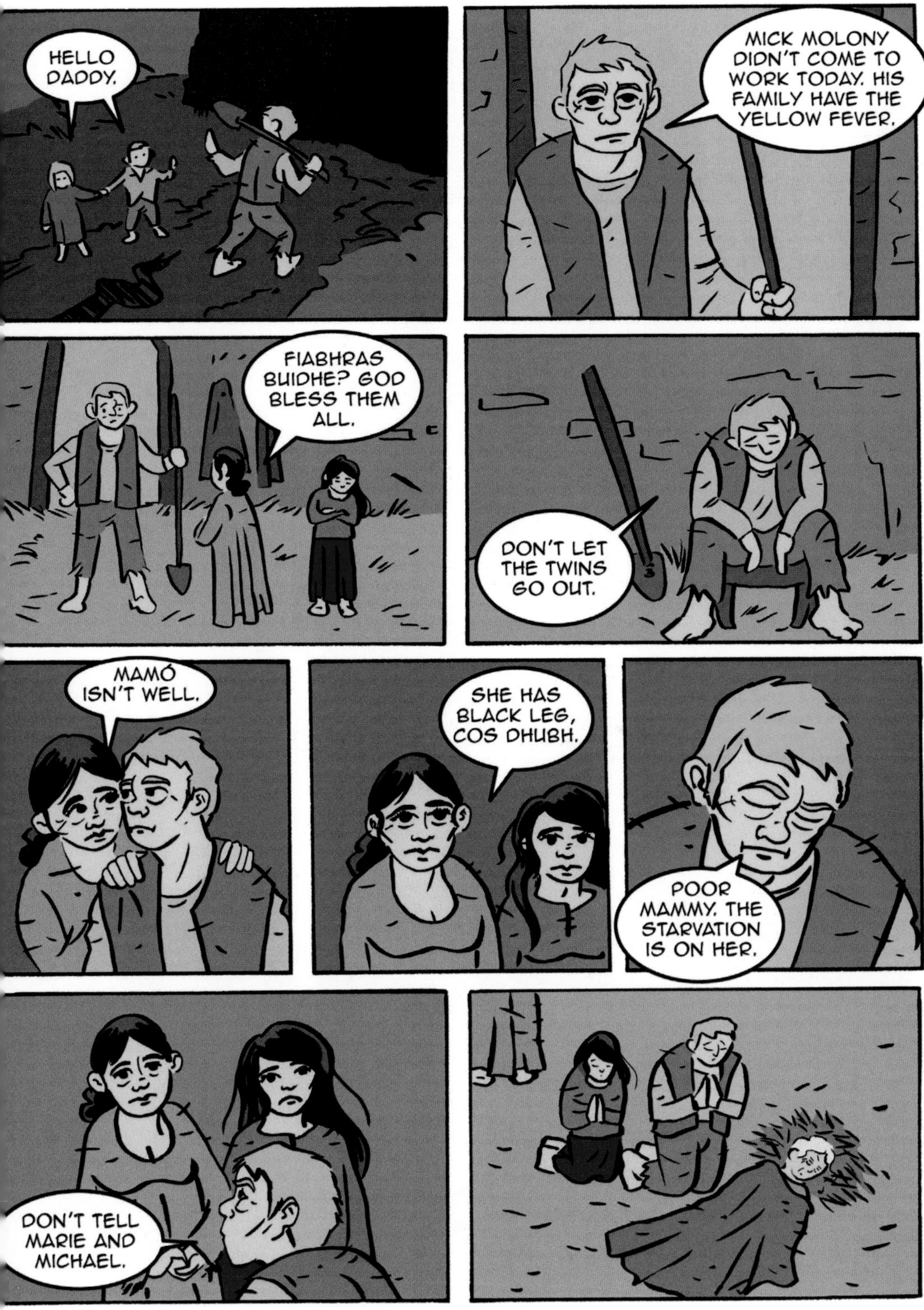
HELLO DADDY.
MICK MOLONY DIDN'T COME TO WORK TODAY. HIS FAMILY HAVE THE YELLOW FEVER.
FIABHRAS BUIDHE? GOD BLESS THEM ALL.
DON'T LET THE TWINS GO OUT.
MAMÓ ISN'T WELL.
SHE HAS BLACK LEG, COS DHUBH.
POOR MAMMY. THE STARVATION IS ON HER.
DON'T TELL MARIE AND MICHAEL.

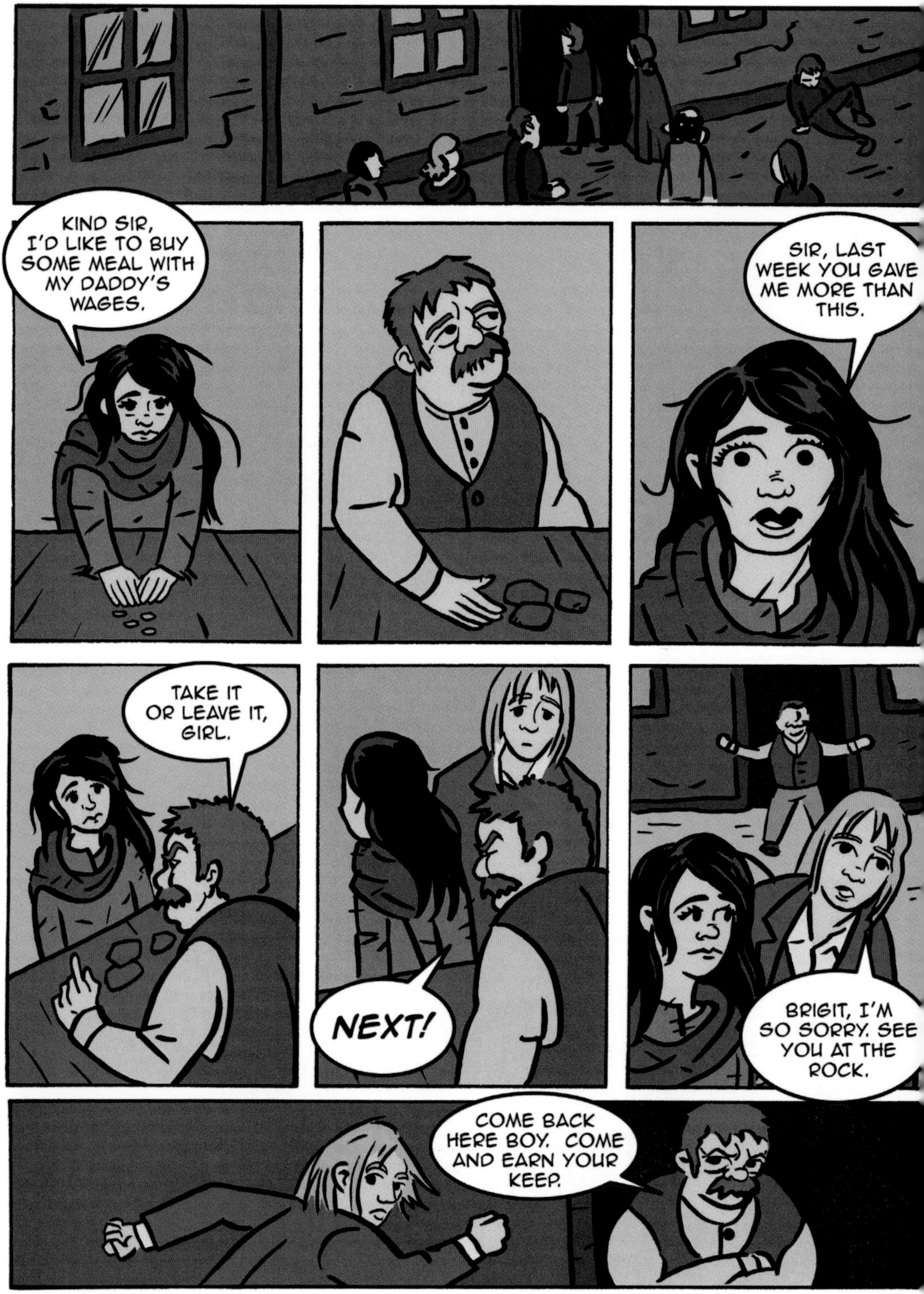
KIND SIR, I'D LIKE TO BUY SOME MEAL WITH MY DADDY'S WAGES.
SIR, LAST WEEK YOU GAVE ME MORE THAN THIS.
TAKE IT OR LEAVE IT, GIRL.
NEXT!
BRIGIT, I'M SO SORRY. SEE YOU AT THE ROCK.
COME BACK HERE BOY. COME AND EARN YOUR KEEP.

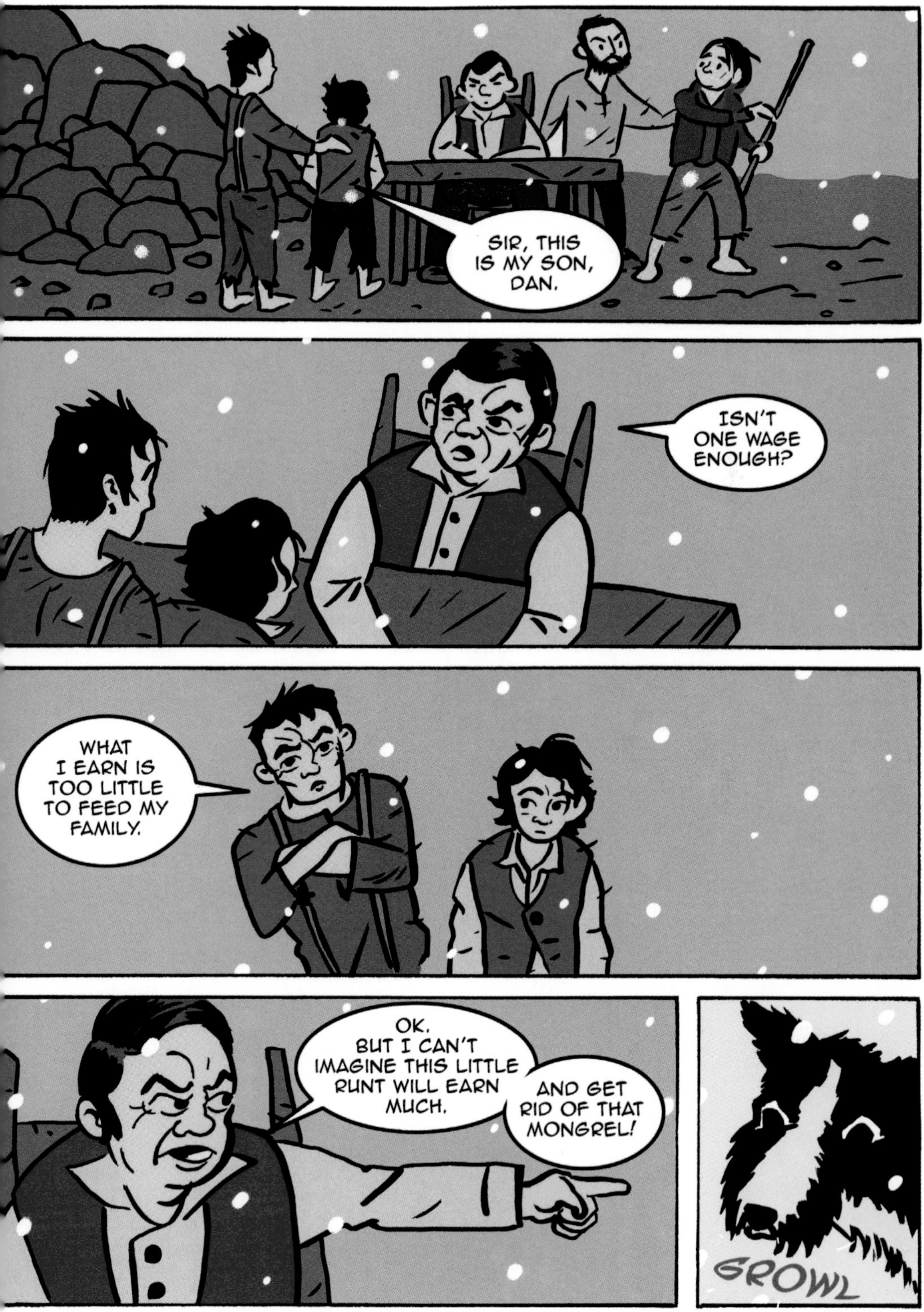
SIR, THIS IS MY SON, DAN.
ISN'T ONE WAGE ENOUGH?
WHAT I EARN IS TOO LITTLE TO FEED MY FAMILY.
OK. BUT I CAN'T IMAGINE THIS LITTLE RUNT WILL EARN MUCH.
AND GET RID OF THAT MONGREL!
GROWL

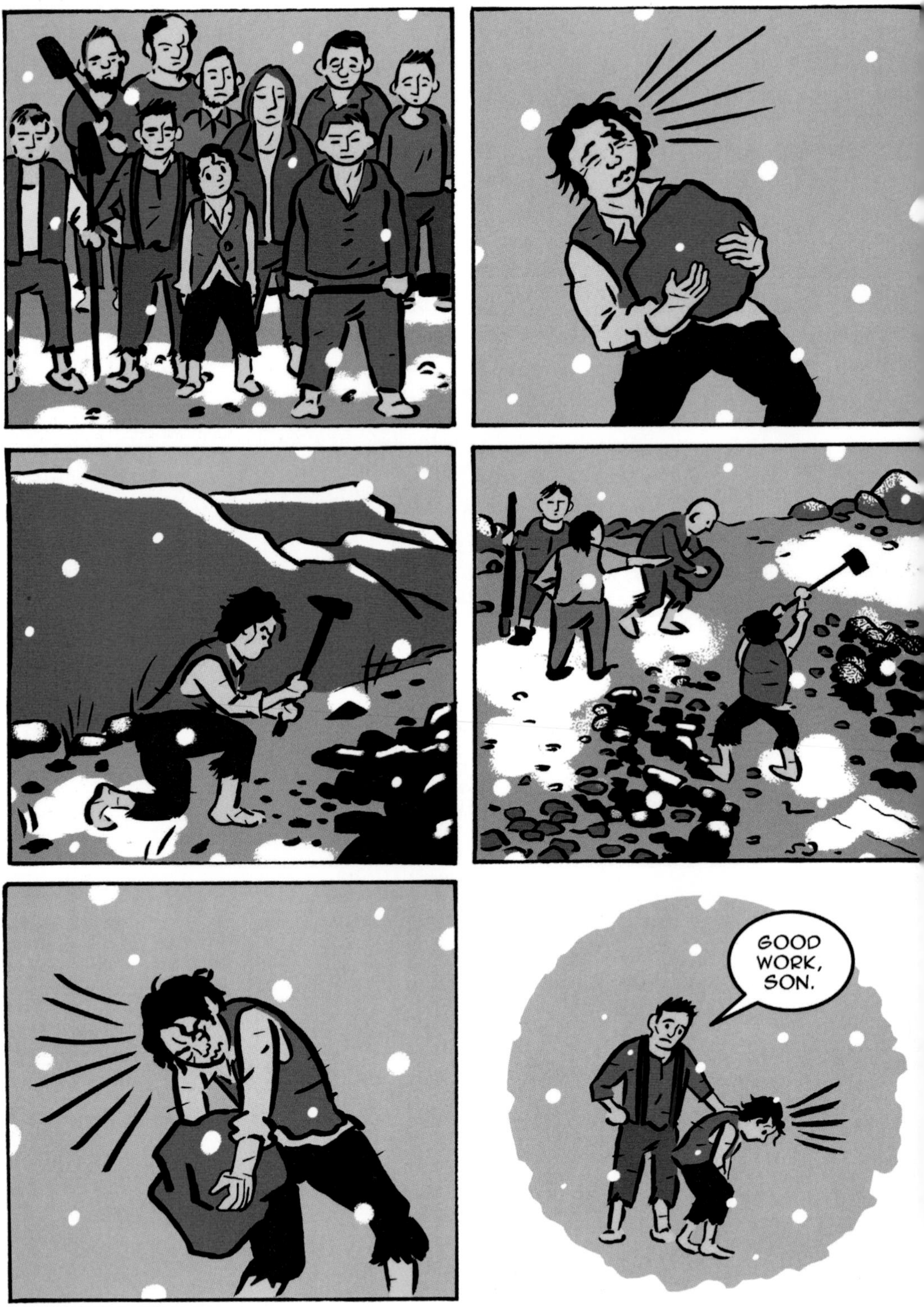
GOOD WORK, SON.

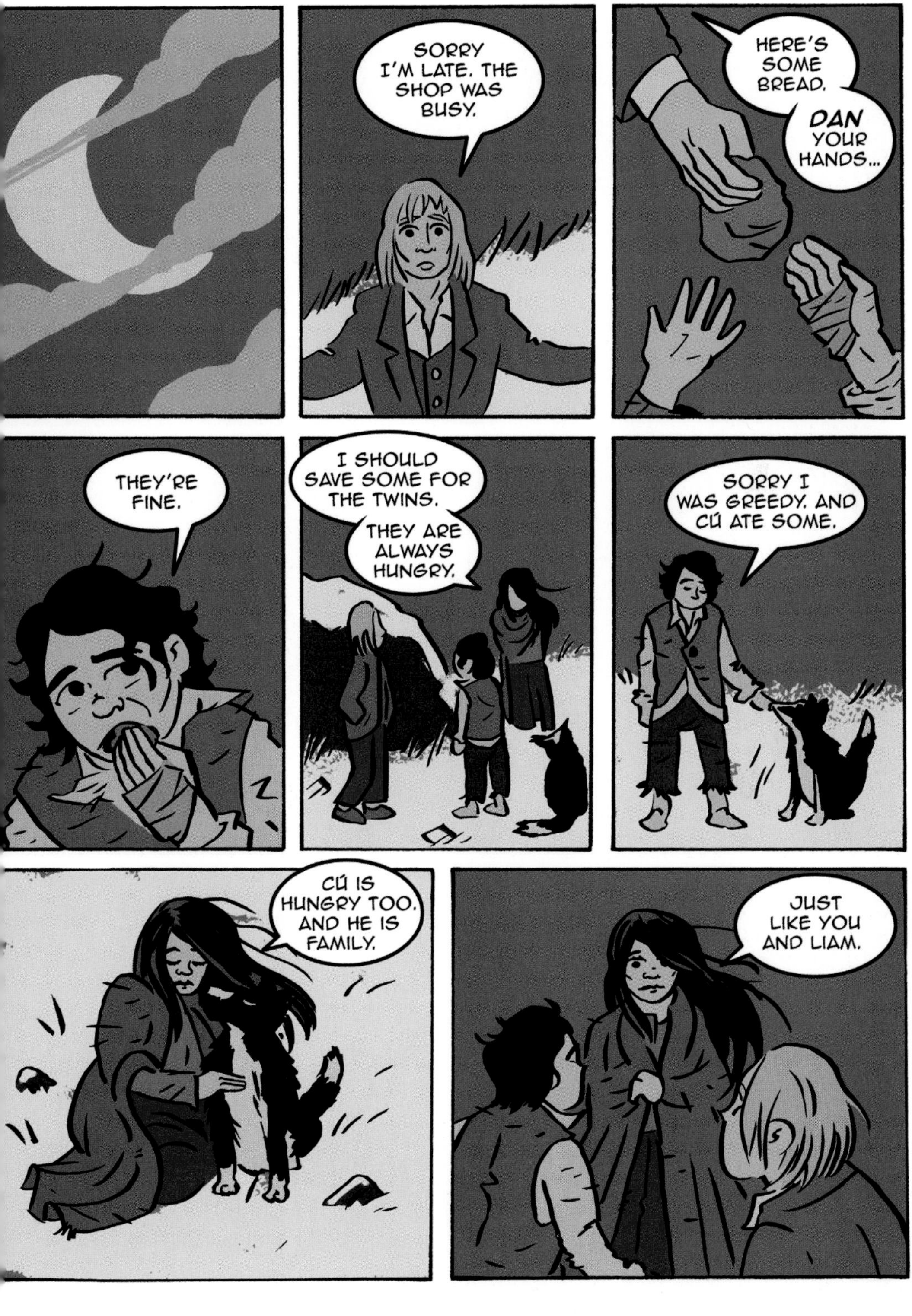
SORRY I'M LATE. THE SHOP WAS BUSY.
HERE'S SOME BREAD.
DAN YOUR HANDS...
THEY'RE FINE.
I SHOULD SAVE SOME FOR THE TWINS.
THEY ARE ALWAYS HUNGRY.
SORRY I WAS GREEDY. AND CÚ ATE SOME.
CÚ IS HUNGRY TOO. AND HE IS FAMILY.
JUST LIKE YOU AND LIAM.

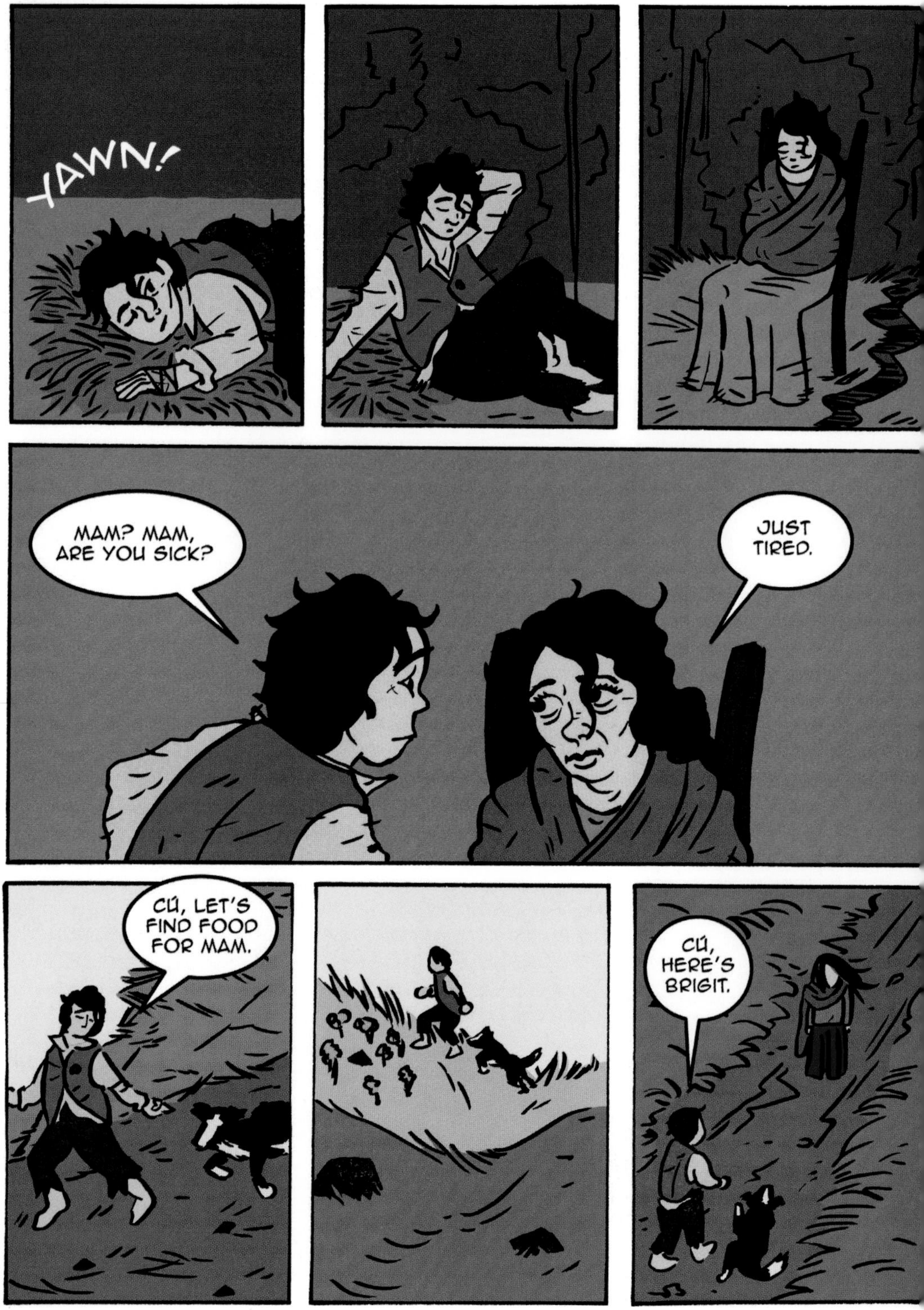
YAWN!
MAM? MAM, ARE YOU SICK?
JUST TIRED.
CÚ, LET'S FIND FOOD FOR MAM.
CÚ, HERE'S BRIGIT.

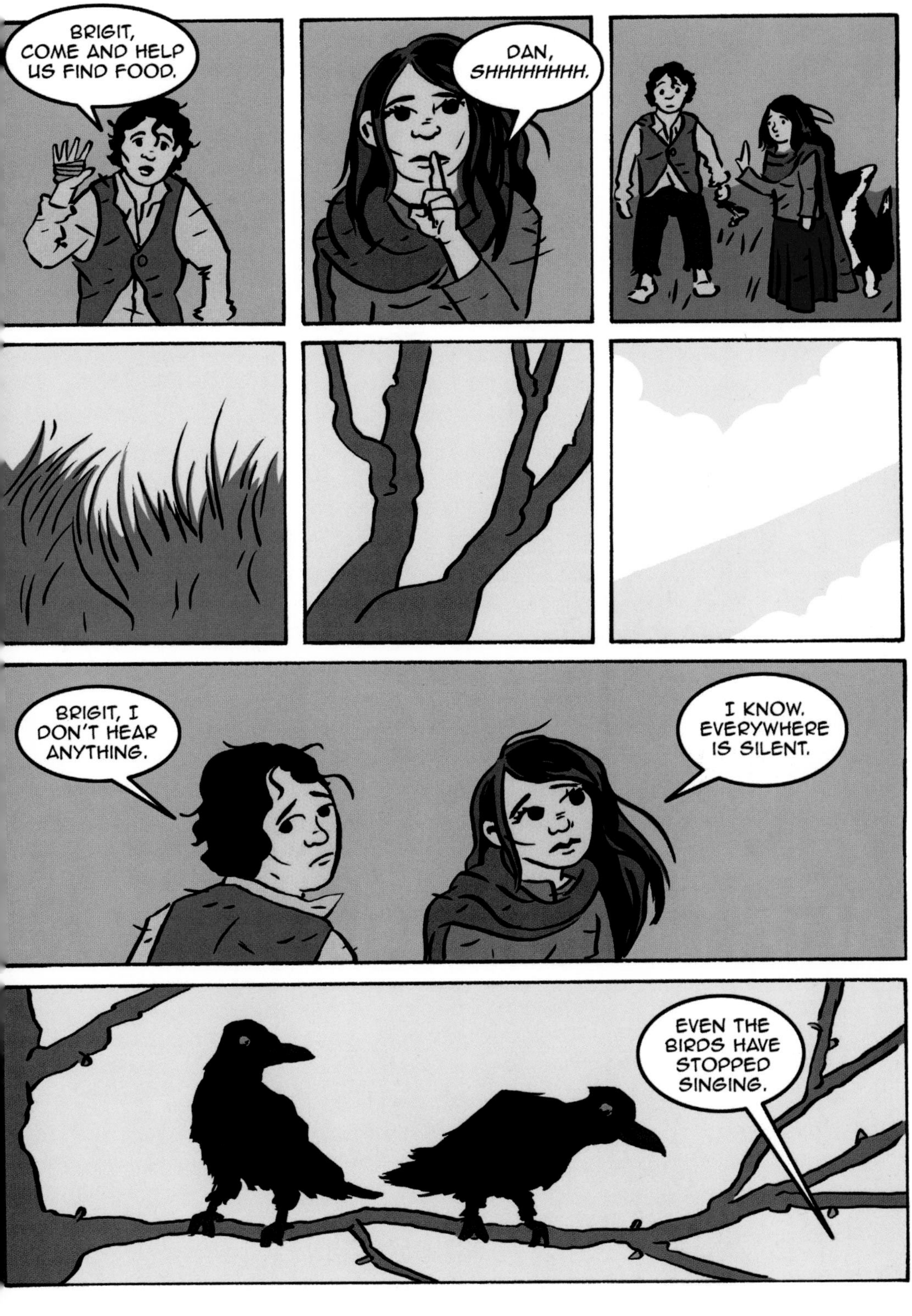
BRIGIT, COME AND HELP US FIND FOOD.
DAN, SHHHHHHHH.
BRIGIT, I DON'T HEAR ANYTHING.
I KNOW. EVERYWHERE IS SILENT.
EVEN THE BIRDS HAVE STOPPED SINGING.

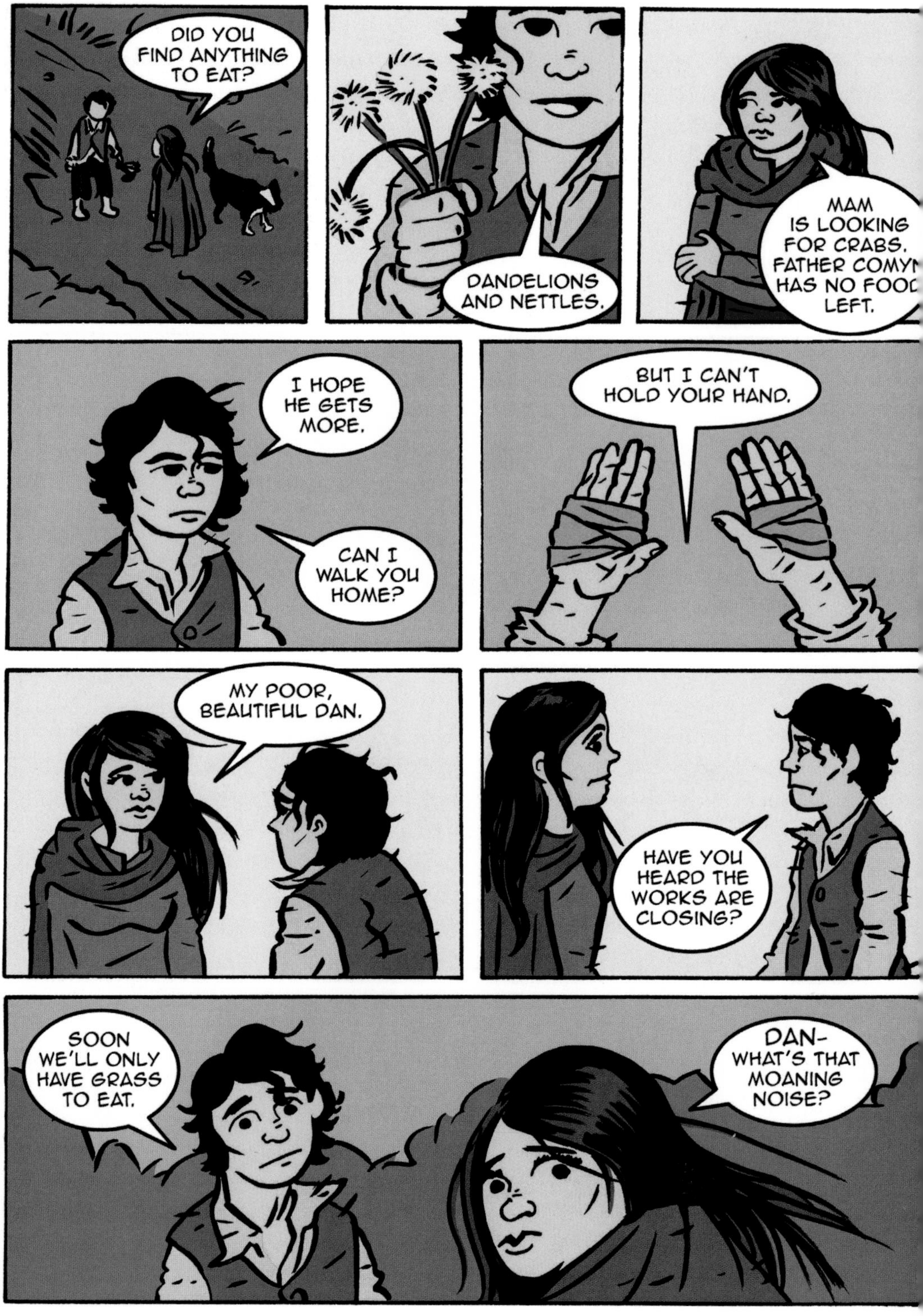
DID YOU FIND ANYTHING TO EAT?
DANDELIONS AND NETTLES.
MAM IS LOOKING FOR CRABS. FATHER COMYN HAS NO FOOD LEFT.
I HOPE HE GETS MORE.
CAN I WALK YOU HOME?
BUT I CAN'T HOLD YOUR HAND.
MY POOR, BEAUTIFUL DAN.
HAVE YOU HEARD THE WORKS ARE CLOSING?
SOON WE'LL ONLY HAVE GRASS TO EAT.
DAN- WHAT'S THAT MOANING NOISE?

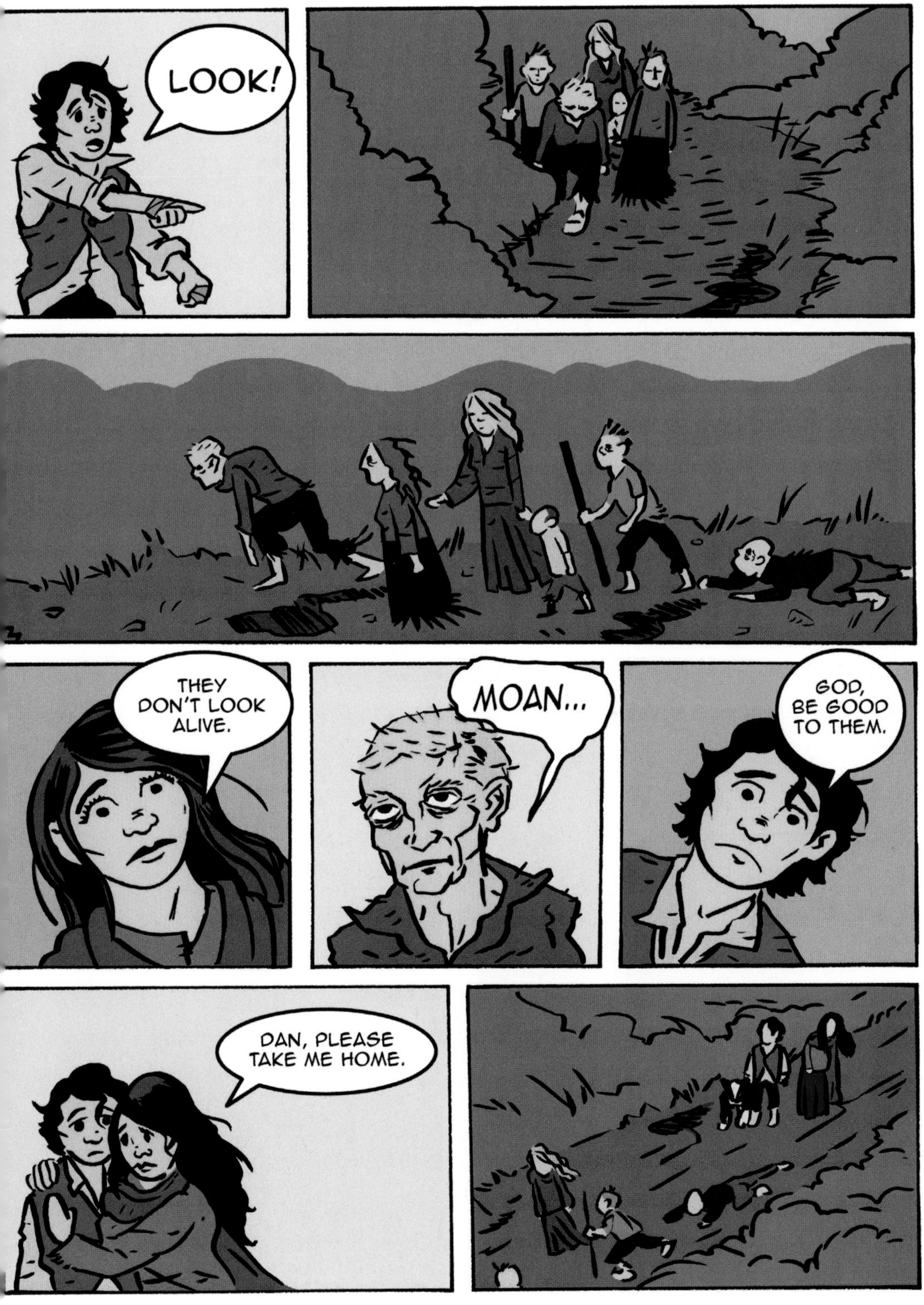
LOOK!
THEY DON'T LOOK ALIVE.
MOAN...
GOD, BE GOOD TO THEM.
DAN, PLEASE TAKE ME HOME.

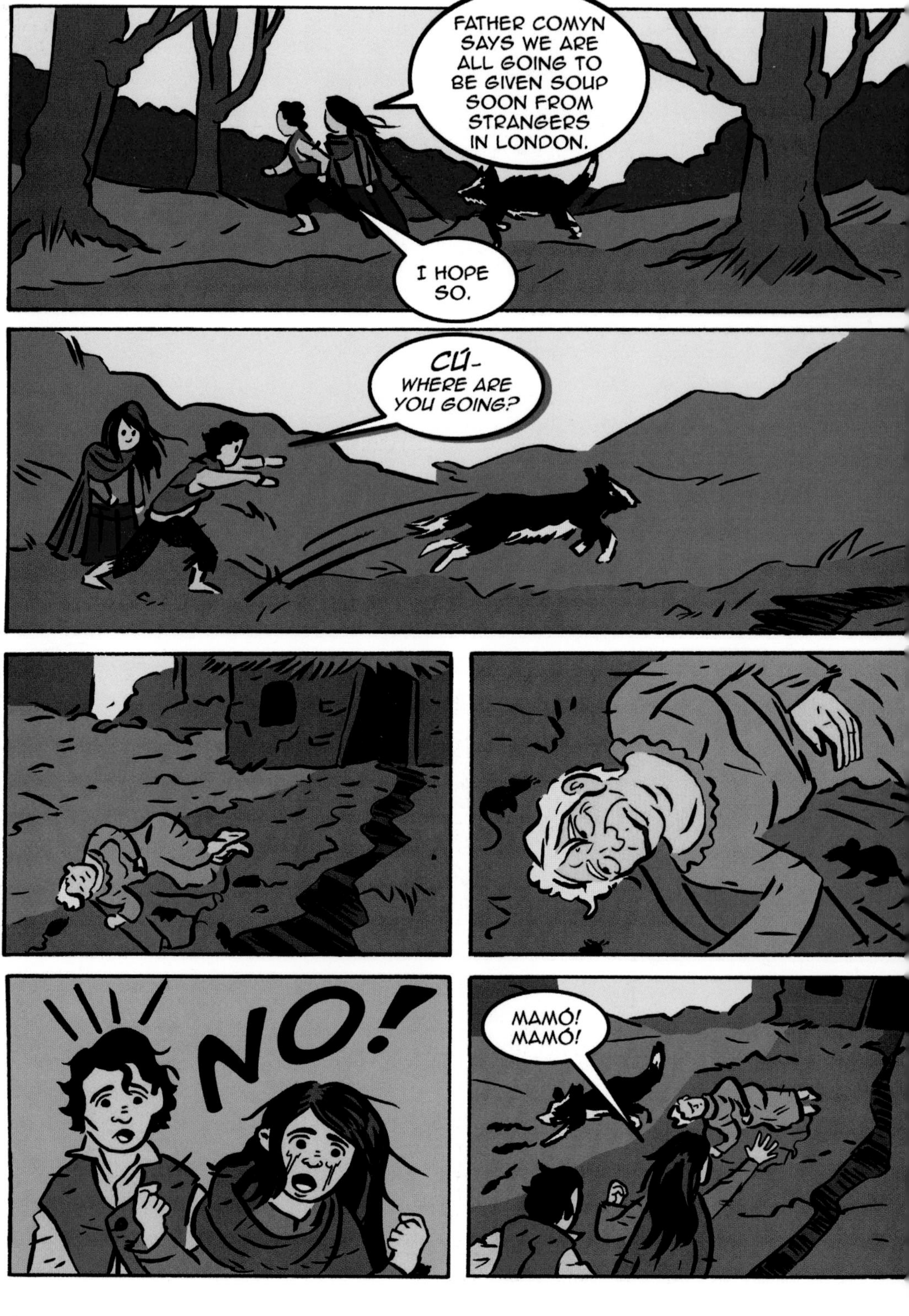
FATHER COMYN SAYS WE ARE ALL GOING TO BE GIVEN SOUP SOON FROM STRANGERS IN LONDON.
I HOPE SO.
CÚ- WHERE ARE YOU GOING?
NO!
MAMÓ! MAMÓ!

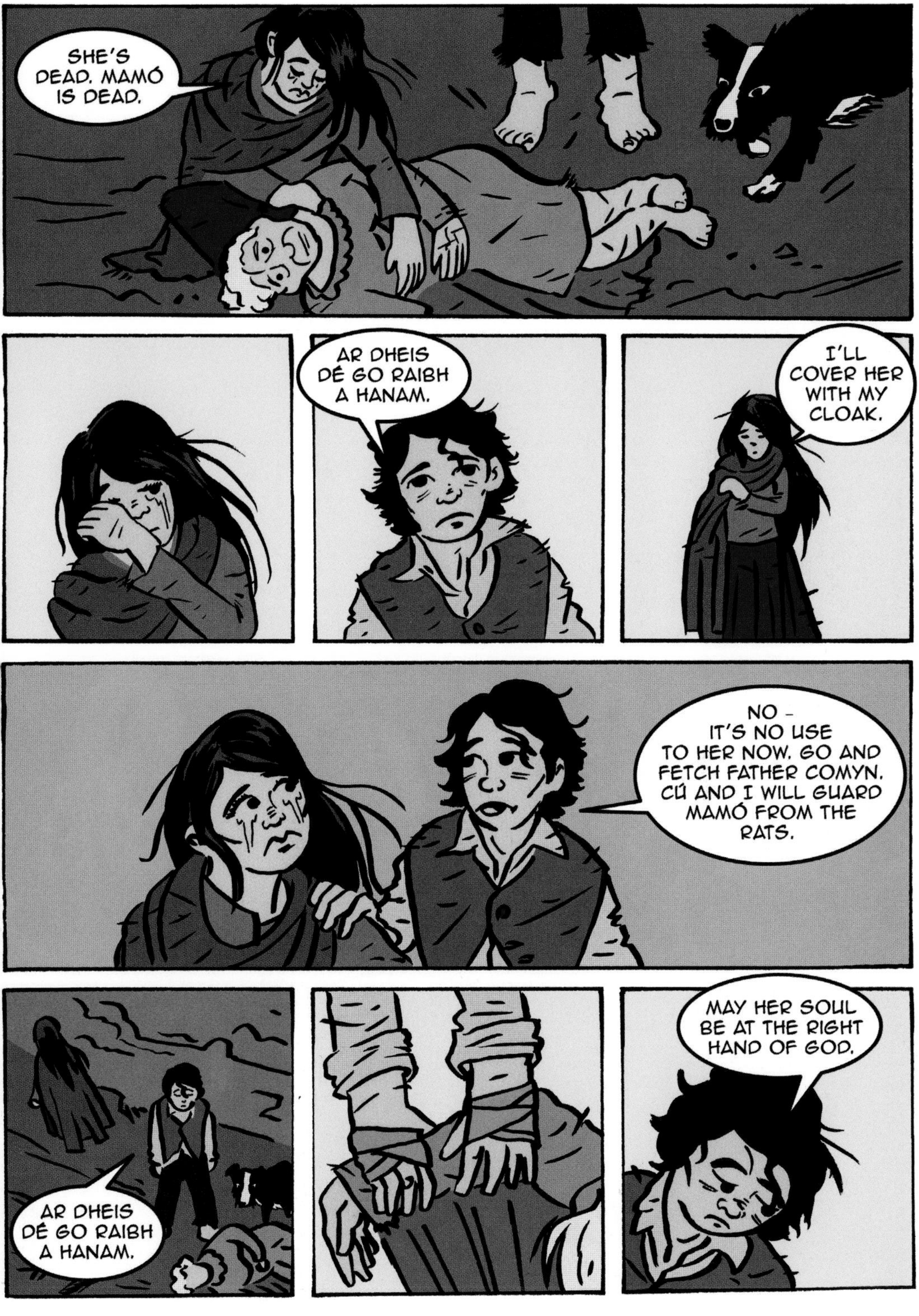
SHE'S DEAD. MAMÓ IS DEAD.
AR DHEIS DÉ GO RAIBH A HANAM.
I'LL COVER HER WITH MY CLOAK.
NO – IT'S NO USE TO HER NOW. GO AND FETCH FATHER COMYN. CÚ AND I WILL GUARD MAMÓ FROM THE RATS.
AR DHEIS DÉ GO RAIBH A HANAM.
MAY HER SOUL BE AT THE RIGHT HAND OF GOD.

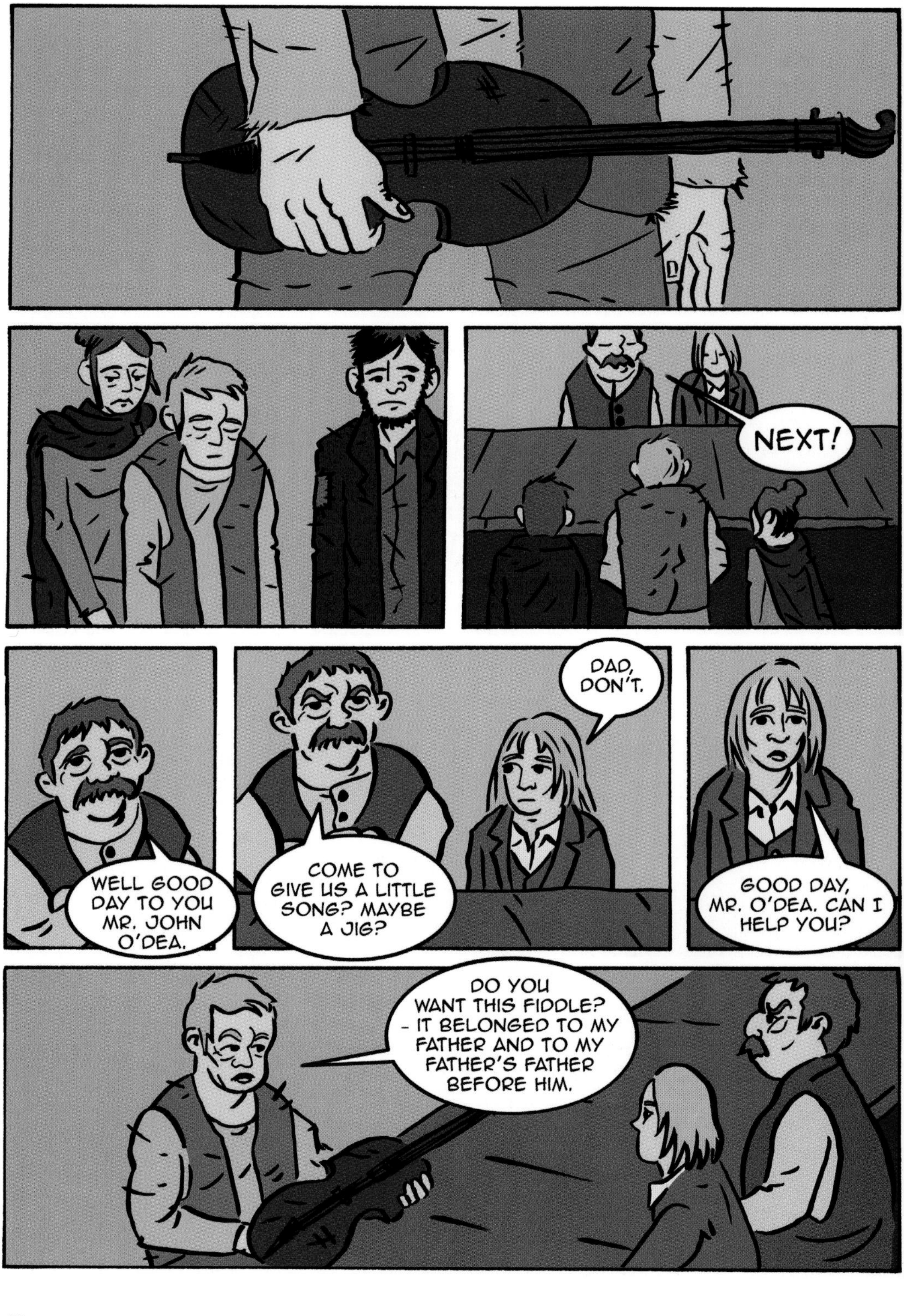
NEXT!
WELL GOOD DAY TO YOU MR. JOHN O'DEA.
COME TO GIVE US A LITTLE SONG? MAYBE A JIG?
DAD, DON'T.
GOOD DAY, MR. O'DEA. CAN I HELP YOU?
DO YOU WANT THIS FIDDLE? - IT BELONGED TO MY FATHER AND TO MY FATHER'S FATHER BEFORE HIM.

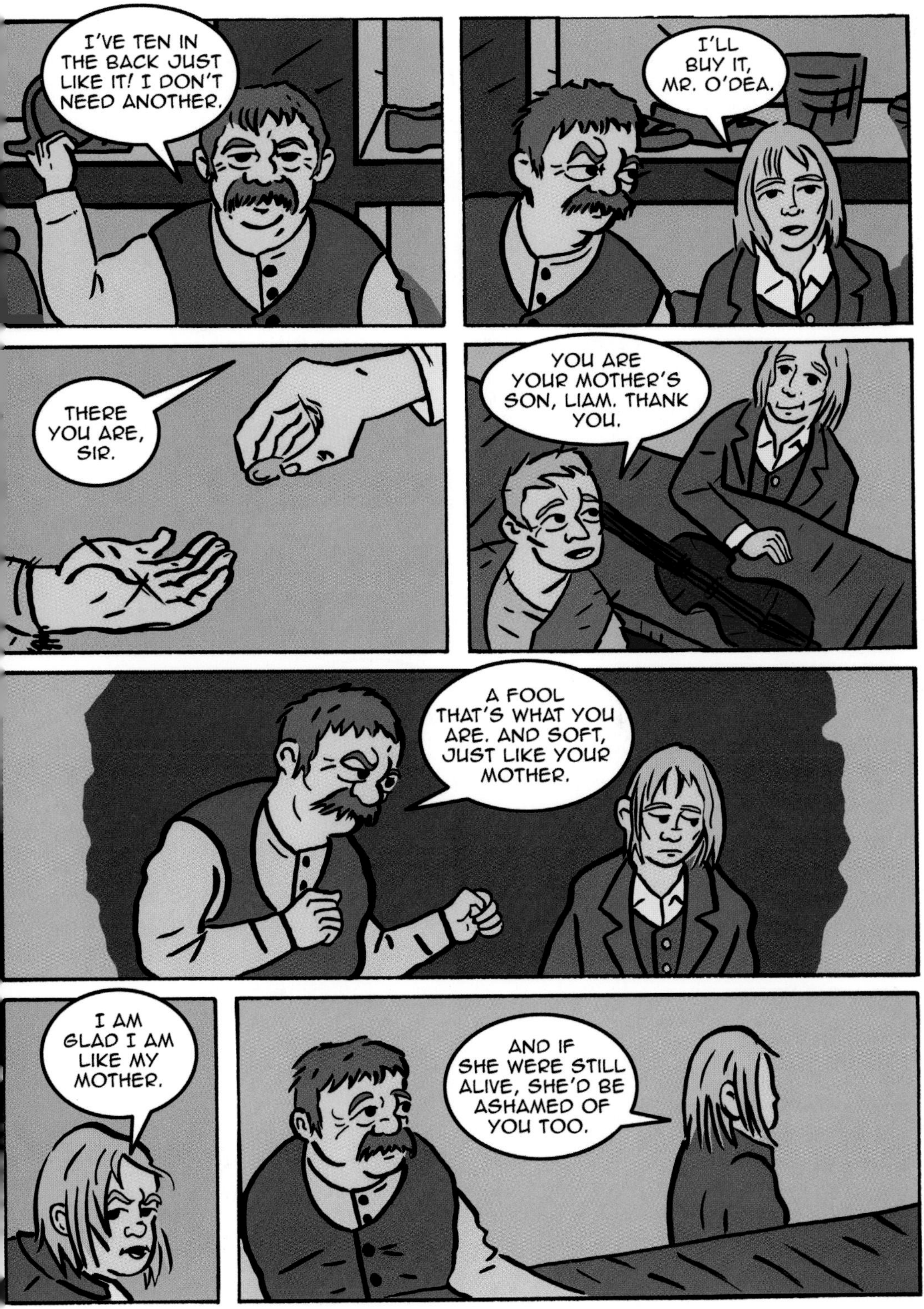
I'VE TEN IN THE BACK JUST LIKE IT! I DON'T NEED ANOTHER.
I'LL BUY IT, MR. O'DEA.
THERE YOU ARE, SIR.
YOU ARE YOUR MOTHER'S SON, LIAM. THANK YOU.
A FOOL THAT'S WHAT YOU ARE. AND SOFT, JUST LIKE YOUR MOTHER.
I AM GLAD I AM LIKE MY MOTHER.
AND IF SHE WERE STILL ALIVE, SHE'D BE ASHAMED OF YOU TOO.

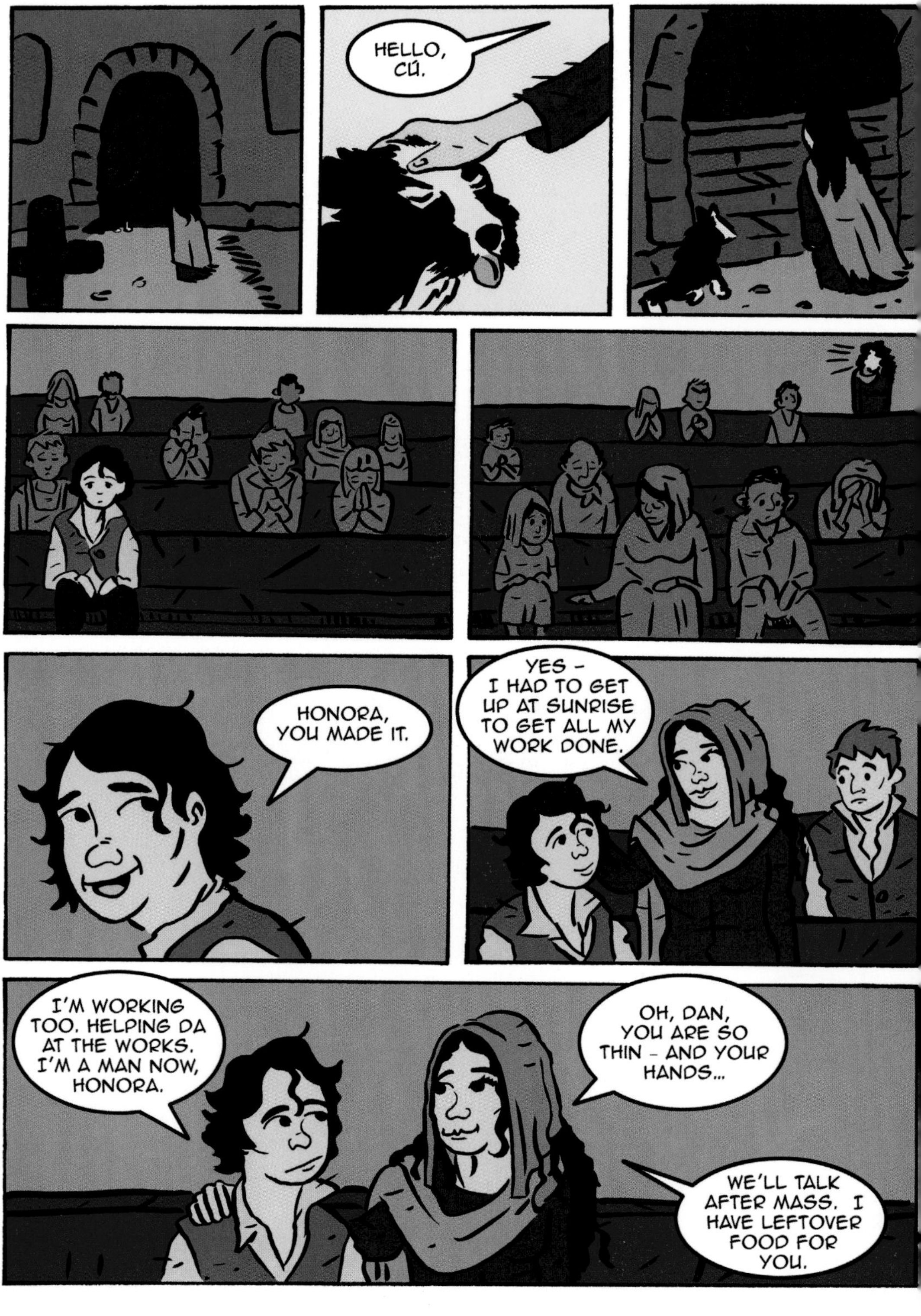
HELLO, CÚ.
HONORA, YOU MADE IT.
YES – I HAD TO GET UP AT SUNRISE TO GET ALL MY WORK DONE.
I'M WORKING TOO. HELPING DA AT THE WORKS. I'M A MAN NOW, HONORA.
OH, DAN, YOU ARE SO THIN – AND YOUR HANDS...
WE'LL TALK AFTER MASS. I HAVE LEFTOVER FOOD FOR YOU.

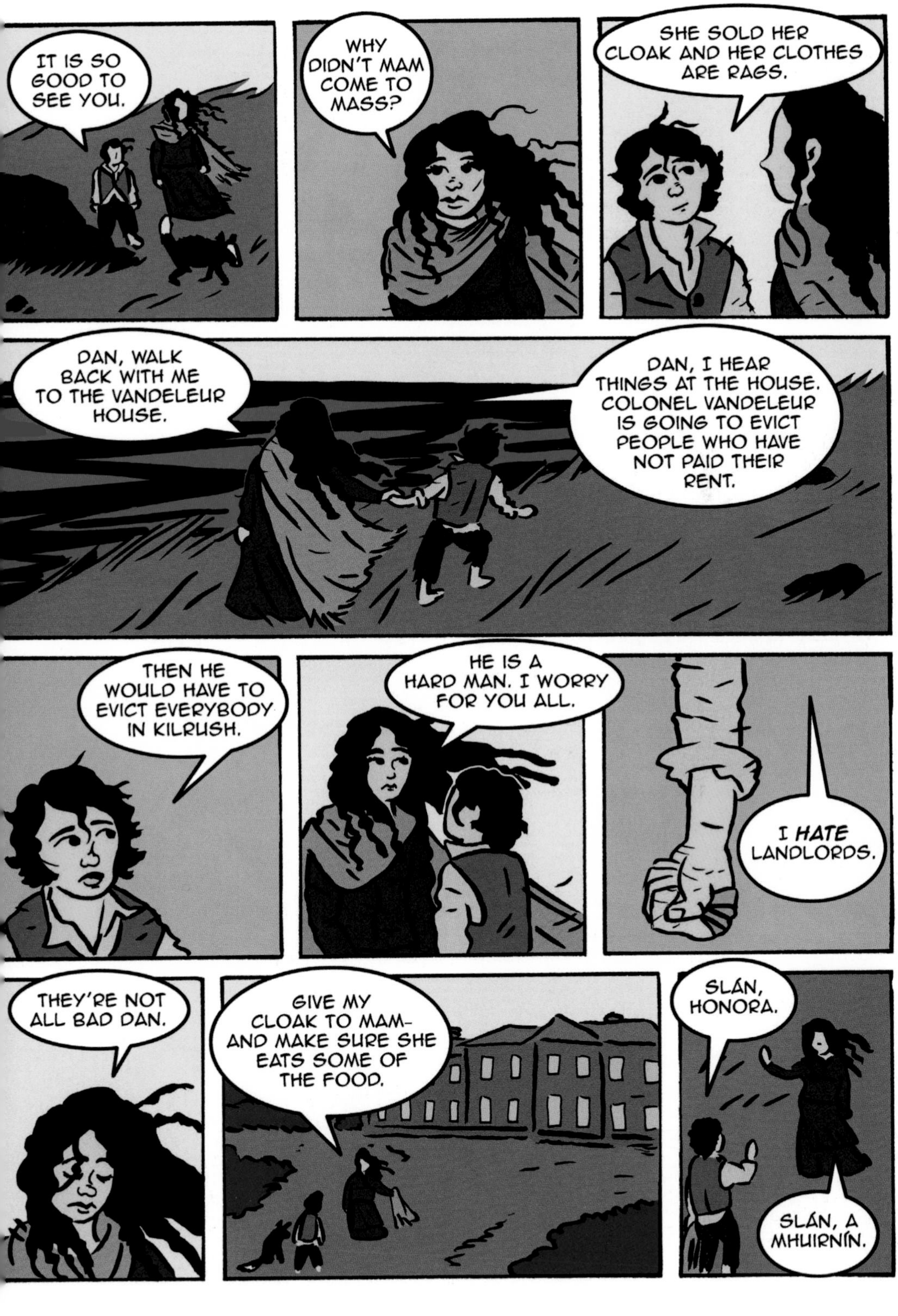
IT IS SO GOOD TO SEE YOU.
WHY DIDN'T MAM COME TO MASS?
SHE SOLD HER CLOAK AND HER CLOTHES ARE RAGS.
DAN, WALK BACK WITH ME TO THE VANDELEUR HOUSE.
DAN, I HEAR THINGS AT THE HOUSE. COLONEL VANDELEUR IS GOING TO EVICT PEOPLE WHO HAVE NOT PAID THEIR RENT.
THEN HE WOULD HAVE TO EVICT EVERYBODY IN KILRUSH.
HE IS A HARD MAN. I WORRY FOR YOU ALL.
I *HATE* LANDLORDS.
THEY'RE NOT ALL BAD DAN.
GIVE MY CLOAK TO MAM- AND MAKE SURE SHE EATS SOME OF THE FOOD.
SLÁN, HONORA.
SLÁN, A MHUIRNÍN.

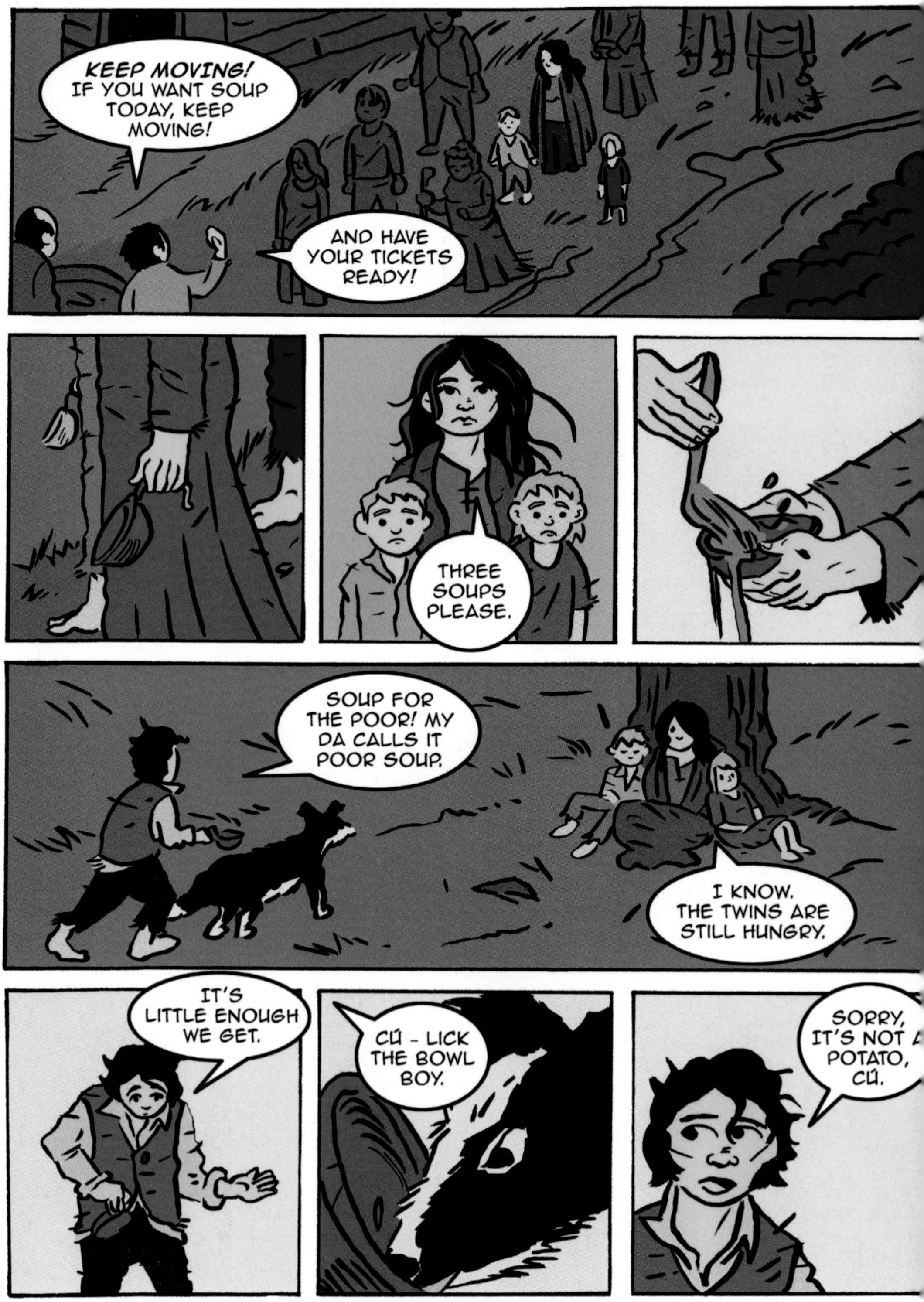
KEEP MOVING! IF YOU WANT SOUP TODAY, KEEP MOVING!
AND HAVE YOUR TICKETS READY!
THREE SOUPS PLEASE.
SOUP FOR THE POOR! MY DA CALLS IT POOR SOUP.
I KNOW. THE TWINS ARE STILL HUNGRY.
IT'S LITTLE ENOUGH WE GET.
CÚ - LICK THE BOWL BOY.
SORRY, IT'S NOT A POTATO, CÚ.

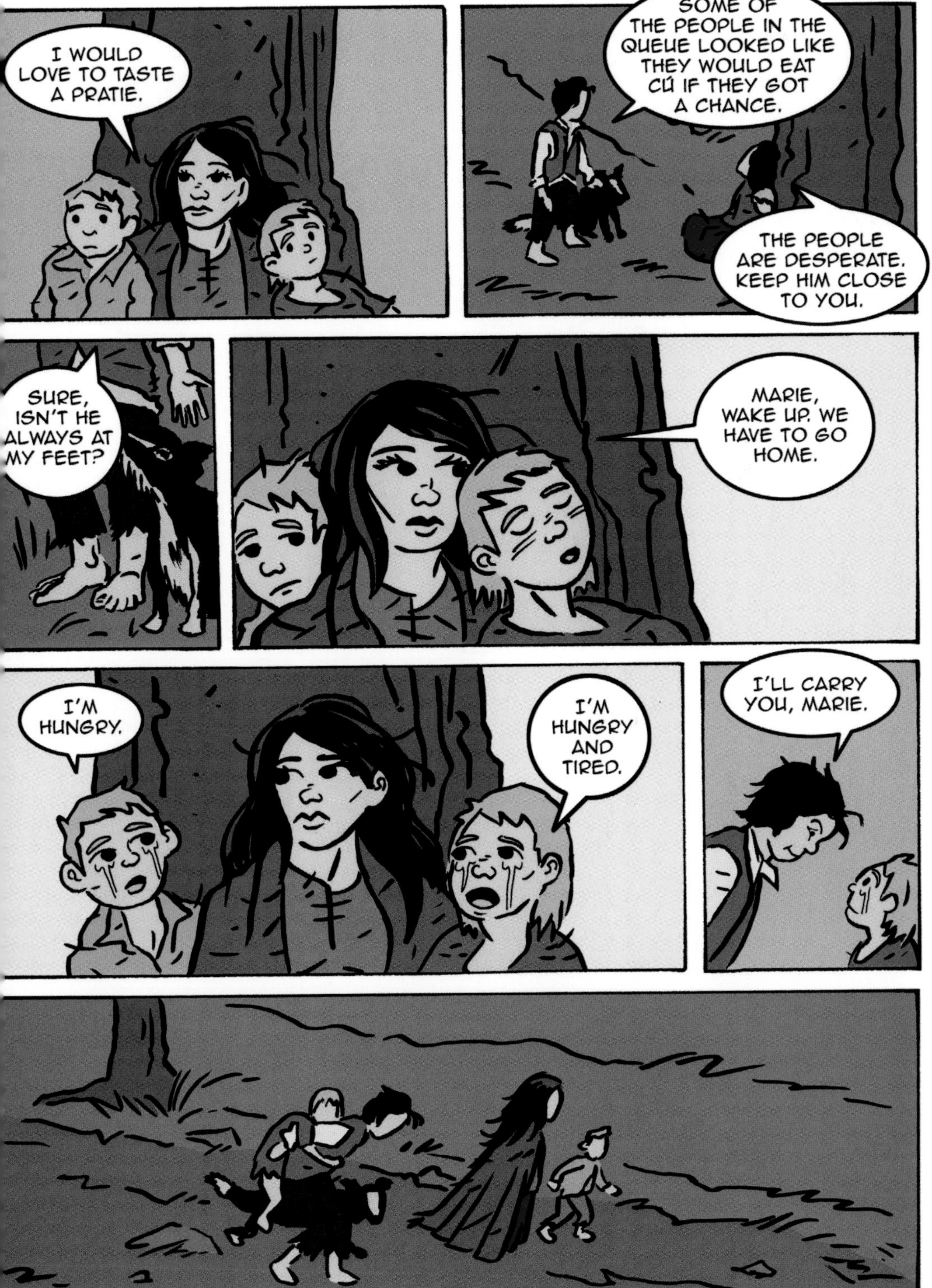
I WOULD LOVE TO TASTE A PRATIE.
SOME OF THE PEOPLE IN THE QUEUE LOOKED LIKE THEY WOULD EAT CÚ IF THEY GOT A CHANCE.
THE PEOPLE ARE DESPERATE. KEEP HIM CLOSE TO YOU.
SURE, ISN'T HE ALWAYS AT MY FEET?
MARIE, WAKE UP. WE HAVE TO GO HOME.
I'M HUNGRY.
I'M HUNGRY AND TIRED.
I'LL CARRY YOU, MARIE.

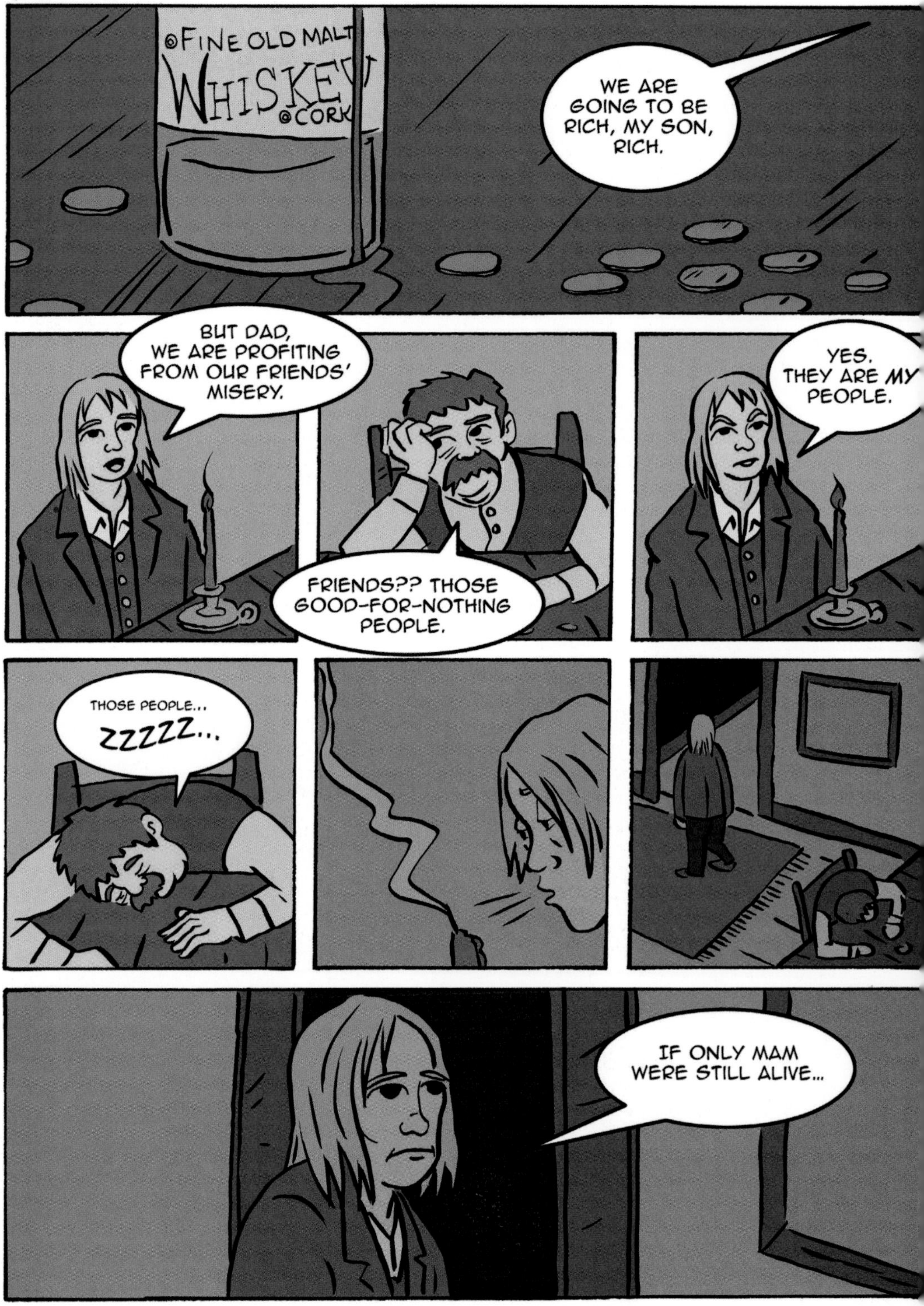

©FINE OLD MALT
WHISKEY
©CORK
WE ARE GOING TO BE RICH, MY SON, RICH.
BUT DAD, WE ARE PROFITING FROM OUR FRIENDS' MISERY.
FRIENDS?? THOSE GOOD-FOR-NOTHING PEOPLE.
YES. THEY ARE *MY* PEOPLE.
THOSE PEOPLE... ZZZZZ...
IF ONLY MAM WERE STILL ALIVE...

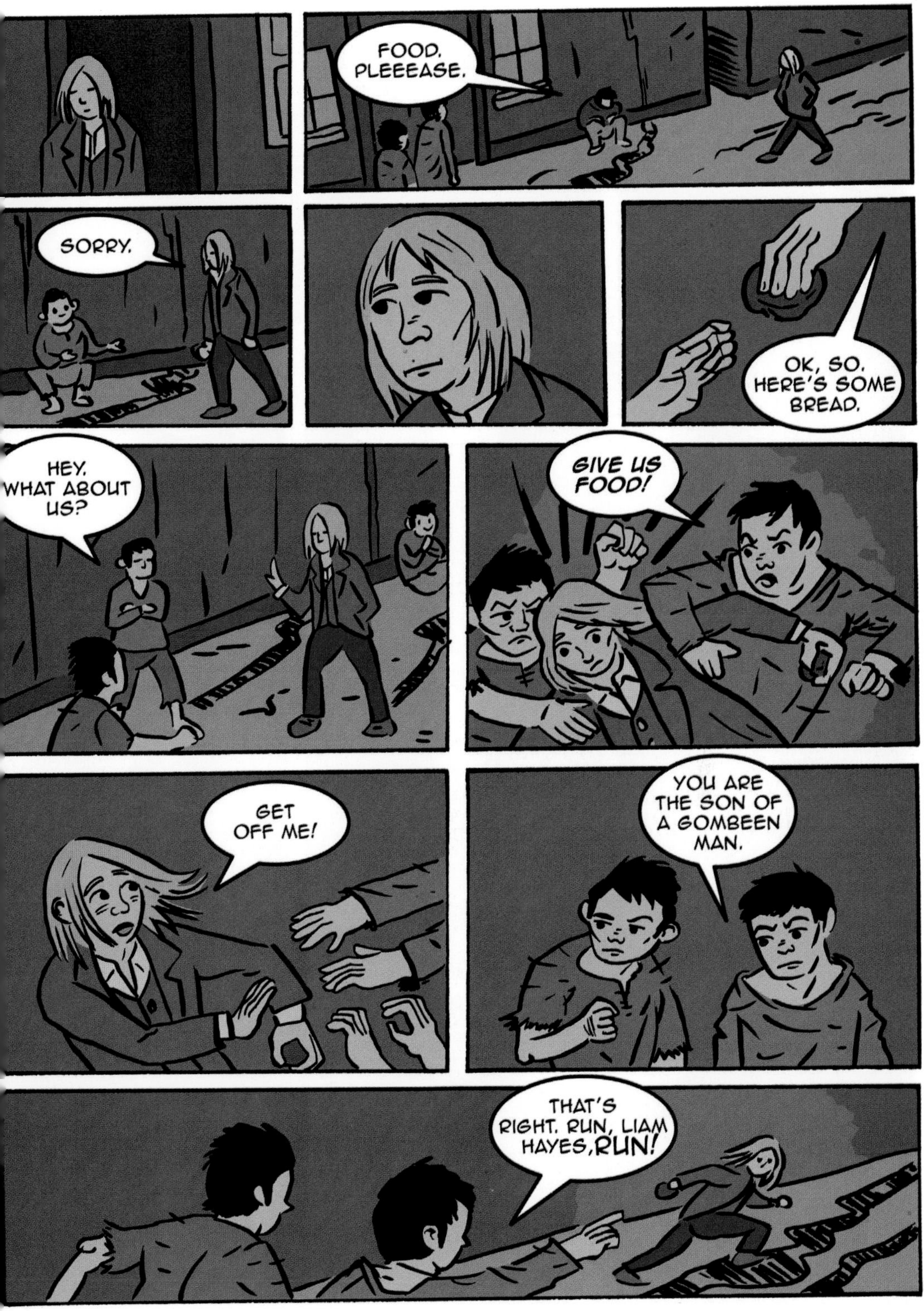
FOOD. PLEEEASE.
SORRY.
OK, SO. HERE'S SOME BREAD.
HEY. WHAT ABOUT US?
GIVE US FOOD!
GET OFF ME!
YOU ARE THE SON OF A GOMBEEN MAN.
THAT'S RIGHT. RUN, LIAM HAYES, RUN!

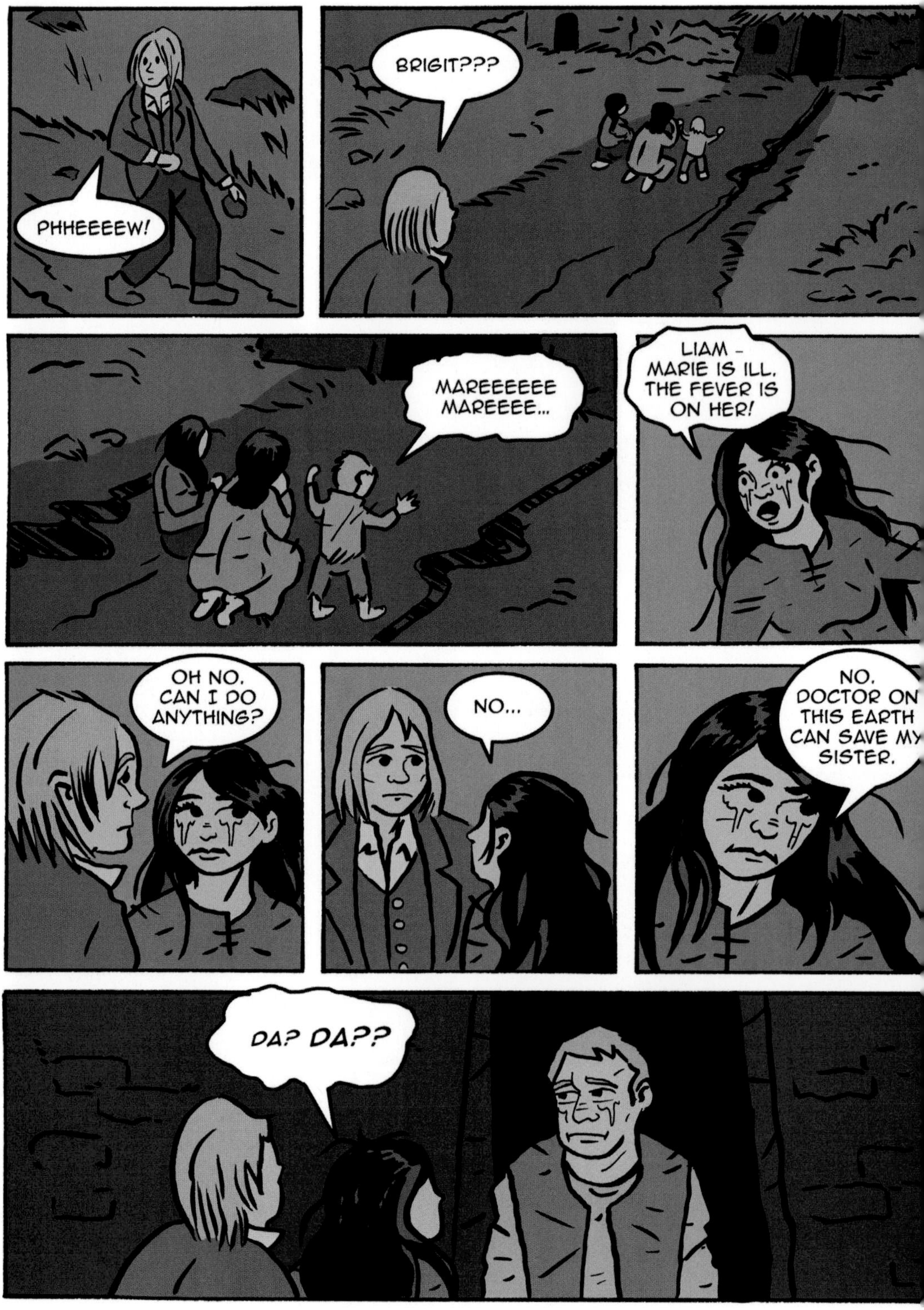
PHHEEEEW!
BRIGIT???
MAREEEEEE MAREEEE...
LIAM - MARIE IS ILL. THE FEVER IS ON HER!
OH NO. CAN I DO ANYTHING?
NO...
NO. DOCTOR ON THIS EARTH CAN SAVE MY SISTER.
DA? DA??

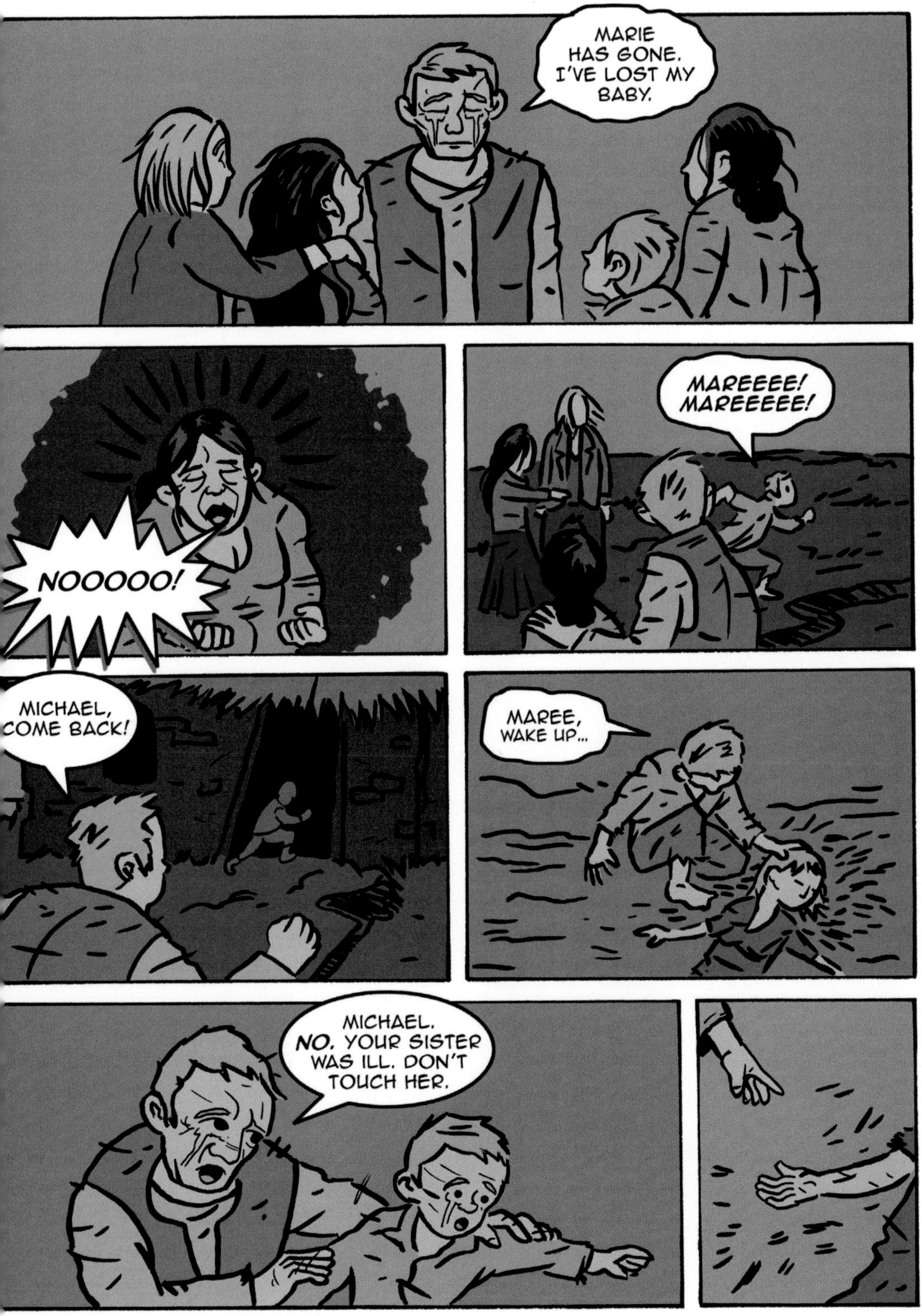
MARIE HAS GONE. I'VE LOST MY BABY.
NOOOOO!
MAREEEE! MAREEEEEE!
MICHAEL, COME BACK!
MAREE, WAKE UP...
MICHAEL. NO. YOUR SISTER WAS ILL. DON'T TOUCH HER.

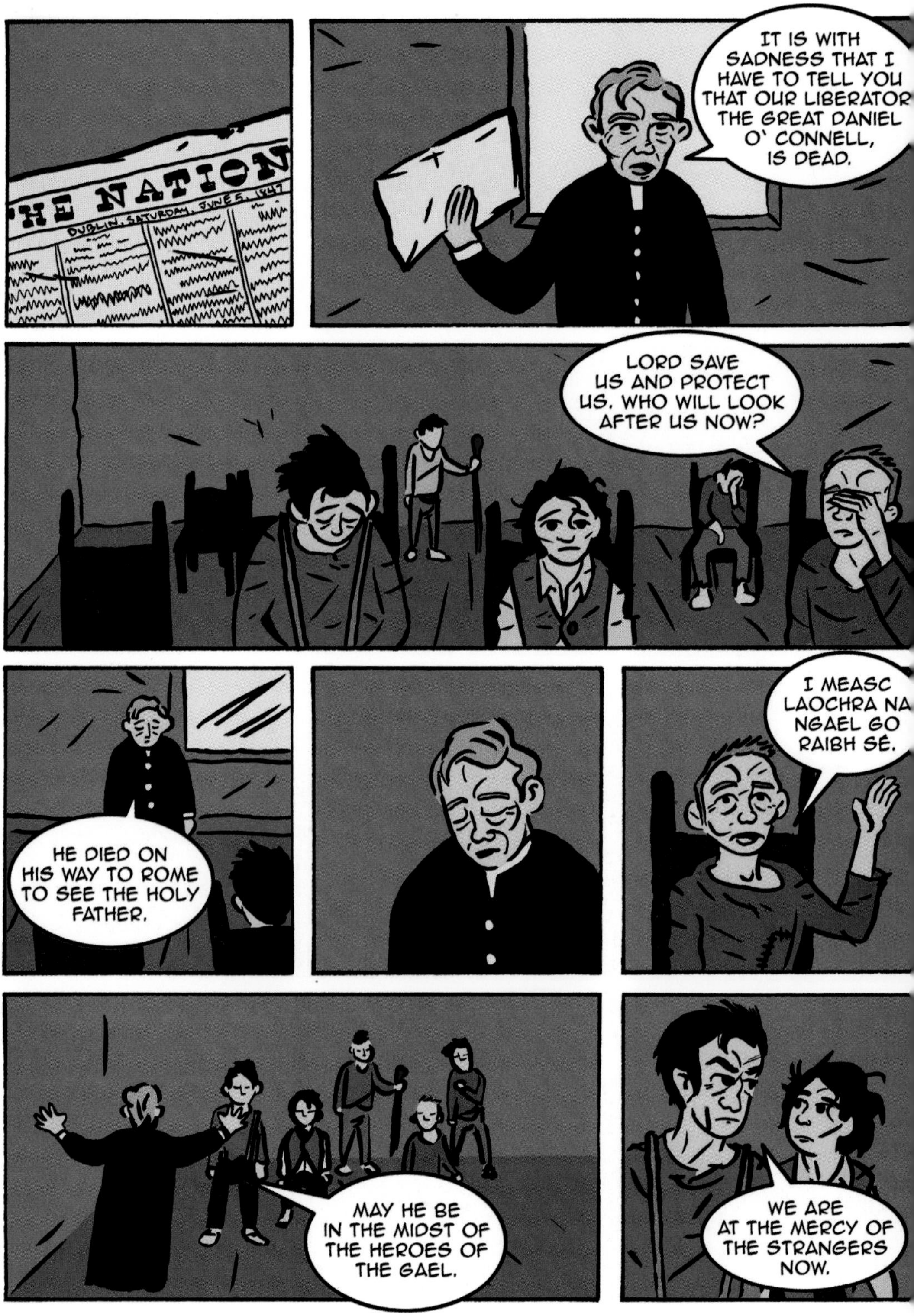
THE NATION
DUBLIN, SATURDAY, JUNE 5, 1847
IT IS WITH SADNESS THAT I HAVE TO TELL YOU THAT OUR LIBERATOR THE GREAT DANIEL O' CONNELL, IS DEAD.
LORD SAVE US AND PROTECT US. WHO WILL LOOK AFTER US NOW?
HE DIED ON HIS WAY TO ROME TO SEE THE HOLY FATHER.
I MEASC LAOCHRA NA NGAEL GO RAIBH SÉ.
MAY HE BE IN THE MIDST OF THE HEROES OF THE GAEL.
WE ARE AT THE MERCY OF THE STRANGERS NOW.

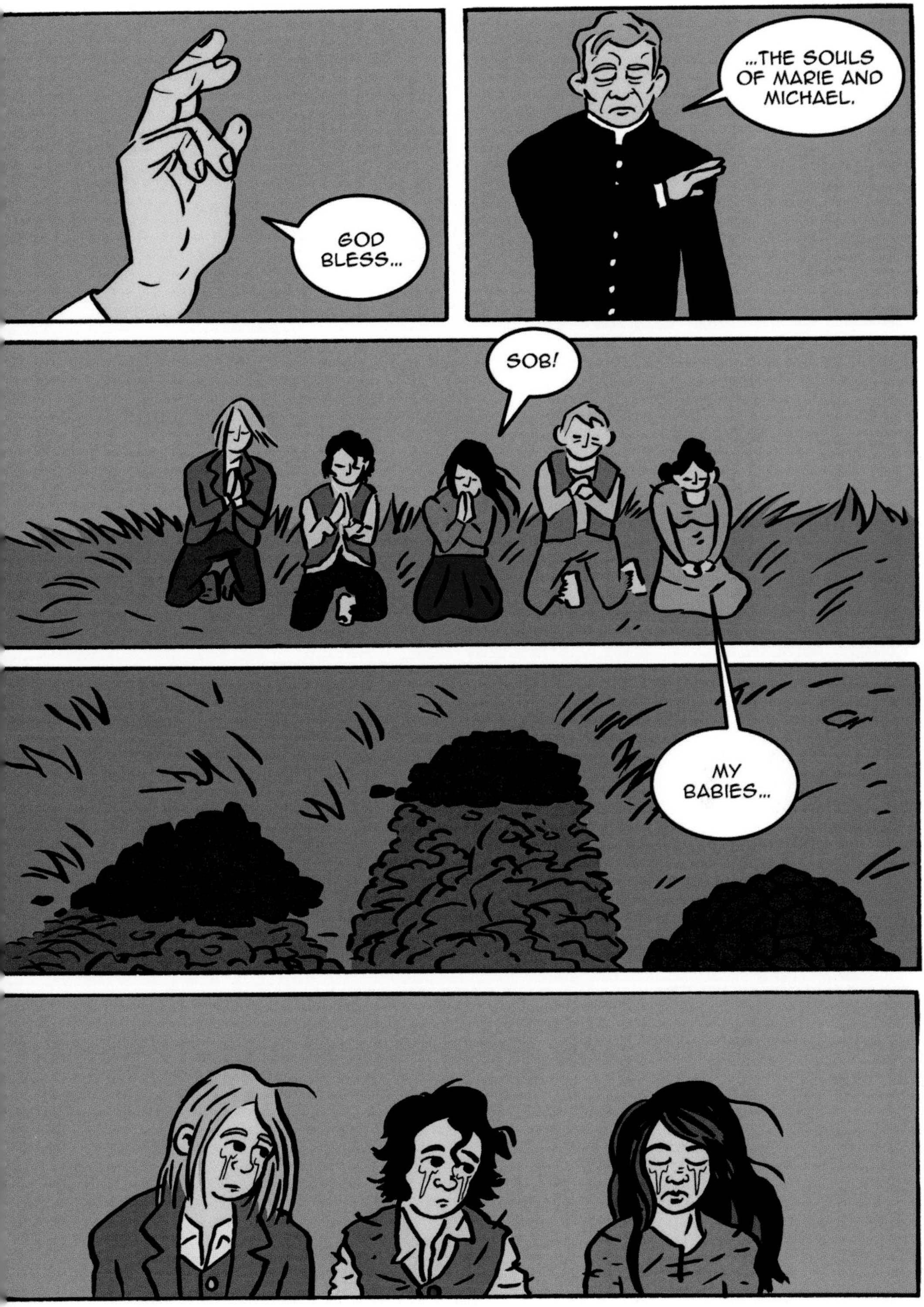
GOD BLESS...
...THE SOULS OF MARIE AND MICHAEL.
SOB!
MY BABIES...

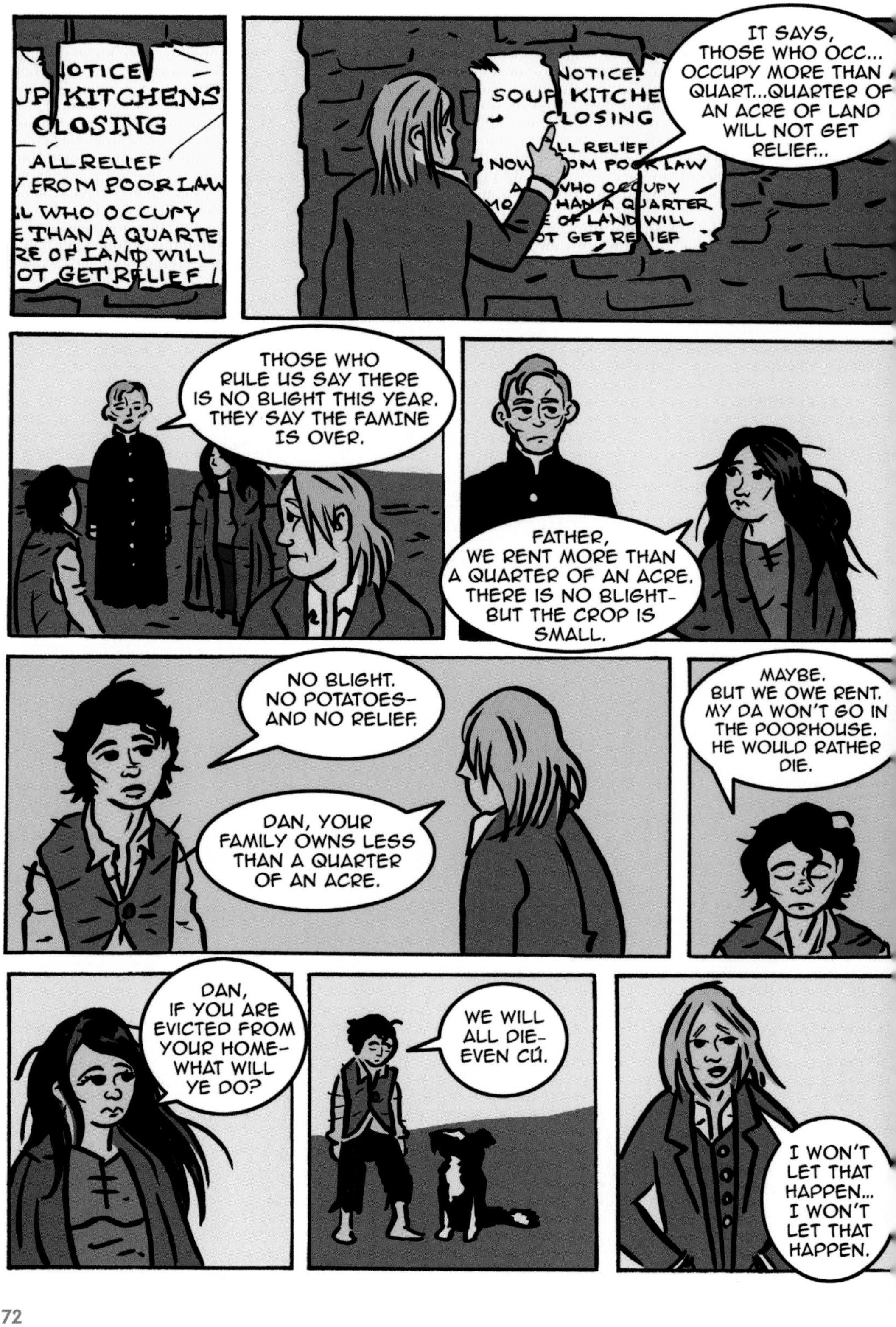
NOTICE
UP KITCHENS
CLOSING
ALL RELIEF
FROM POOR LAW
L WHO OCCUPY
E THAN A QUARTE
RE OF LAND WILL
OT GET RELIEF
IT SAYS, THOSE WHO OCC... OCCUPY MORE THAN QUART...QUARTER OF AN ACRE OF LAND WILL NOT GET RELIEF...
THOSE WHO RULE US SAY THERE IS NO BLIGHT THIS YEAR. THEY SAY THE FAMINE IS OVER.
FATHER, WE RENT MORE THAN A QUARTER OF AN ACRE. THERE IS NO BLIGHT- BUT THE CROP IS SMALL.
NO BLIGHT. NO POTATOES- AND NO RELIEF.
DAN, YOUR FAMILY OWNS LESS THAN A QUARTER OF AN ACRE.
MAYBE. BUT WE OWE RENT. MY DA WON'T GO IN THE POORHOUSE. HE WOULD RATHER DIE.
DAN, IF YOU ARE EVICTED FROM YOUR HOME- WHAT WILL YE DO?
WE WILL ALL DIE- EVEN CÚ.
I WON'T LET THAT HAPPEN... I WON'T LET THAT HAPPEN.

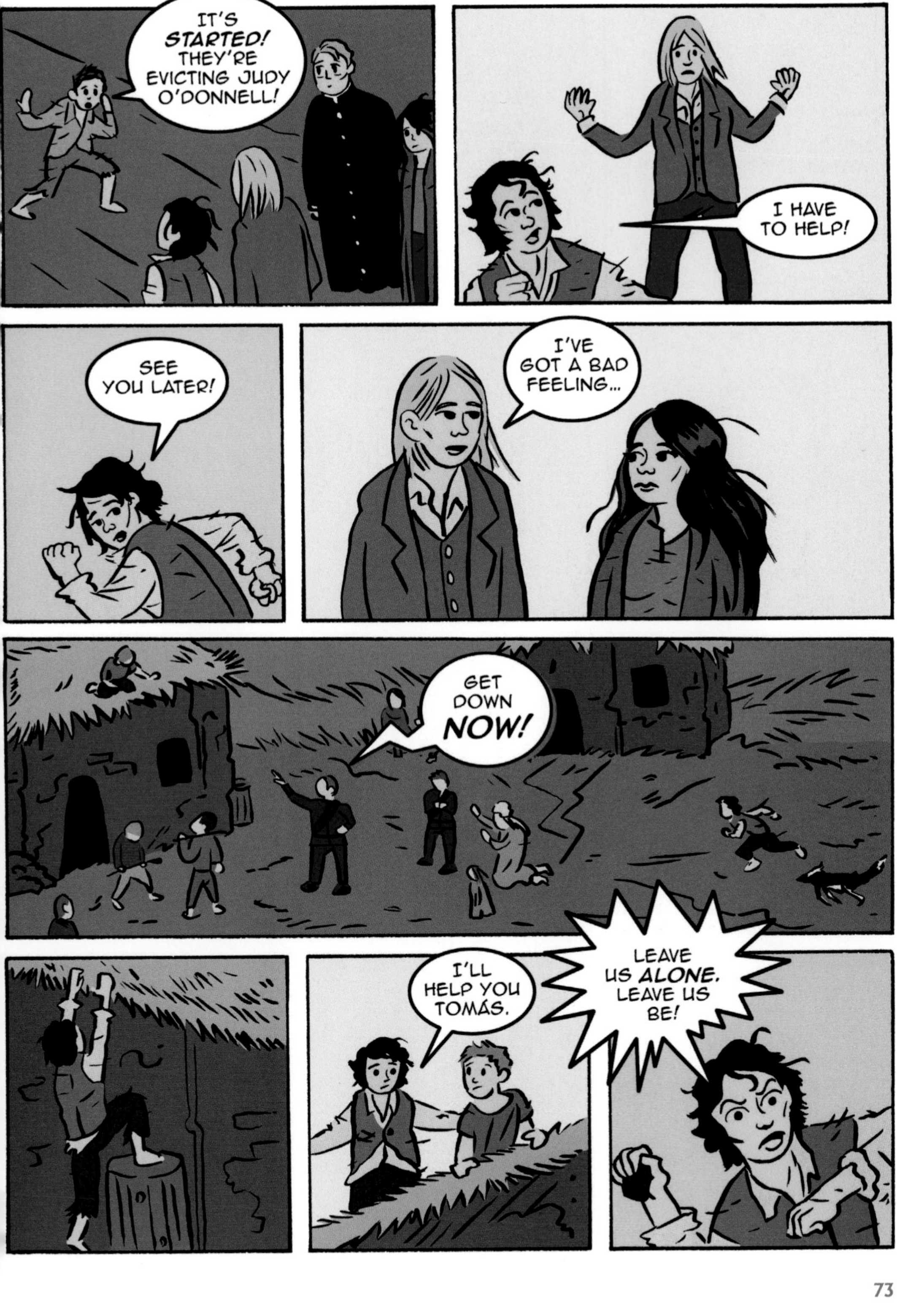
IT'S *STARTED!* THEY'RE EVICTING JUDY O'DONNELL!
I HAVE TO HELP!
SEE YOU LATER!
I'VE GOT A BAD FEELING...
GET DOWN **NOW!**
I'LL HELP YOU TOMÁS.
LEAVE US **ALONE.** LEAVE US BE!

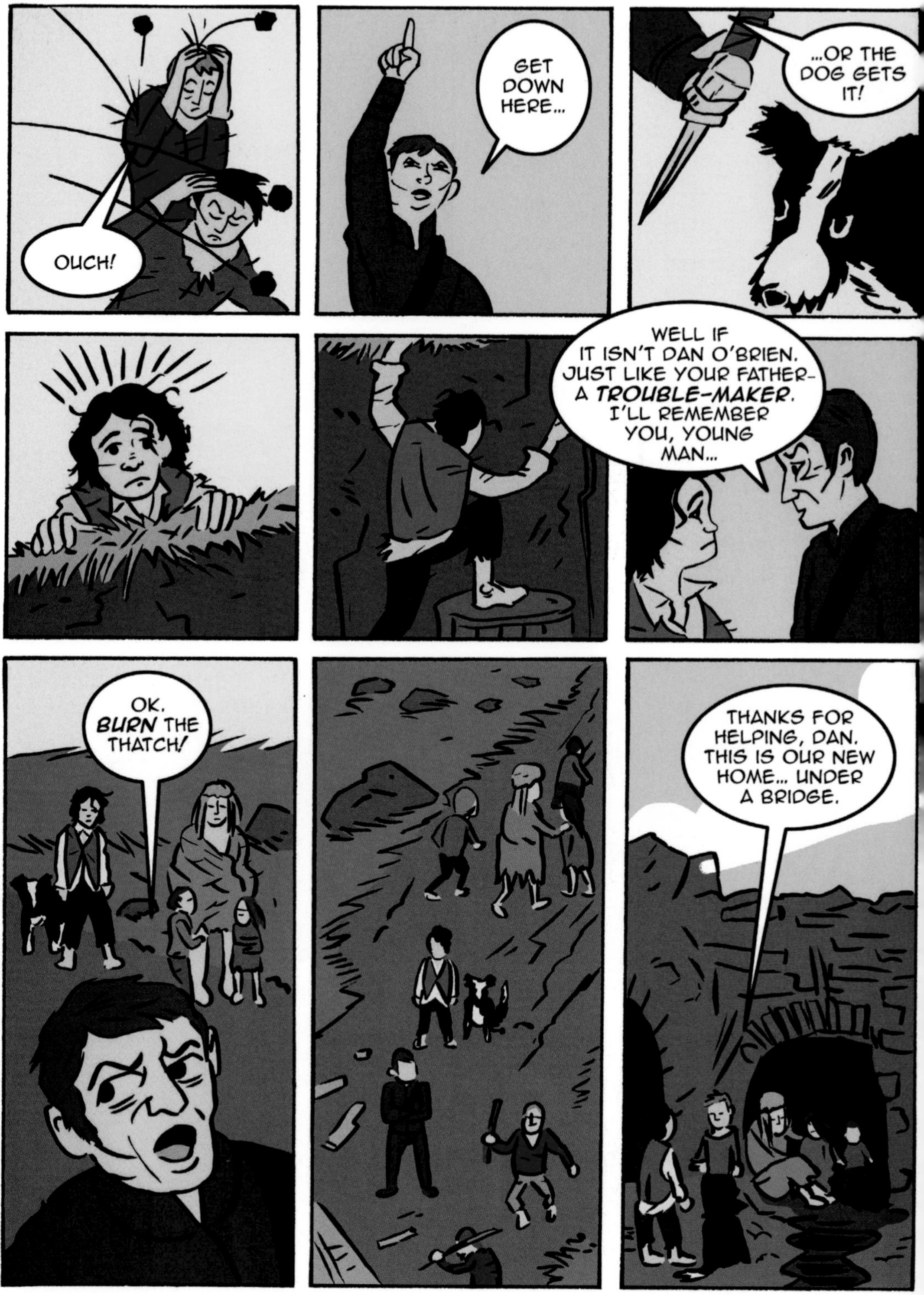
OUCH!
GET DOWN HERE...
...OR THE DOG GETS IT!
WELL IF IT ISN'T DAN O'BRIEN. JUST LIKE YOUR FATHER- A TROUBLE-MAKER. I'LL REMEMBER YOU, YOUNG MAN...
OK. BURN THE THATCH!
THANKS FOR HELPING, DAN. THIS IS OUR NEW HOME... UNDER A BRIDGE.

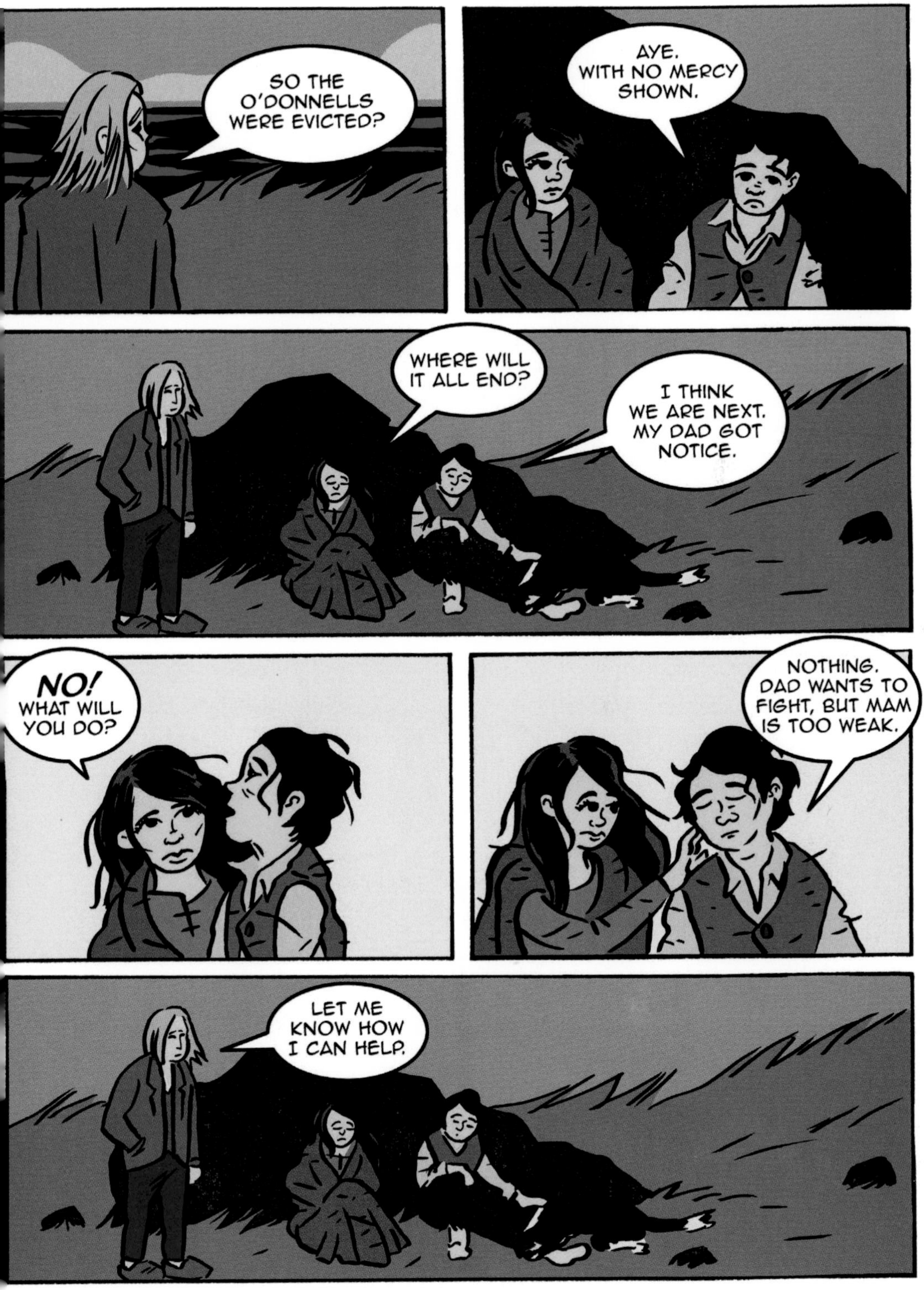

SO THE O'DONNELLS WERE EVICTED?
AYE. WITH NO MERCY SHOWN.
WHERE WILL IT ALL END?
I THINK WE ARE NEXT. MY DAD GOT NOTICE.
NO! WHAT WILL YOU DO?
NOTHING. DAD WANTS TO FIGHT, BUT MAM IS TOO WEAK.
LET ME KNOW HOW I CAN HELP.

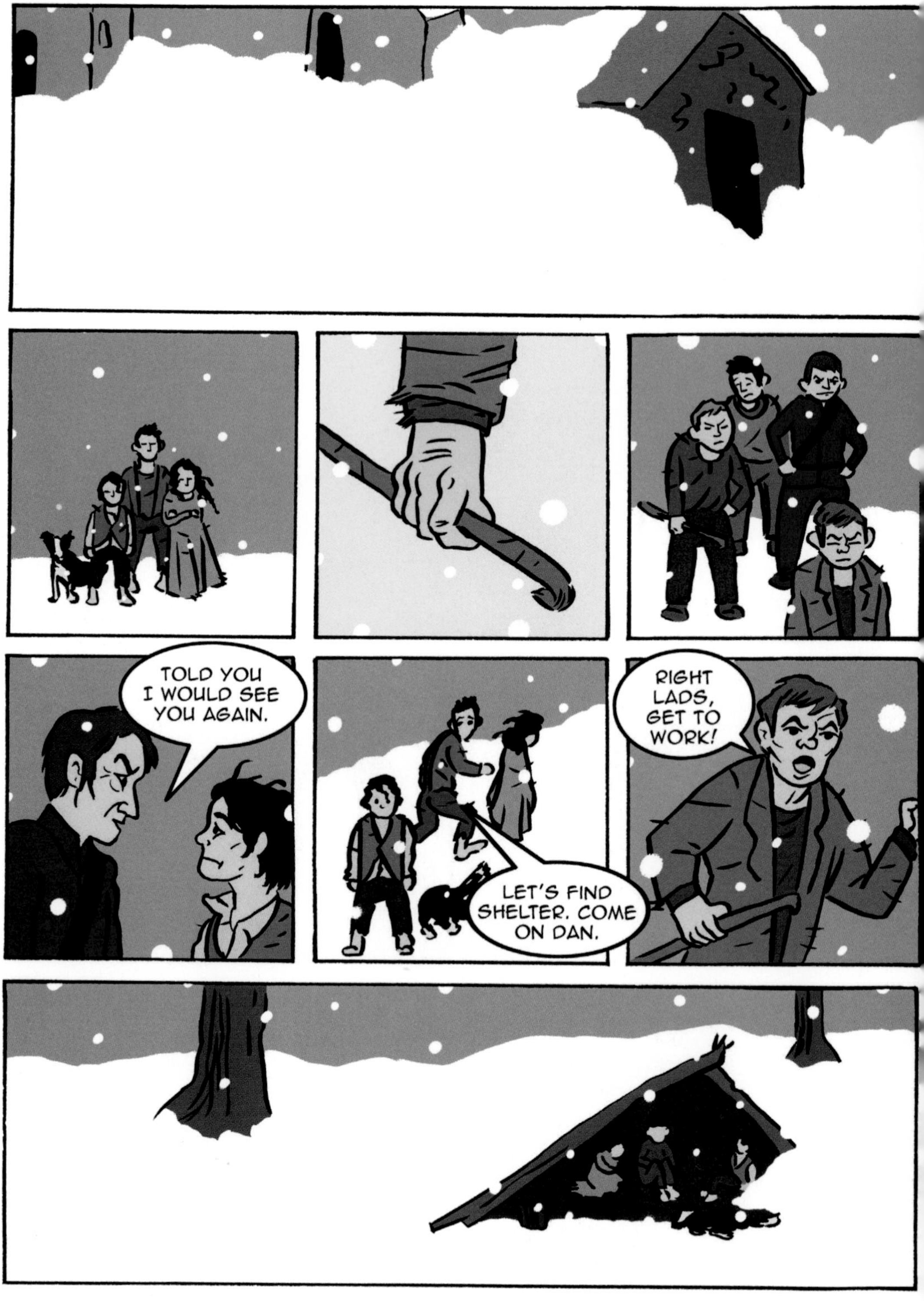
TOLD YOU I WOULD SEE YOU AGAIN.
LET'S FIND SHELTER. COME ON DAN.
RIGHT LADS, GET TO WORK!

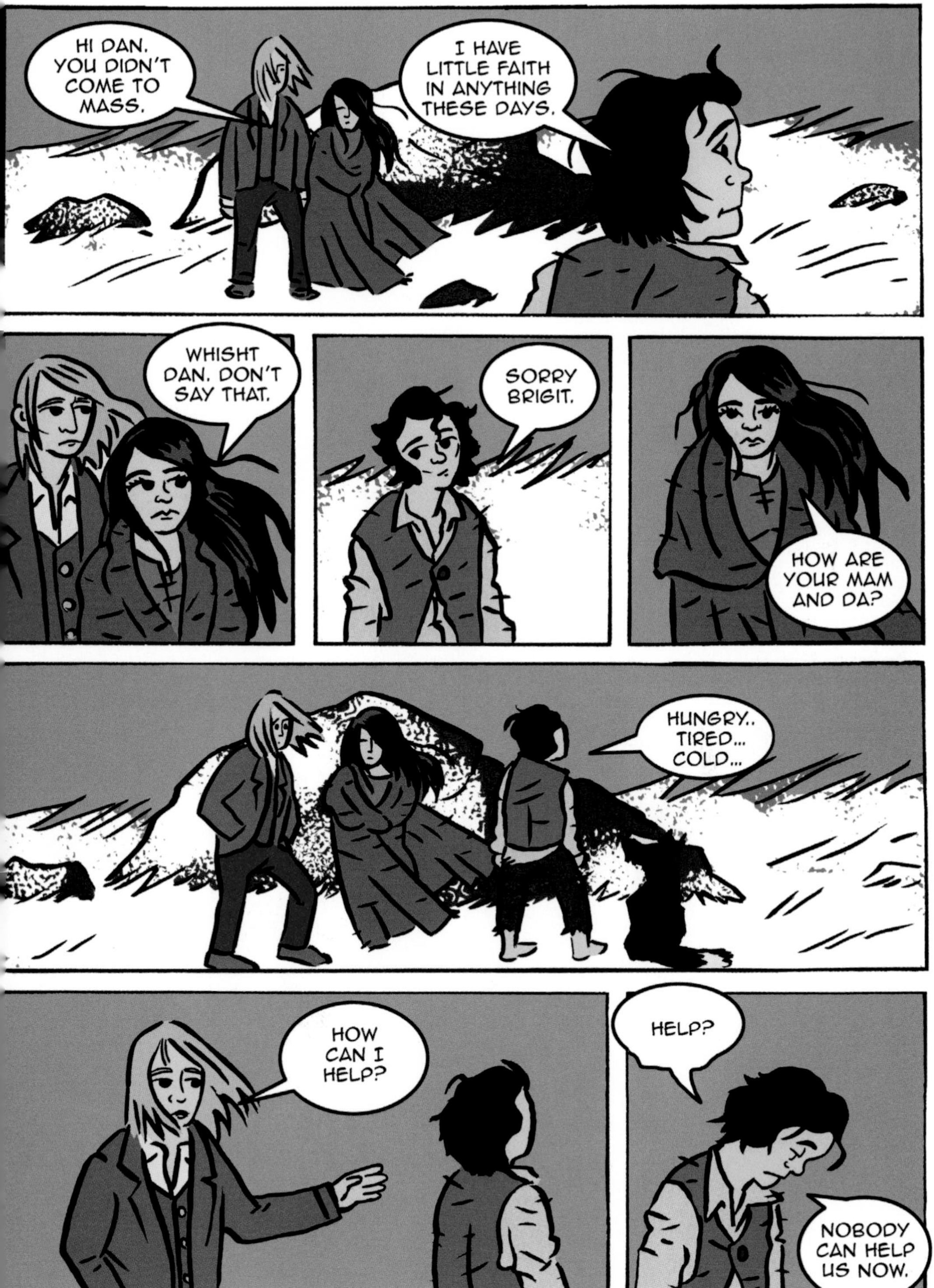
HI DAN. YOU DIDN'T COME TO MASS.
I HAVE LITTLE FAITH IN ANYTHING THESE DAYS.
WHISHT DAN. DON'T SAY THAT.
SORRY BRIGIT.
HOW ARE YOUR MAM AND DA?
HUNGRY.. TIRED... COLD...
HOW CAN I HELP?
HELP?
NOBODY CAN HELP US NOW.

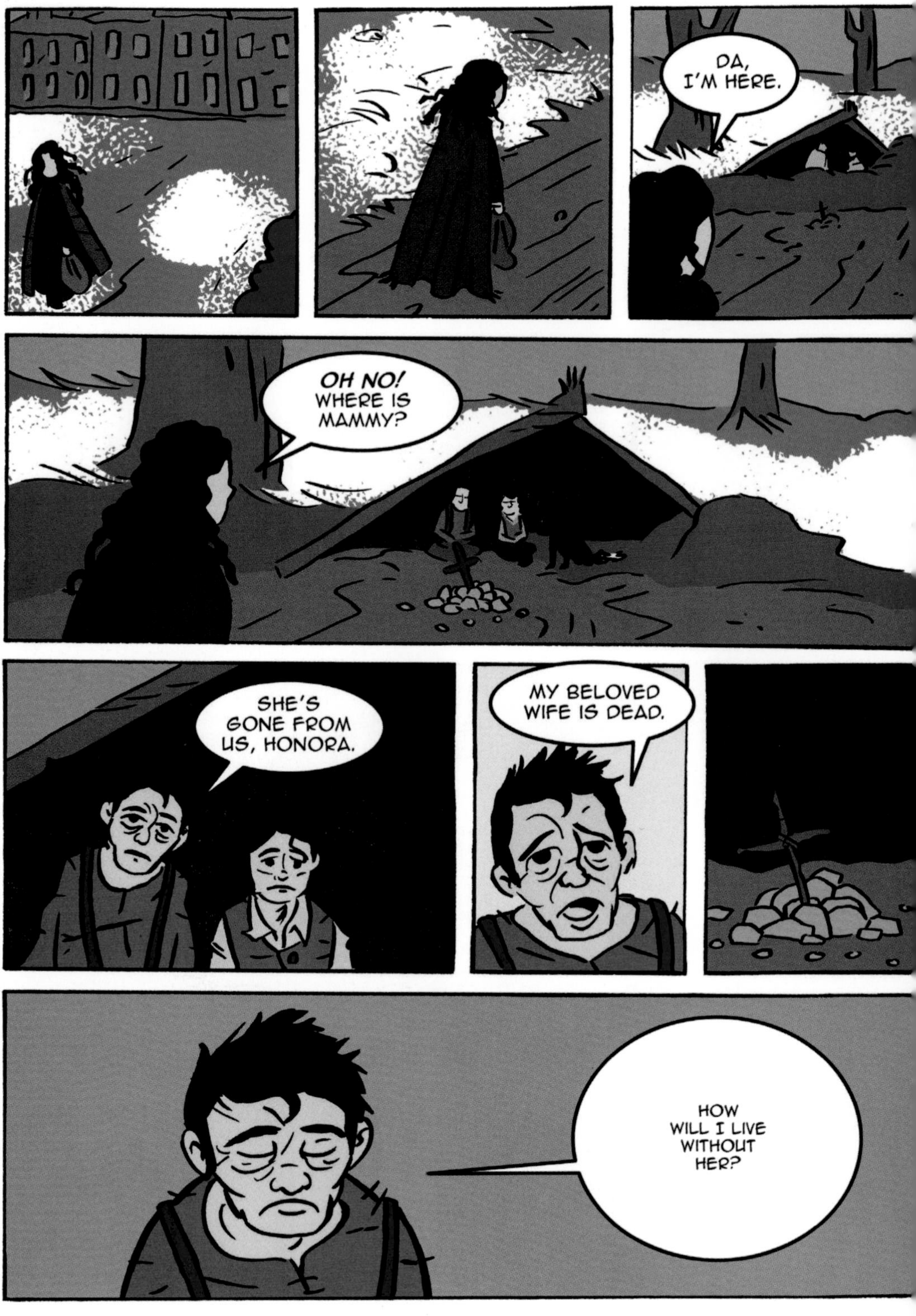
DA, I'M HERE.
OH NO! WHERE IS MAMMY?
SHE'S GONE FROM US, HONORA.
MY BELOVED WIFE IS DEAD.
HOW WILL I LIVE WITHOUT HER?

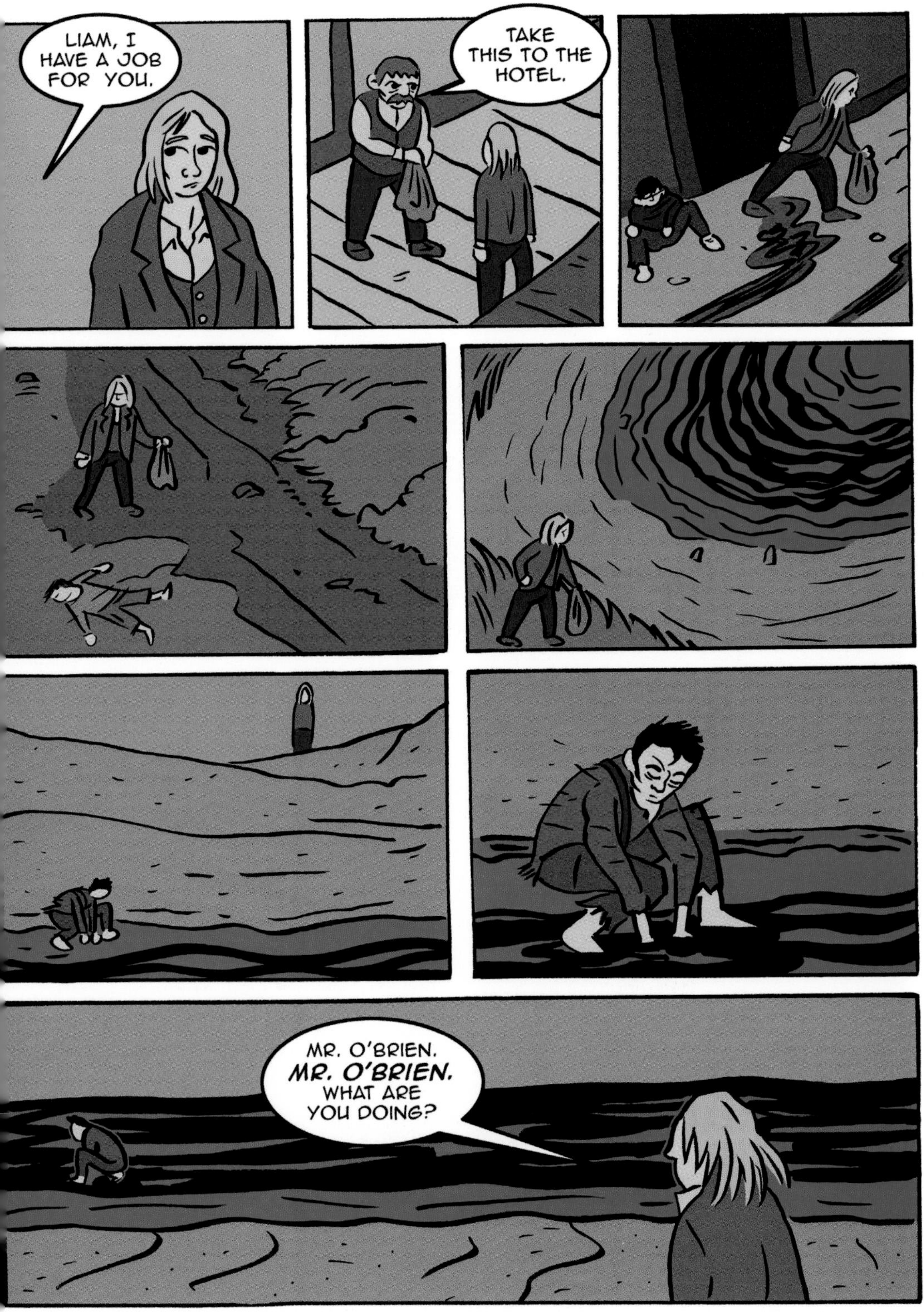
LIAM, I HAVE A JOB FOR YOU.
TAKE THIS TO THE HOTEL.
MR. O'BRIEN. ***MR. O'BRIEN.*** WHAT ARE YOU DOING?

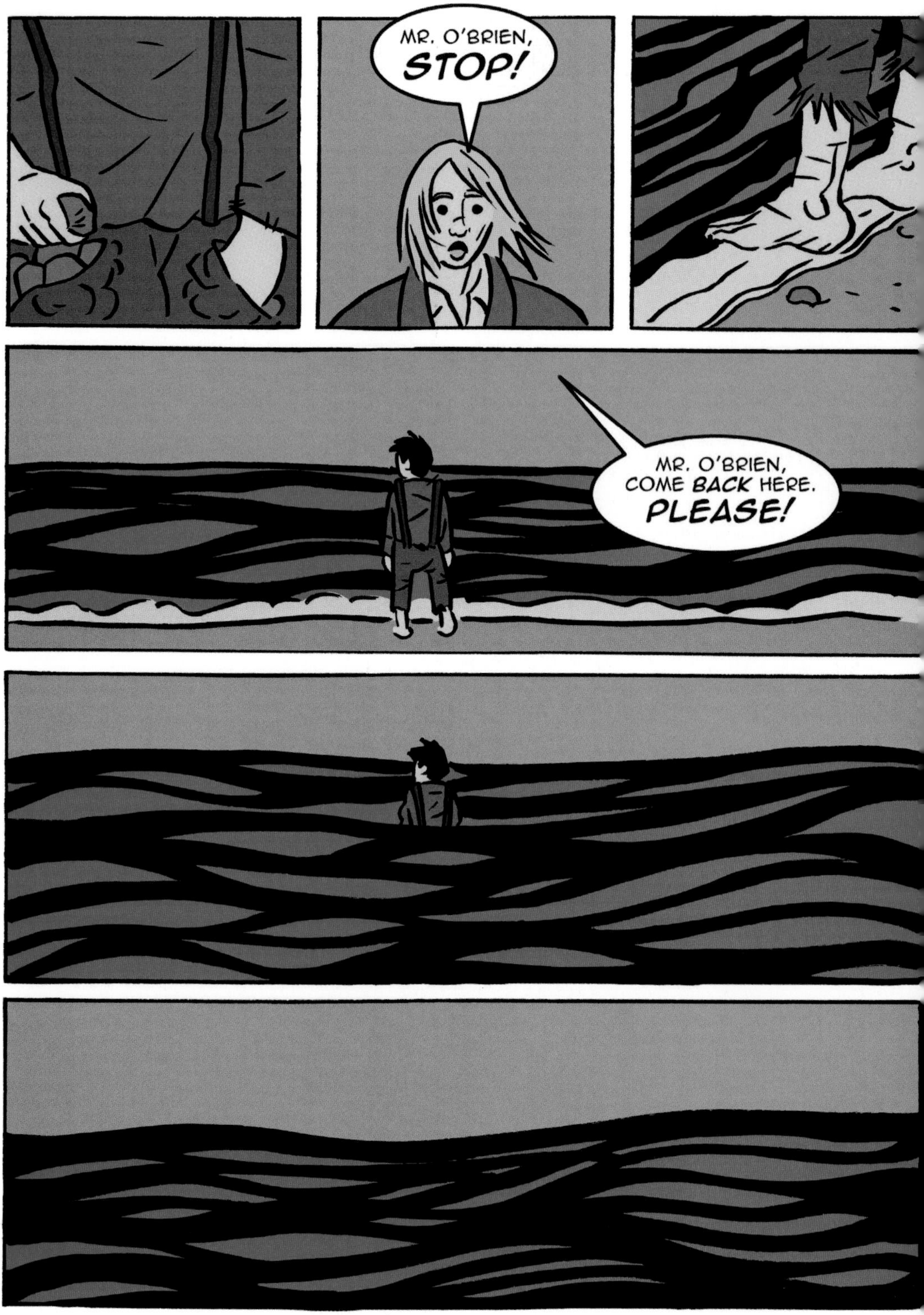
MR. O'BRIEN, STOP!
MR. O'BRIEN, COME BACK HERE. PLEASE!

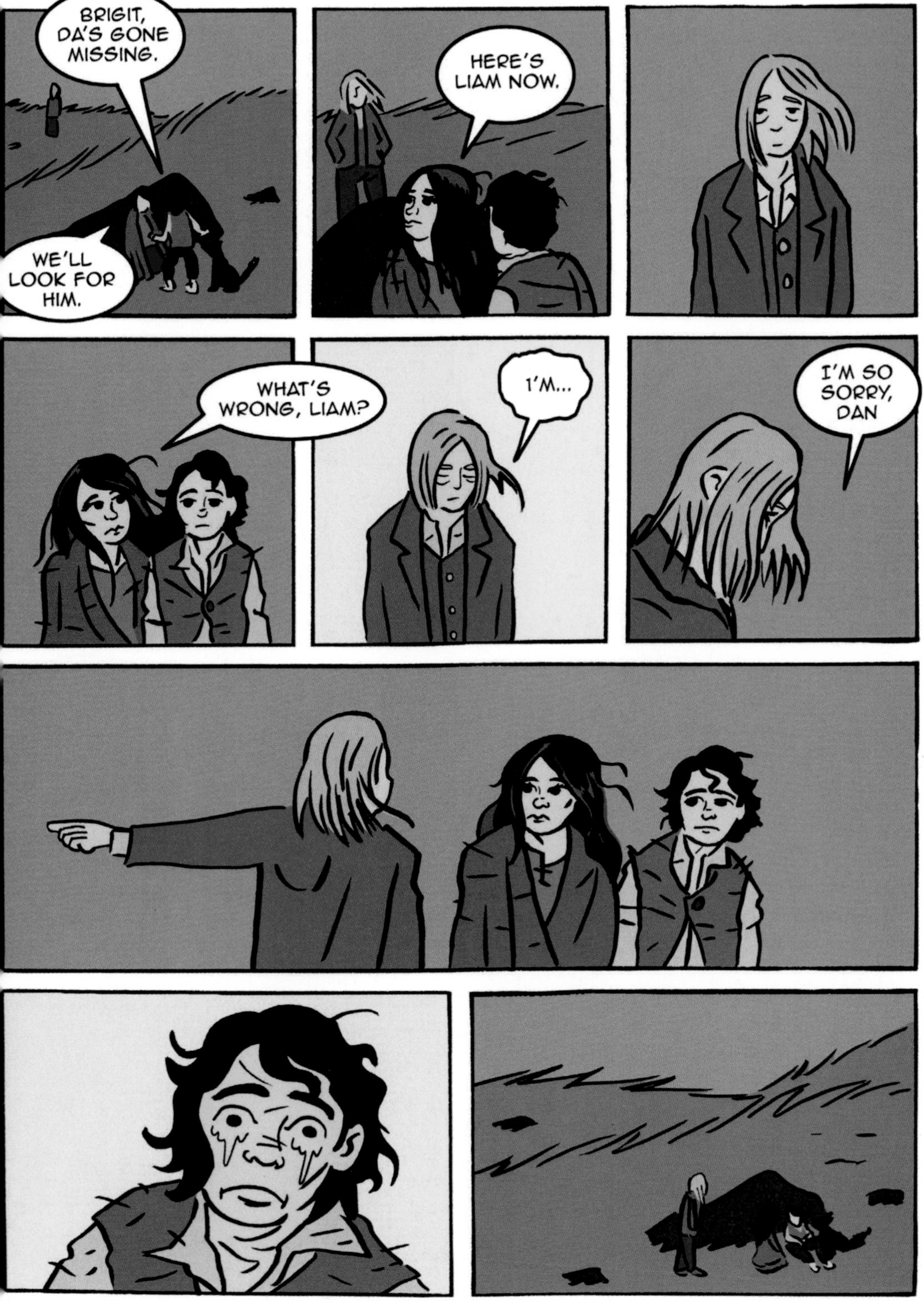
BRIGIT, DA'S GONE MISSING.
WE'LL LOOK FOR HIM.
HERE'S LIAM NOW.
WHAT'S WRONG, LIAM?
I'M...
I'M SO SORRY, DAN

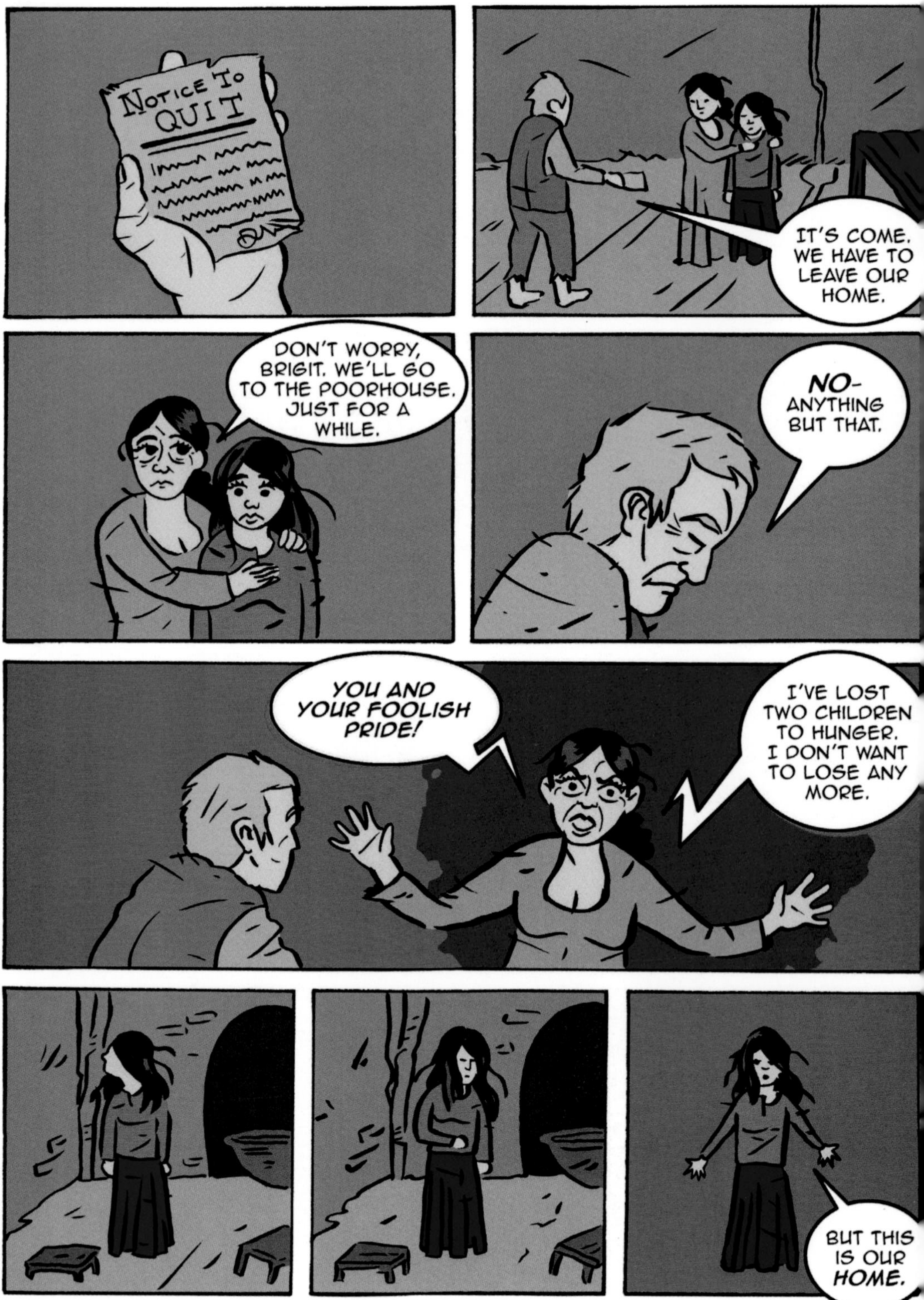
NOTICE TO QUIT
IT'S COME. WE HAVE TO LEAVE OUR HOME.
DON'T WORRY, BRIGIT. WE'LL GO TO THE POORHOUSE. JUST FOR A WHILE.
NO- ANYTHING BUT THAT.
YOU AND YOUR FOOLISH PRIDE!
I'VE LOST TWO CHILDREN TO HUNGER. I DON'T WANT TO LOSE ANY MORE.
BUT THIS IS OUR HOME.

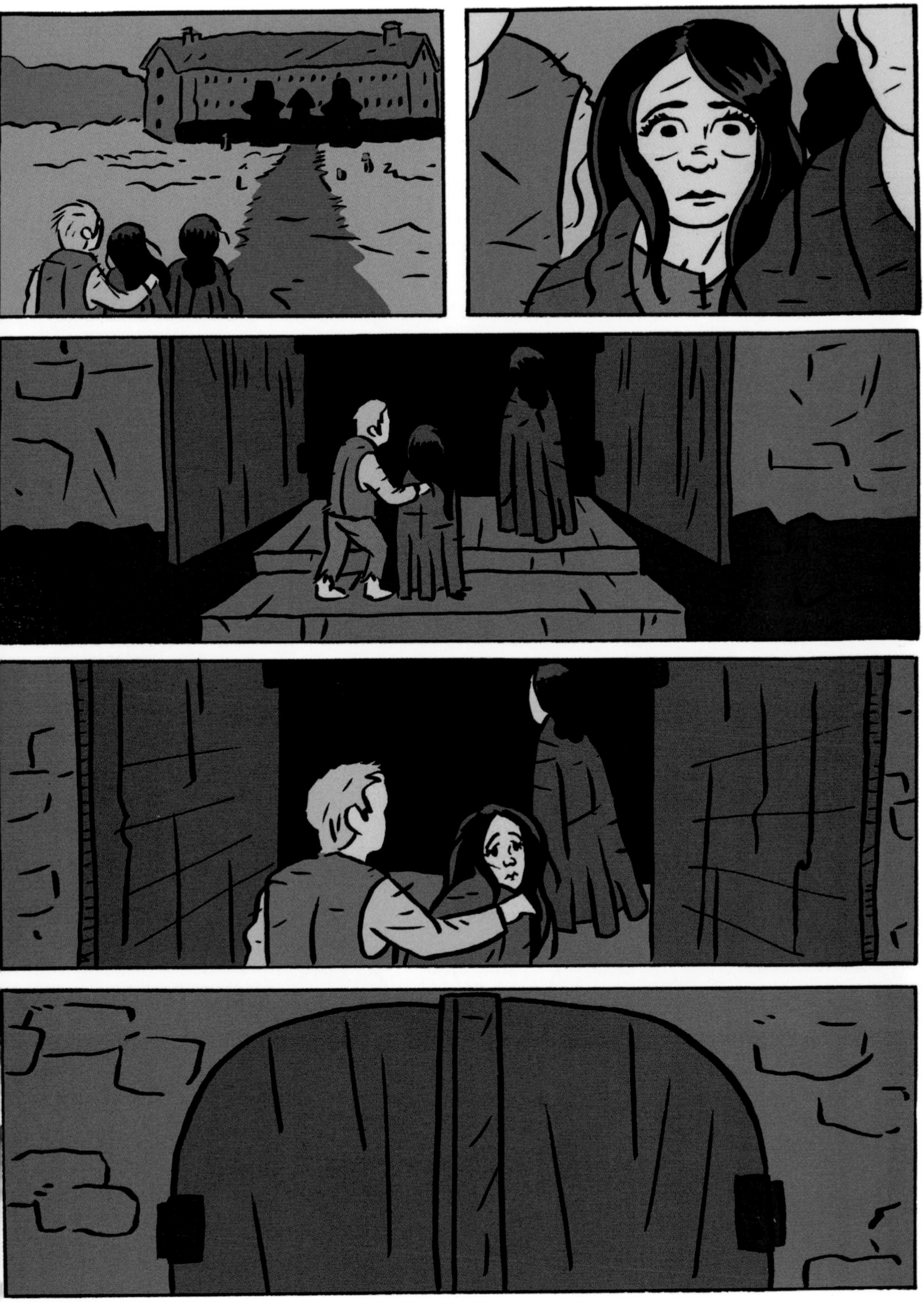

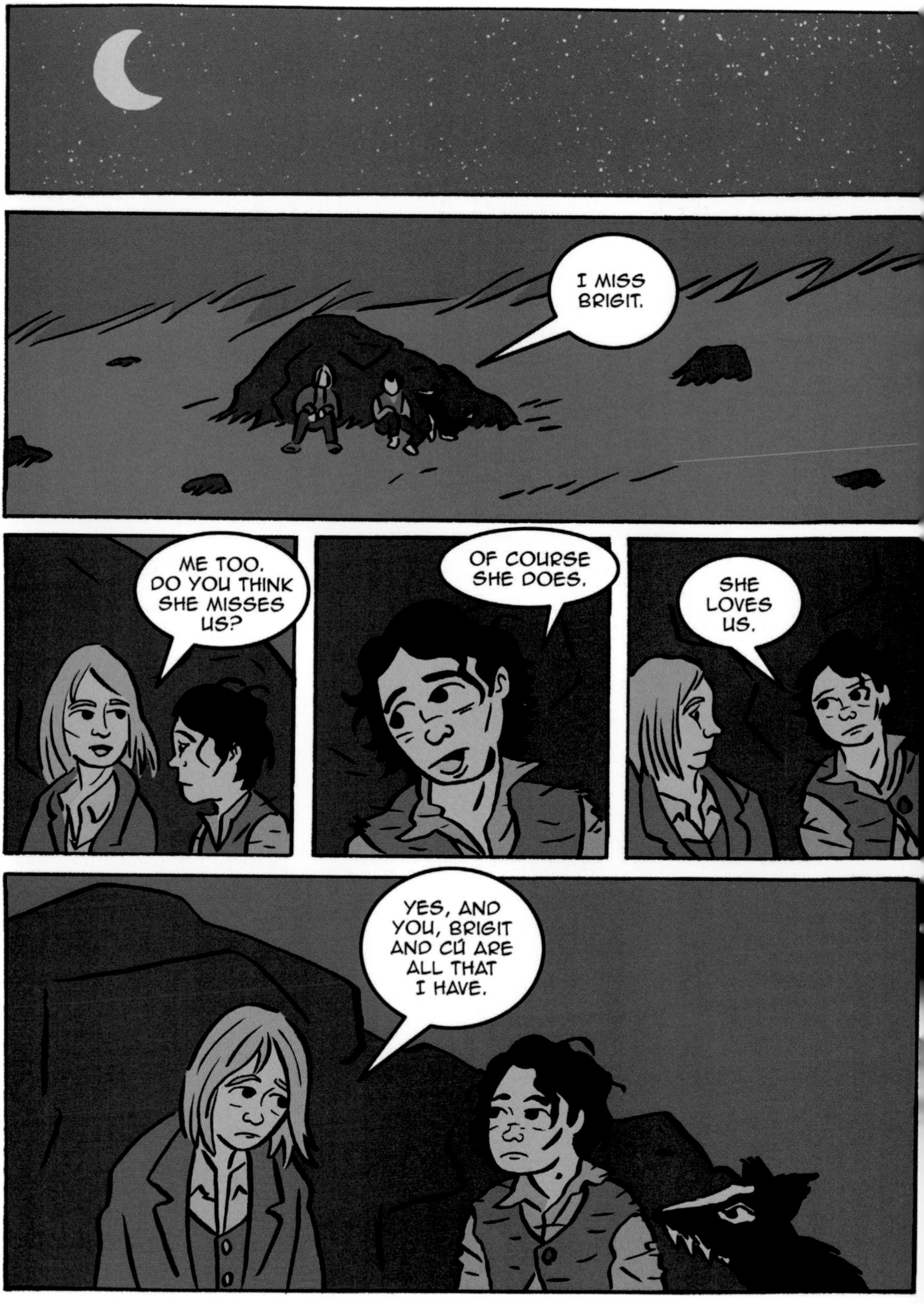
I MISS BRIGIT.
ME TOO. DO YOU THINK SHE MISSES US?
OF COURSE SHE DOES.
SHE LOVES US.
YES, AND YOU, BRIGIT AND CÚ ARE ALL THAT I HAVE.

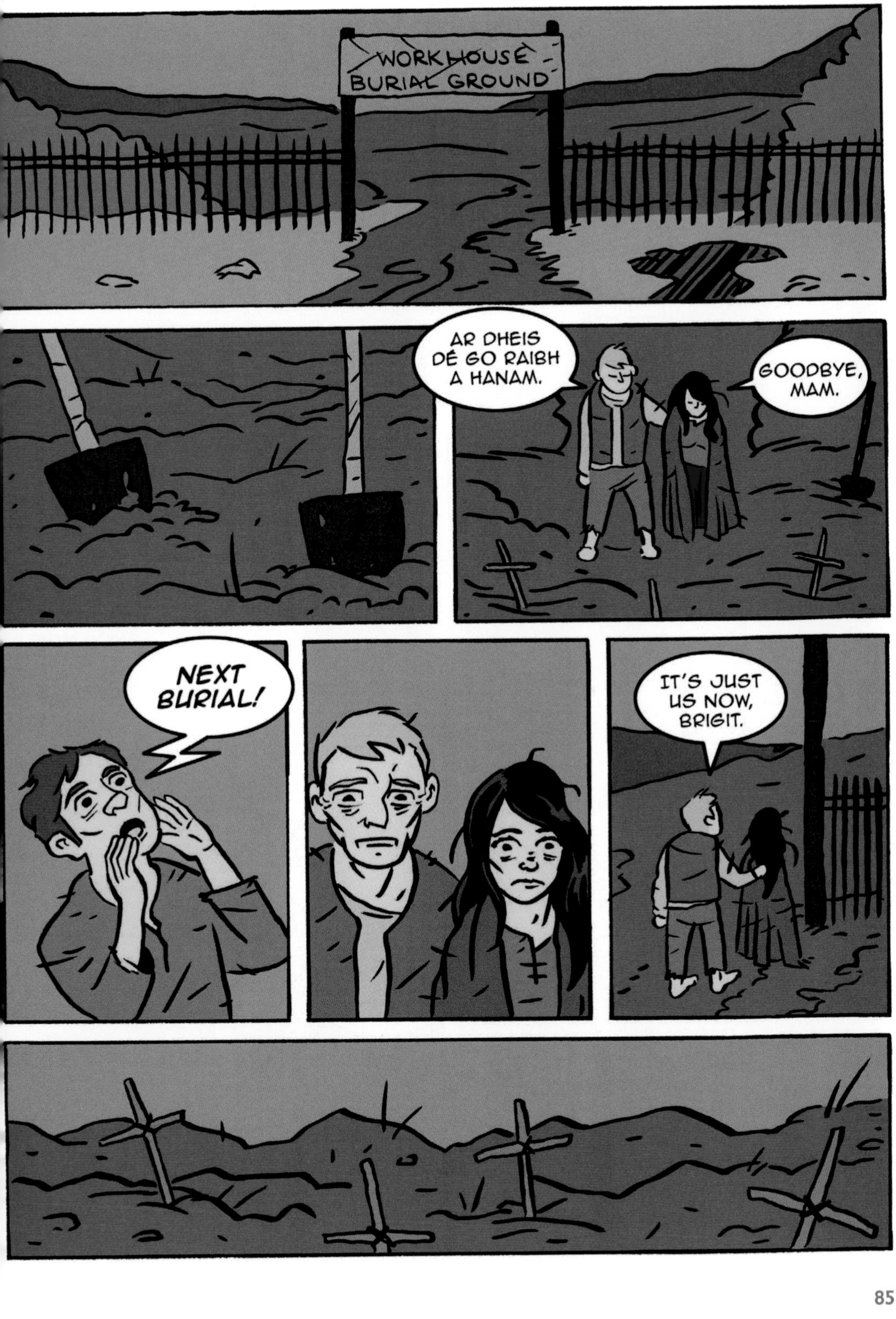
WORKHOUSE
BURIAL GROUND
AR DHEIS DÉ GO RAIBH A HANAM.
GOODBYE, MAM.
NEXT BURIAL!
IT'S JUST US NOW, BRIGIT.

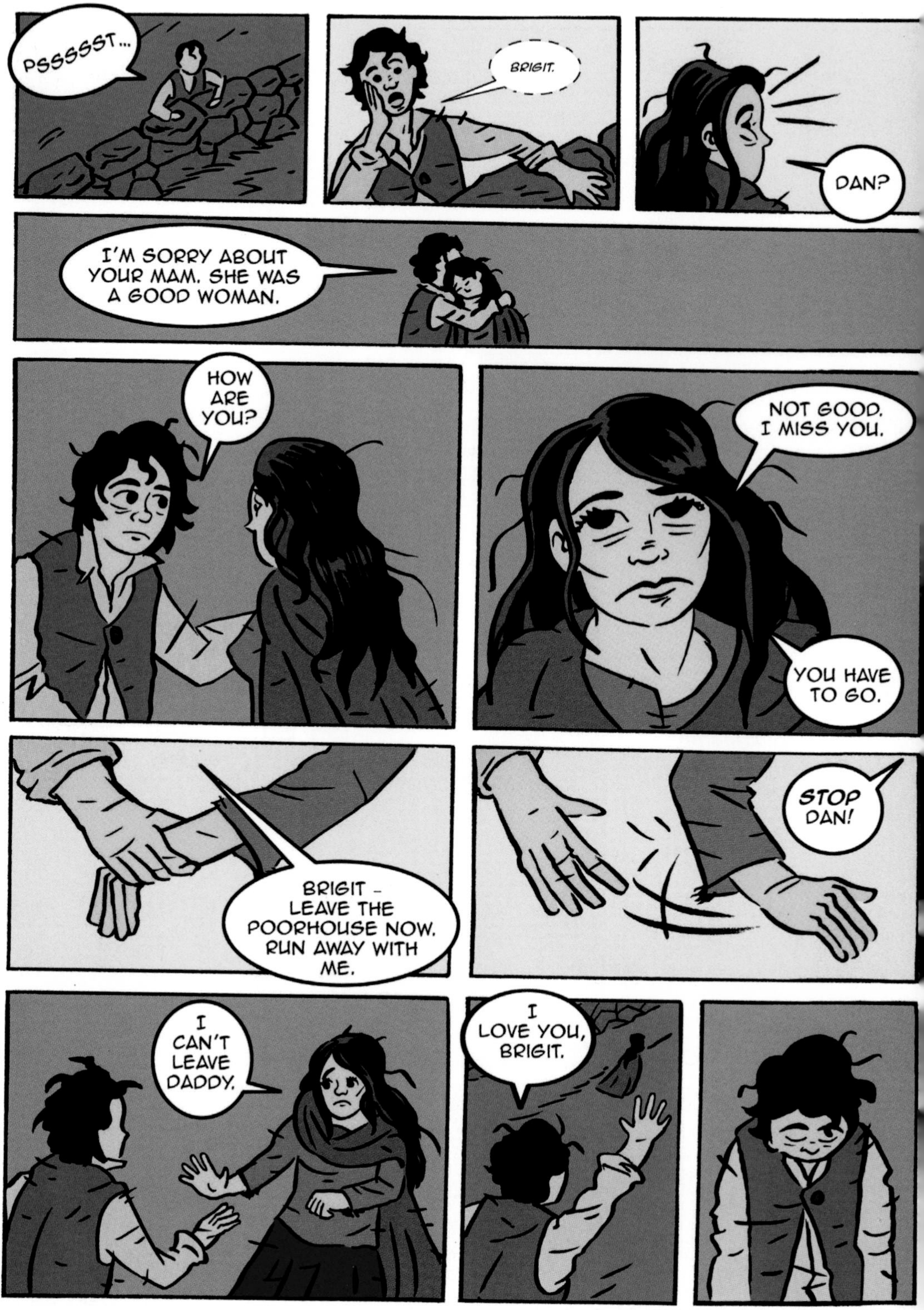
PSSSSST...
BRIGIT.
DAN?
I'M SORRY ABOUT YOUR MAM. SHE WAS A GOOD WOMAN.
HOW ARE YOU?
NOT GOOD. I MISS YOU.
YOU HAVE TO GO.
BRIGIT – LEAVE THE POORHOUSE NOW. RUN AWAY WITH ME.
STOP DAN!
I CAN'T LEAVE DADDY.
I LOVE YOU, BRIGIT.

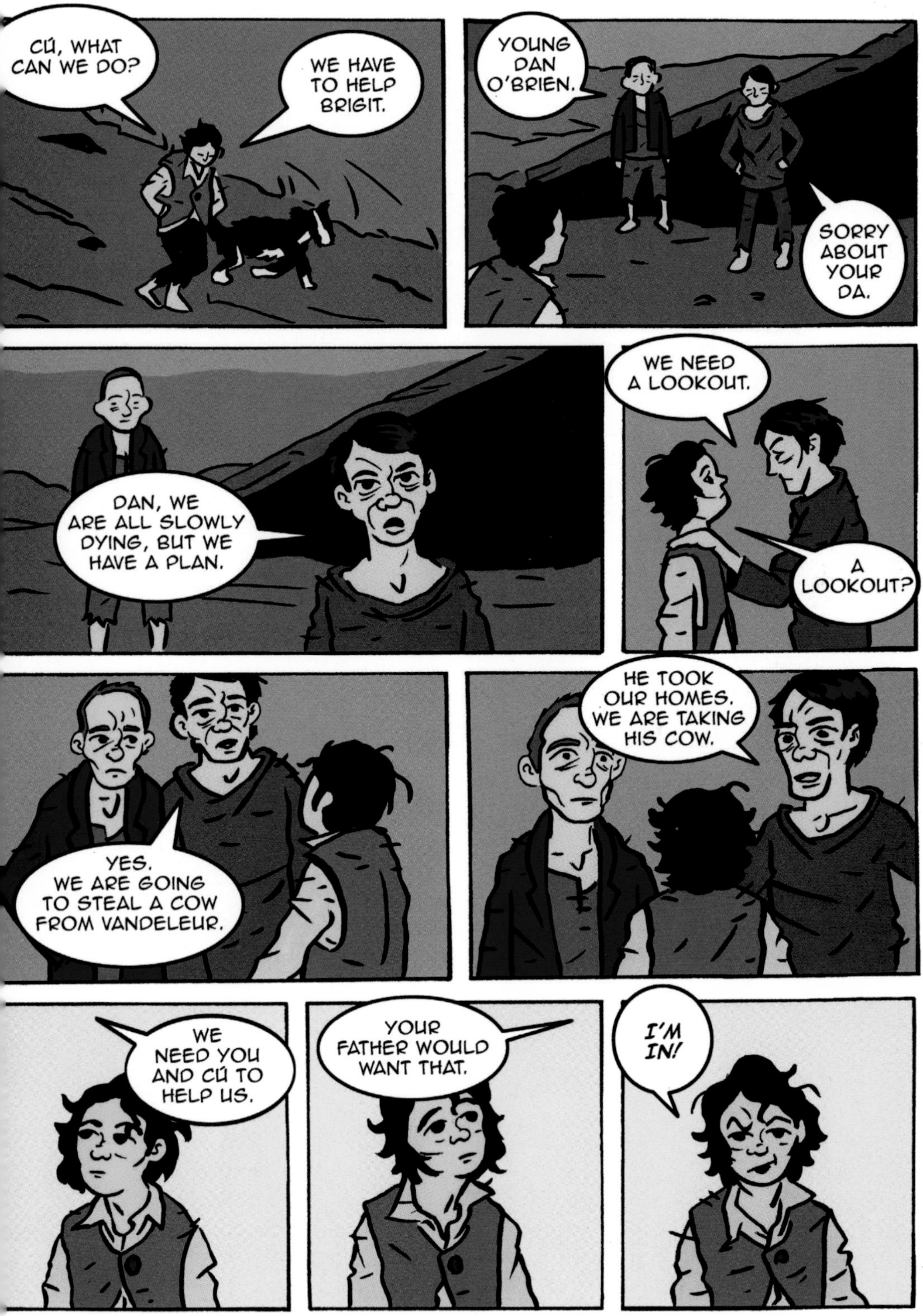

CÚ, WHAT CAN WE DO?
WE HAVE TO HELP BRIGIT.
YOUNG DAN O'BRIEN.
SORRY ABOUT YOUR DA.
DAN, WE ARE ALL SLOWLY DYING, BUT WE HAVE A PLAN.
WE NEED A LOOKOUT.
A LOOKOUT?
YES. WE ARE GOING TO STEAL A COW FROM VANDELEUR.
HE TOOK OUR HOMES. WE ARE TAKING HIS COW.
WE NEED YOU AND CÚ TO HELP US.
YOUR FATHER WOULD WANT THAT.
I'M IN!

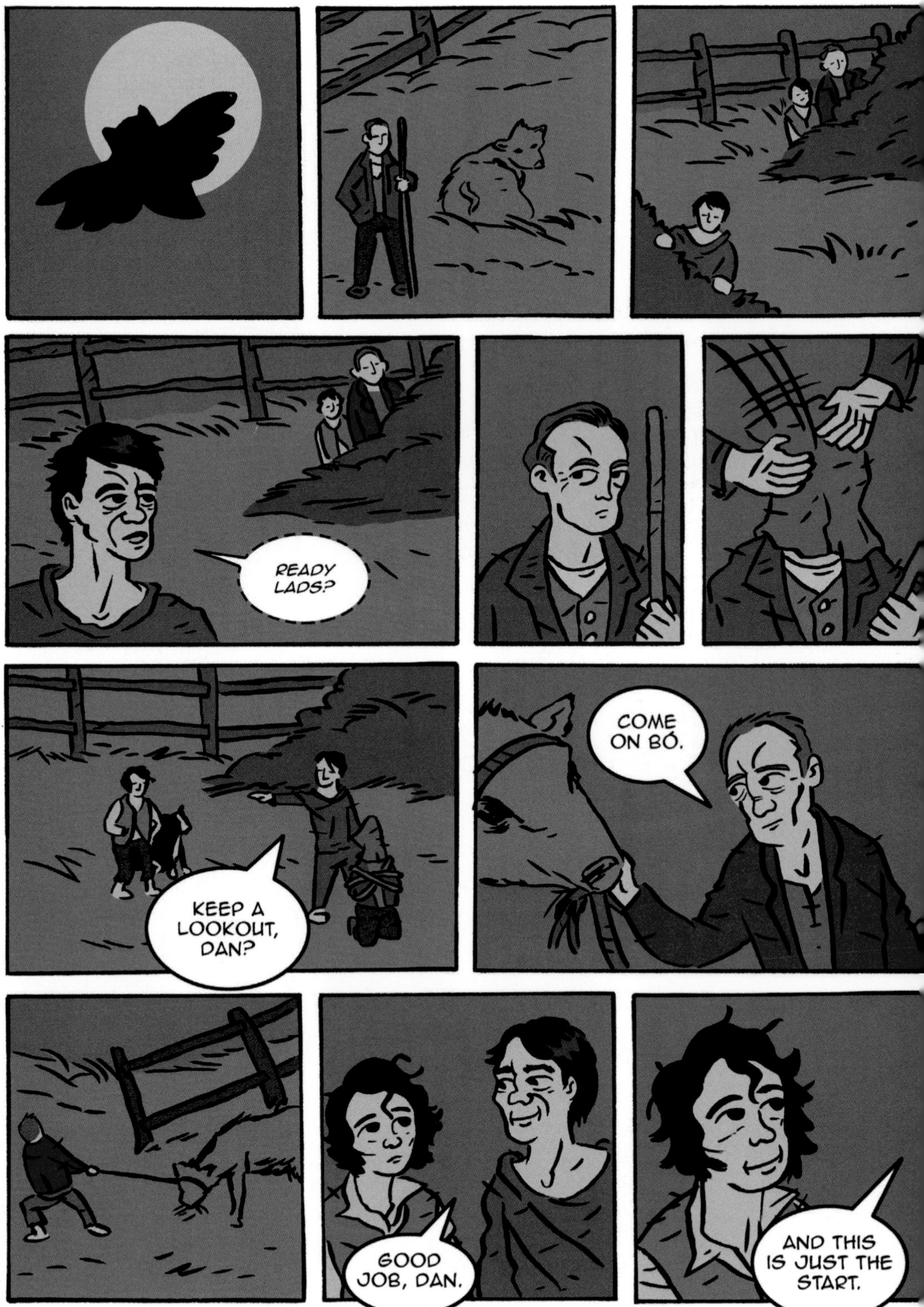
READY LADS?
KEEP A LOOKOUT, DAN?
COME ON BÓ.
GOOD JOB, DAN.
AND THIS IS JUST THE START.

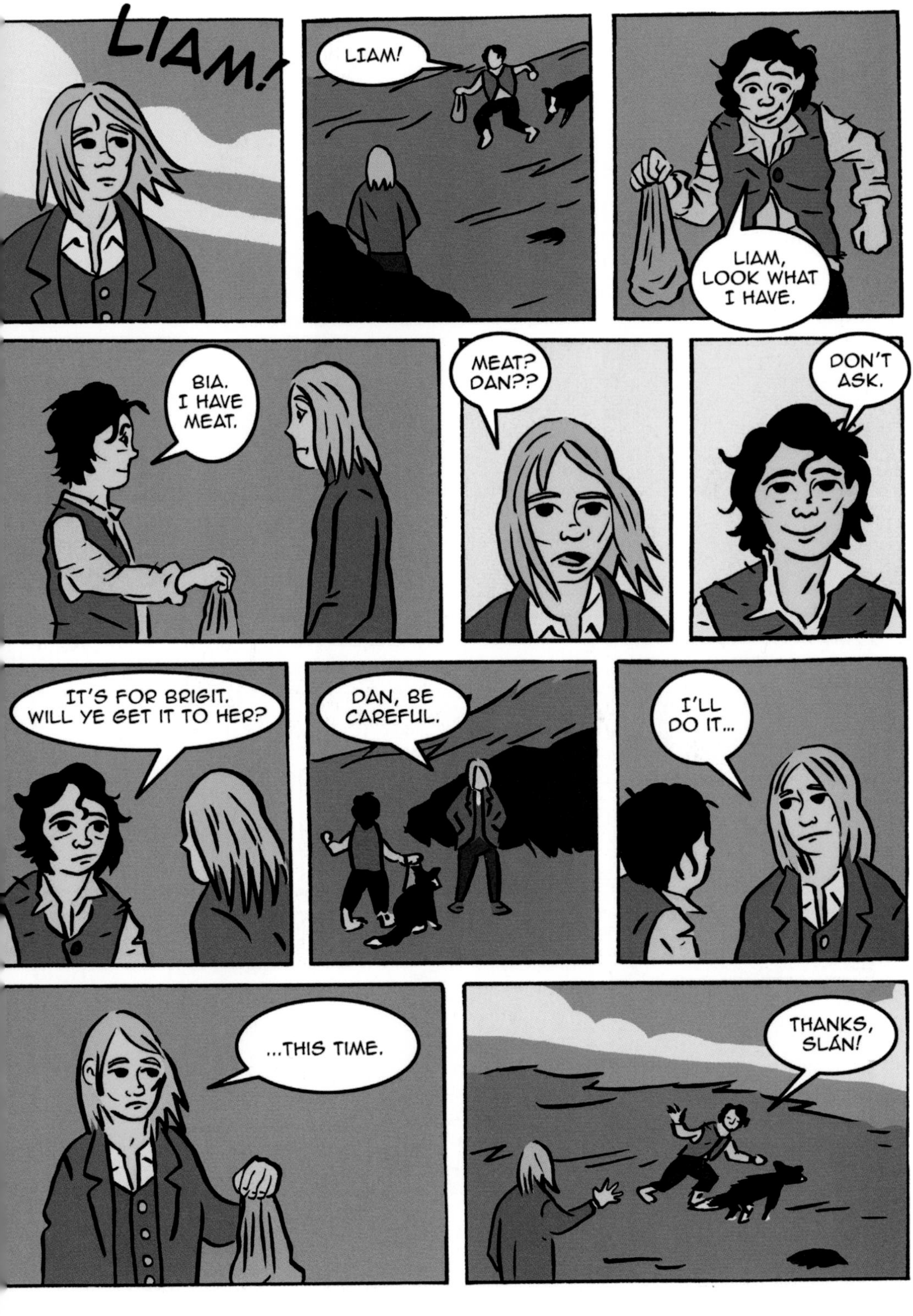
LIAM!
LIAM!
LIAM, LOOK WHAT I HAVE.
BIA. I HAVE MEAT.
MEAT? DAN??
DON'T ASK.
IT'S FOR BRIGIT. WILL YE GET IT TO HER?
DAN, BE CAREFUL.
I'LL DO IT...
...THIS TIME.
THANKS, SLÁN!

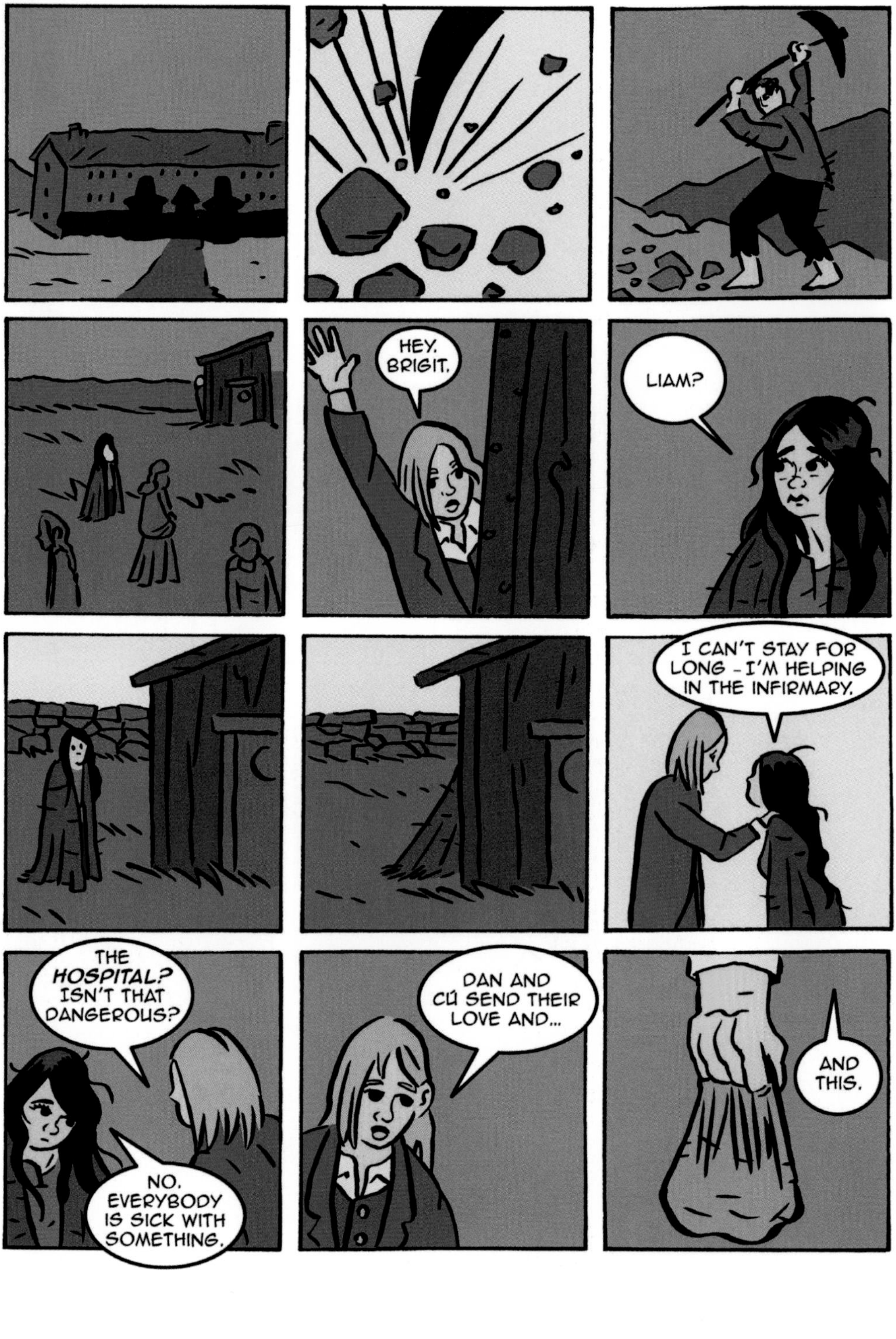
HEY. BRIGIT.
LIAM?
I CAN'T STAY FOR LONG - I'M HELPING IN THE INFIRMARY.
THE HOSPITAL? ISN'T THAT DANGEROUS?
NO. EVERYBODY IS SICK WITH SOMETHING.
DAN AND CÚ SEND THEIR LOVE AND...
AND THIS.

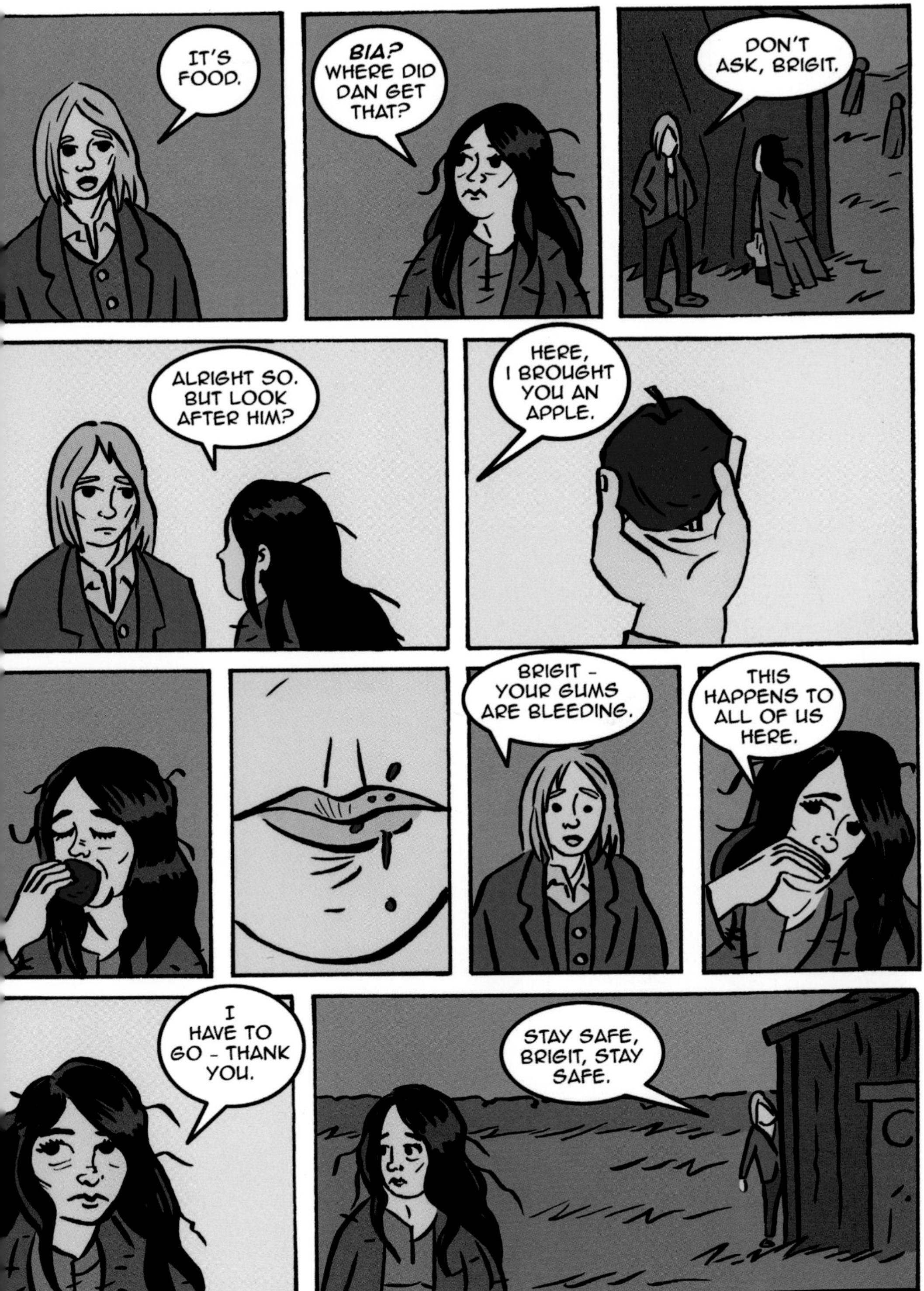
IT'S FOOD.
BIA? WHERE DID DAN GET THAT?
DON'T ASK, BRIGIT.
ALRIGHT SO. BUT LOOK AFTER HIM?
HERE, I BROUGHT YOU AN APPLE.
BRIGIT - YOUR GUMS ARE BLEEDING.
THIS HAPPENS TO ALL OF US HERE.
I HAVE TO GO - THANK YOU.
STAY SAFE, BRIGIT, STAY SAFE.

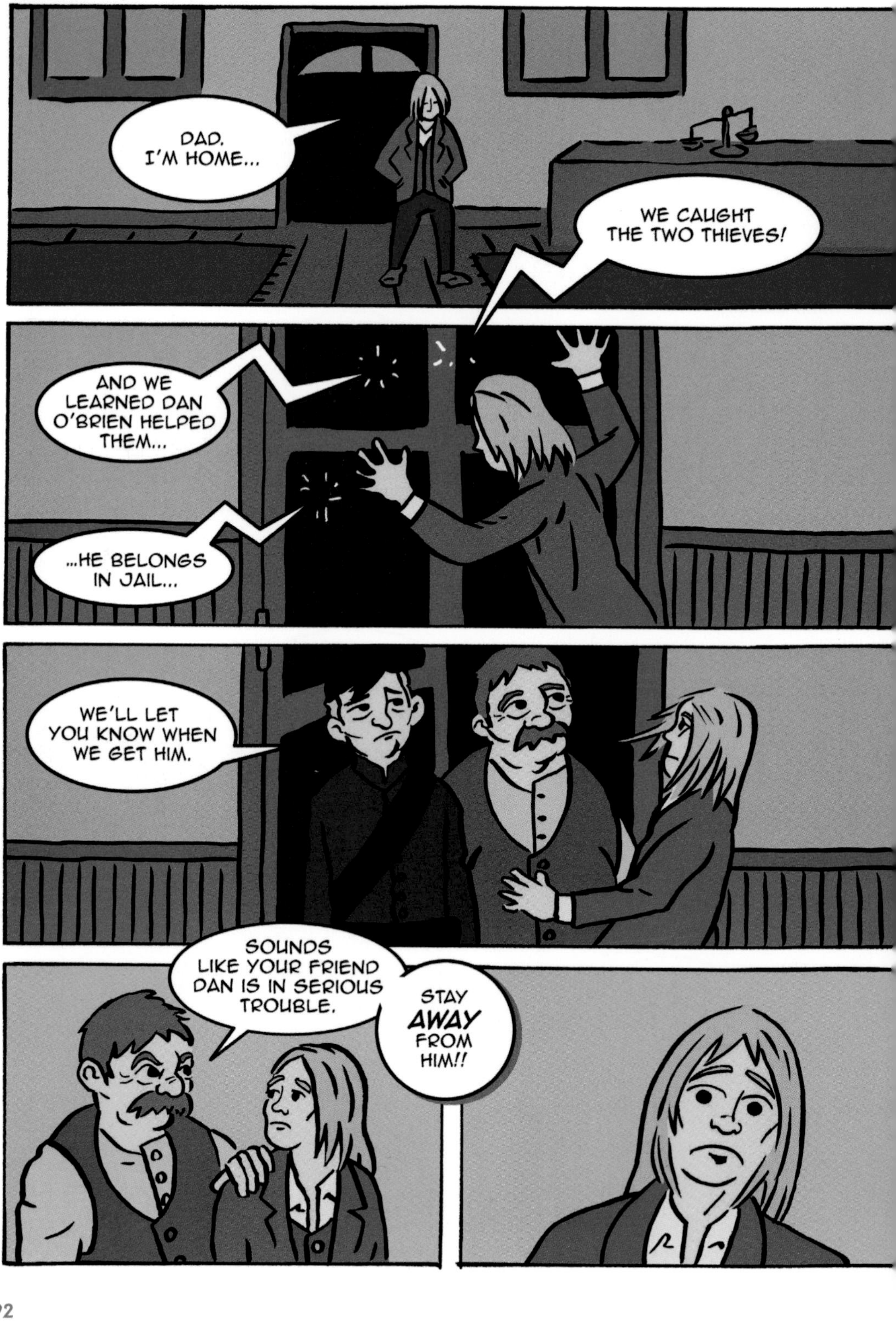
DAD.
I'M HOME...
WE CAUGHT THE TWO THIEVES!
AND WE LEARNED DAN O'BRIEN HELPED THEM...
...HE BELONGS IN JAIL...
WE'LL LET YOU KNOW WHEN WE GET HIM.
SOUNDS LIKE YOUR FRIEND DAN IS IN SERIOUS TROUBLE.
STAY *AWAY* FROM HIM!!

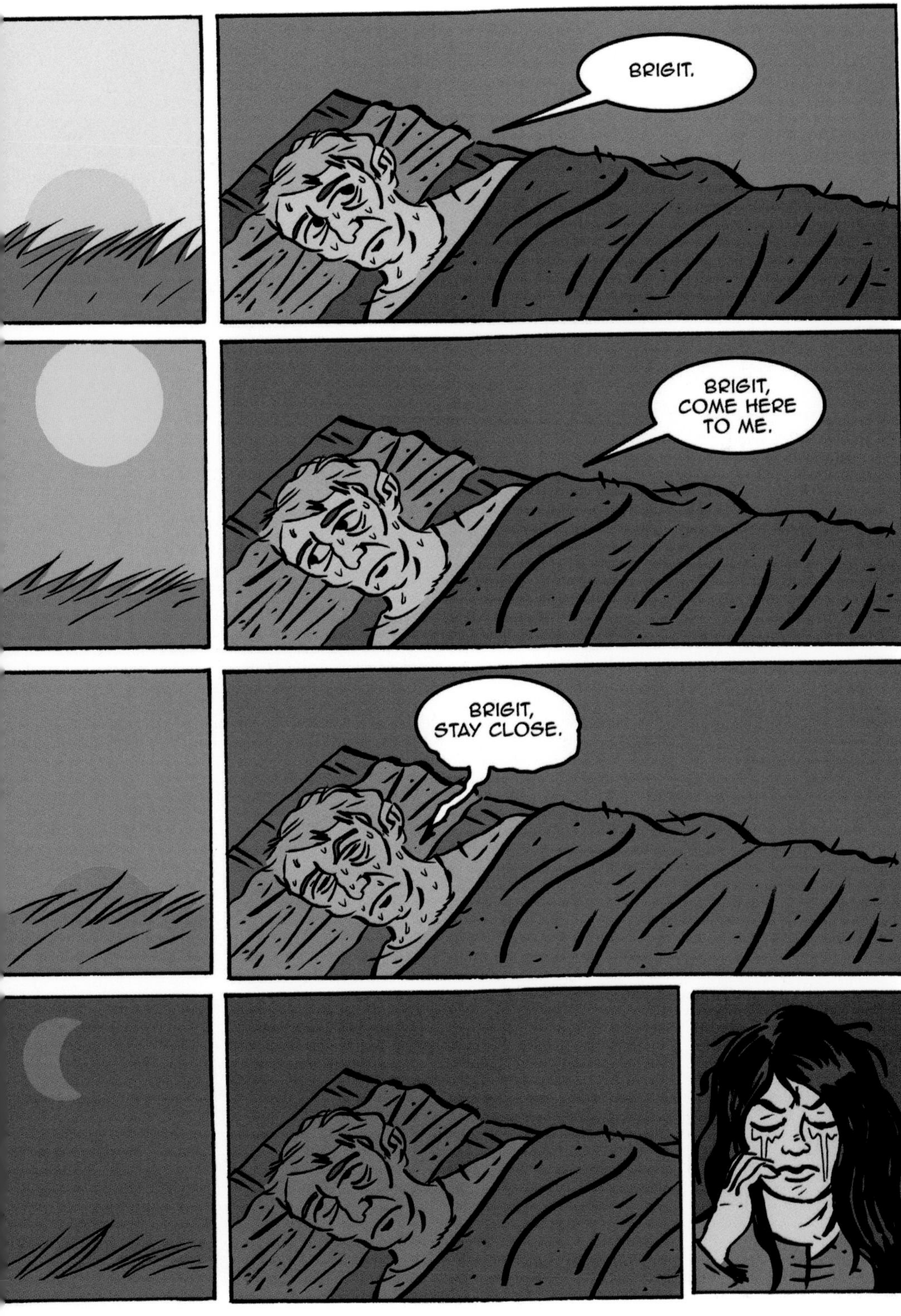
BRIGIT.
BRIGIT, COME HERE TO ME.
BRIGIT, STAY CLOSE.

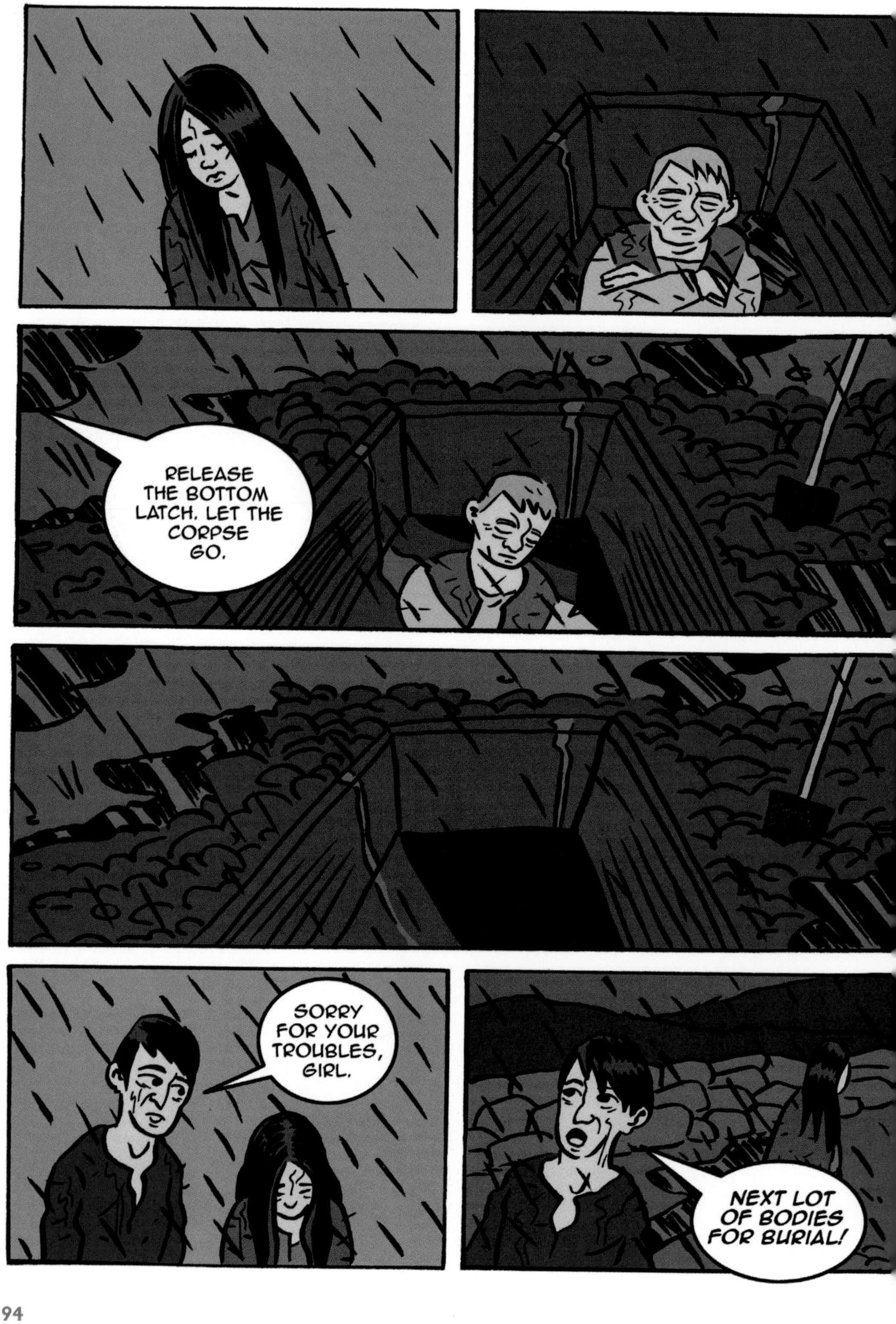
RELEASE THE BOTTOM LATCH. LET THE CORPSE GO.
SORRY FOR YOUR TROUBLES, GIRL.
NEXT LOT OF BODIES FOR BURIAL!

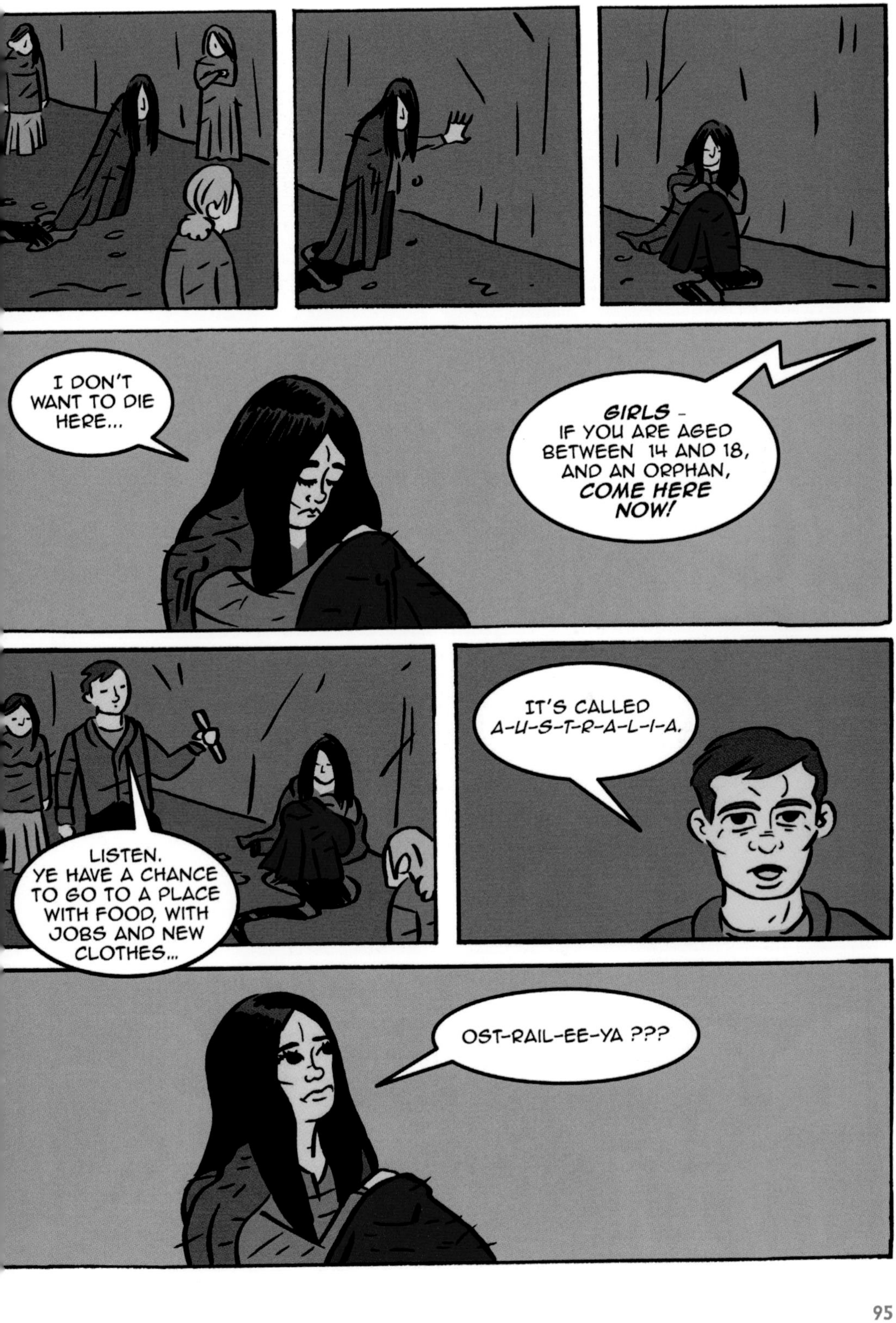
I DON'T WANT TO DIE HERE...
GIRLS - IF YOU ARE AGED BETWEEN 14 AND 18, AND AN ORPHAN, COME HERE NOW!
LISTEN. YE HAVE A CHANCE TO GO TO A PLACE WITH FOOD, WITH JOBS AND NEW CLOTHES...
IT'S CALLED A-U-S-T-R-A-L-I-A.
OST-RAIL-EE-YA ???

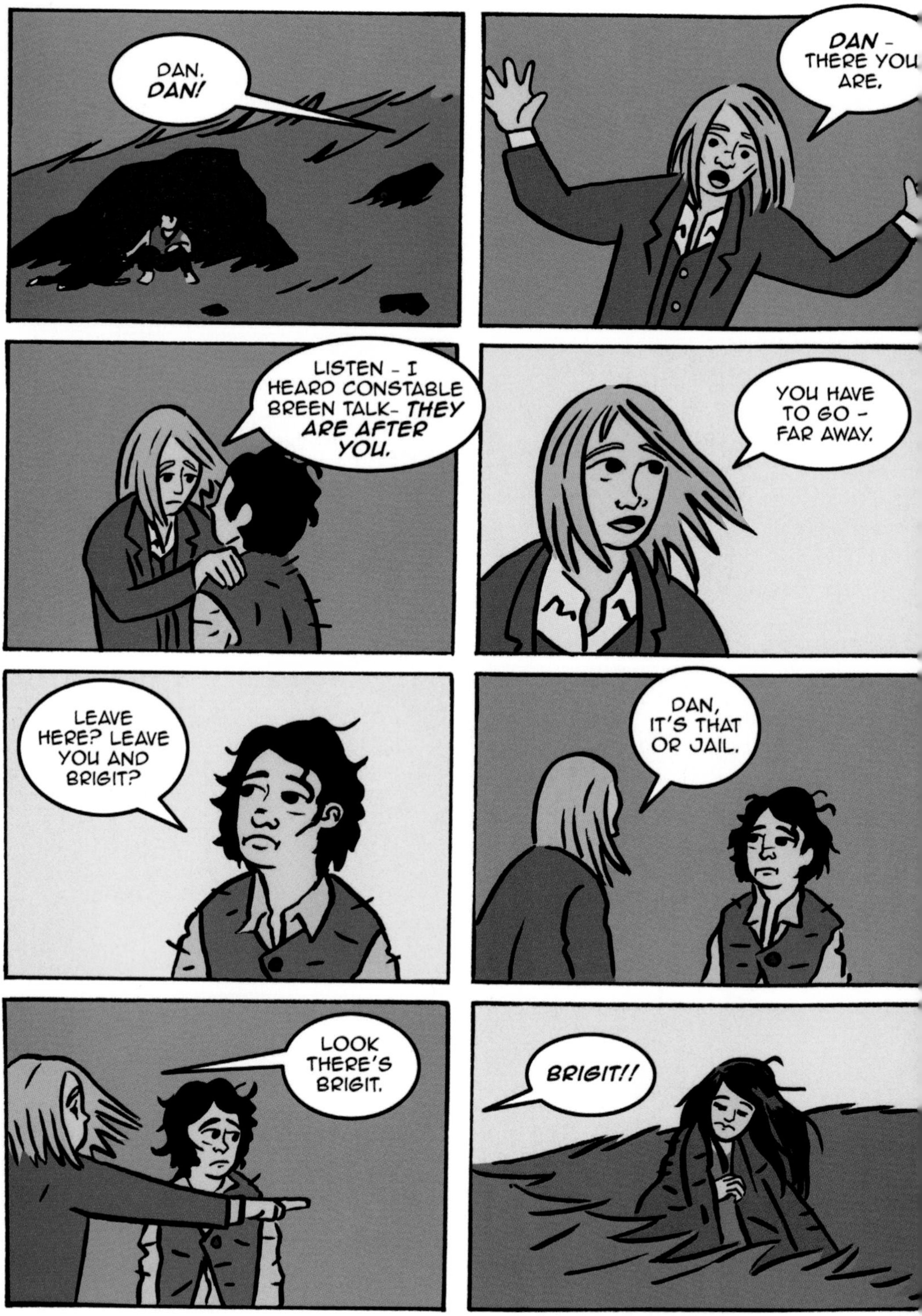
DAN. DAN!
DAN - THERE YOU ARE.
LISTEN - I HEARD CONSTABLE BREEN TALK- THEY ARE AFTER YOU.
YOU HAVE TO GO - FAR AWAY.
LEAVE HERE? LEAVE YOU AND BRIGIT?
DAN, IT'S THAT OR JAIL.
LOOK THERE'S BRIGIT.
BRIGIT!!

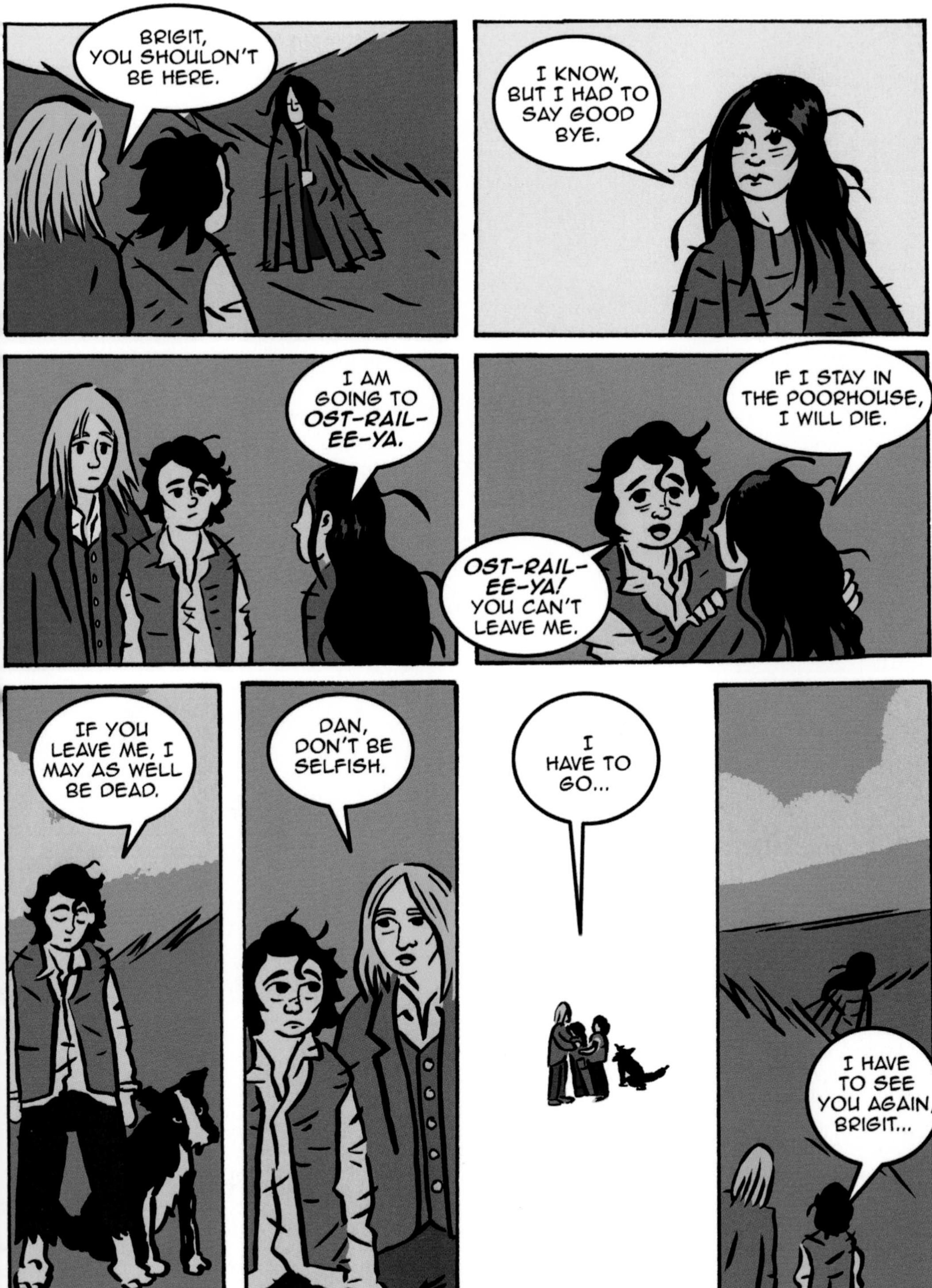
BRIGIT, YOU SHOULDN'T BE HERE.
I KNOW, BUT I HAD TO SAY GOOD BYE.
I AM GOING TO OST-RAIL-EE-YA.
IF I STAY IN THE POORHOUSE, I WILL DIE.
OST-RAIL-EE-YA! YOU CAN'T LEAVE ME.
IF YOU LEAVE ME, I MAY AS WELL BE DEAD.
DAN, DON'T BE SELFISH.
I HAVE TO GO...
I HAVE TO SEE YOU AGAIN, BRIGIT...

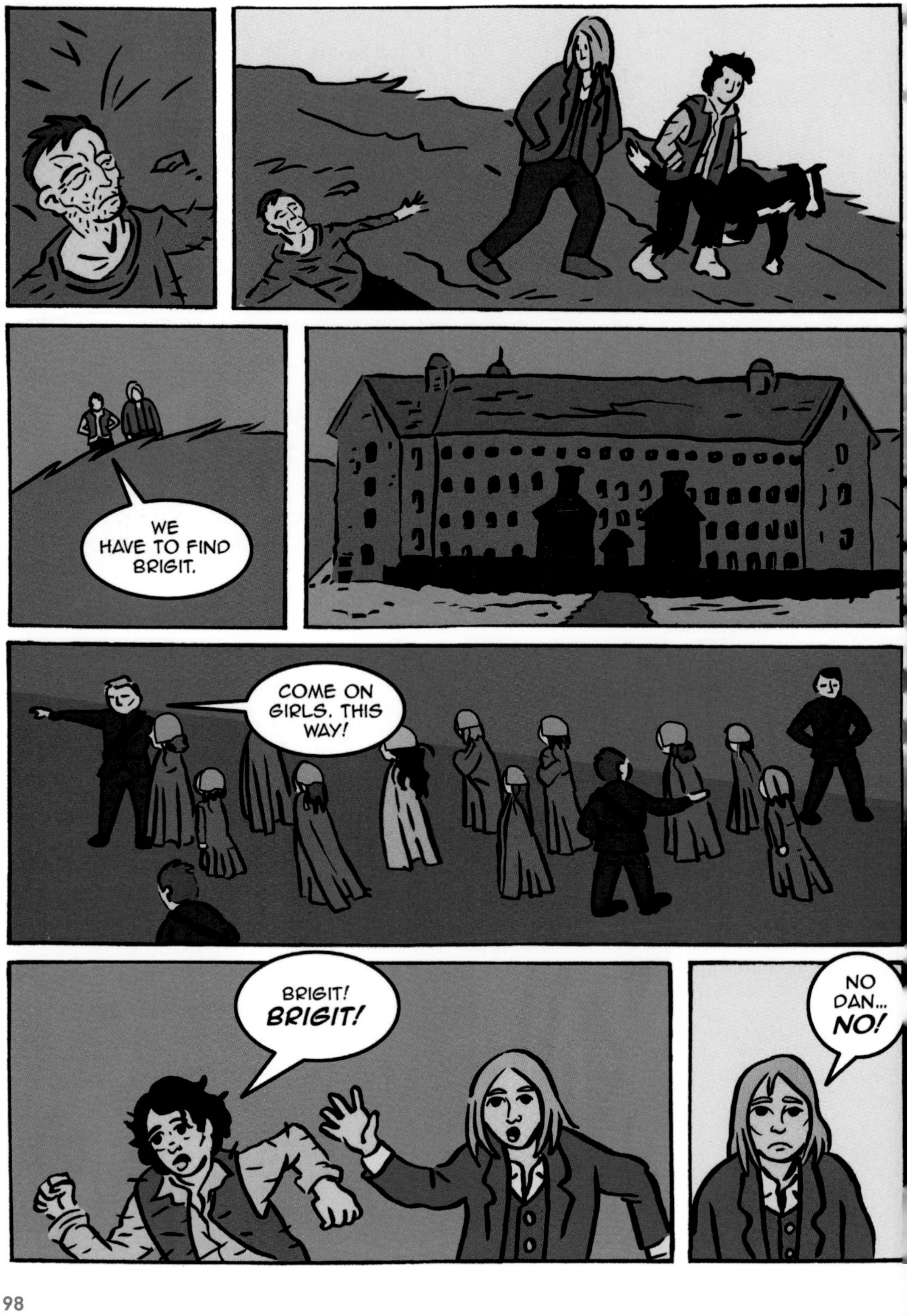
WE HAVE TO FIND BRIGIT.
COME ON GIRLS. THIS WAY!
BRIGIT! BRIGIT!
NO DAN... NO!

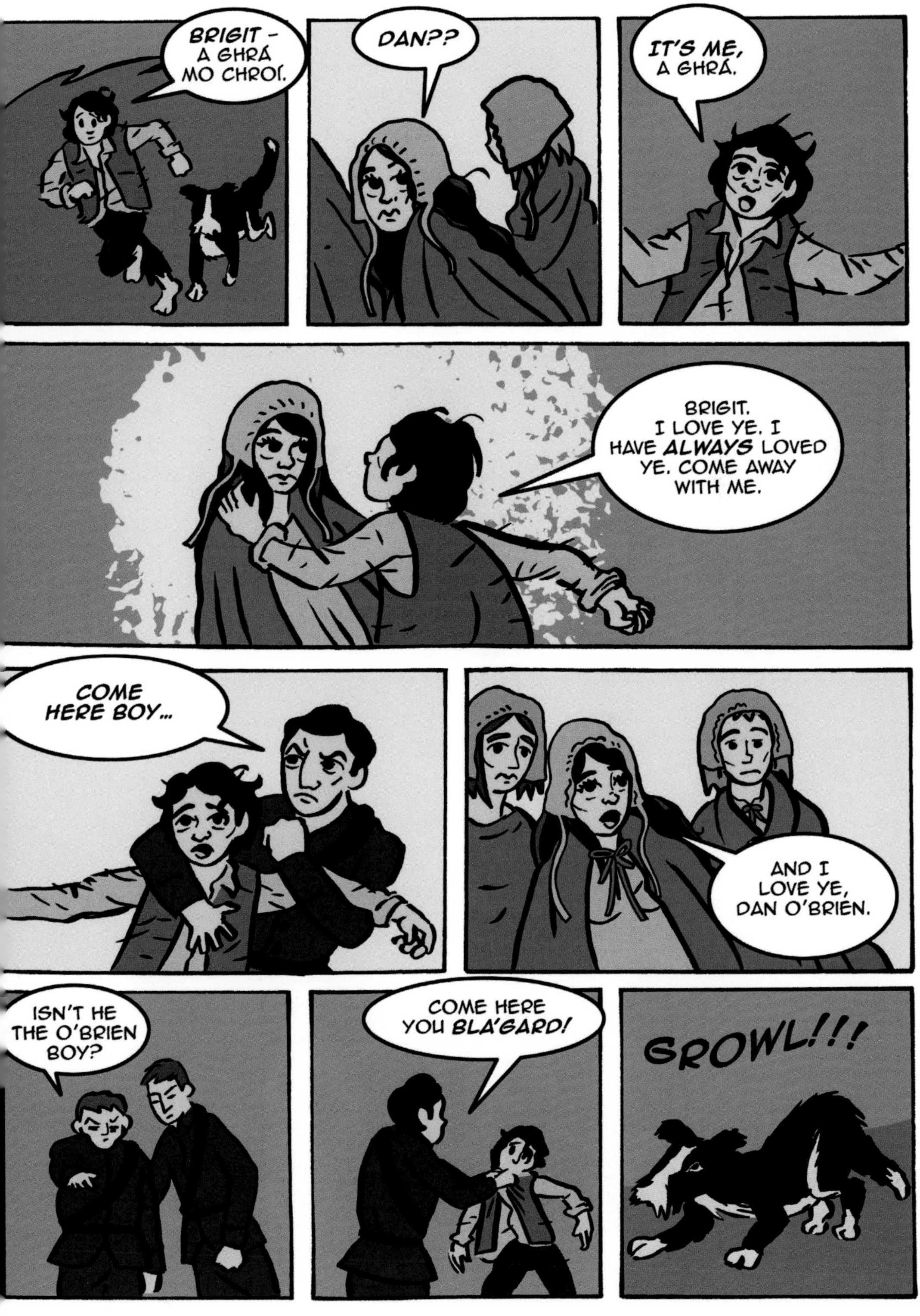
BRIGIT – A GHRÁ MO CHROÍ.
DAN??
IT'S ME, A GHRÁ.
BRIGIT. I LOVE YE. I HAVE ALWAYS LOVED YE. COME AWAY WITH ME.
COME HERE BOY...
AND I LOVE YE, DAN O'BRIEN.
ISN'T HE THE O'BRIEN BOY?
COME HERE YOU BLA'GARD!
GROWL!!!

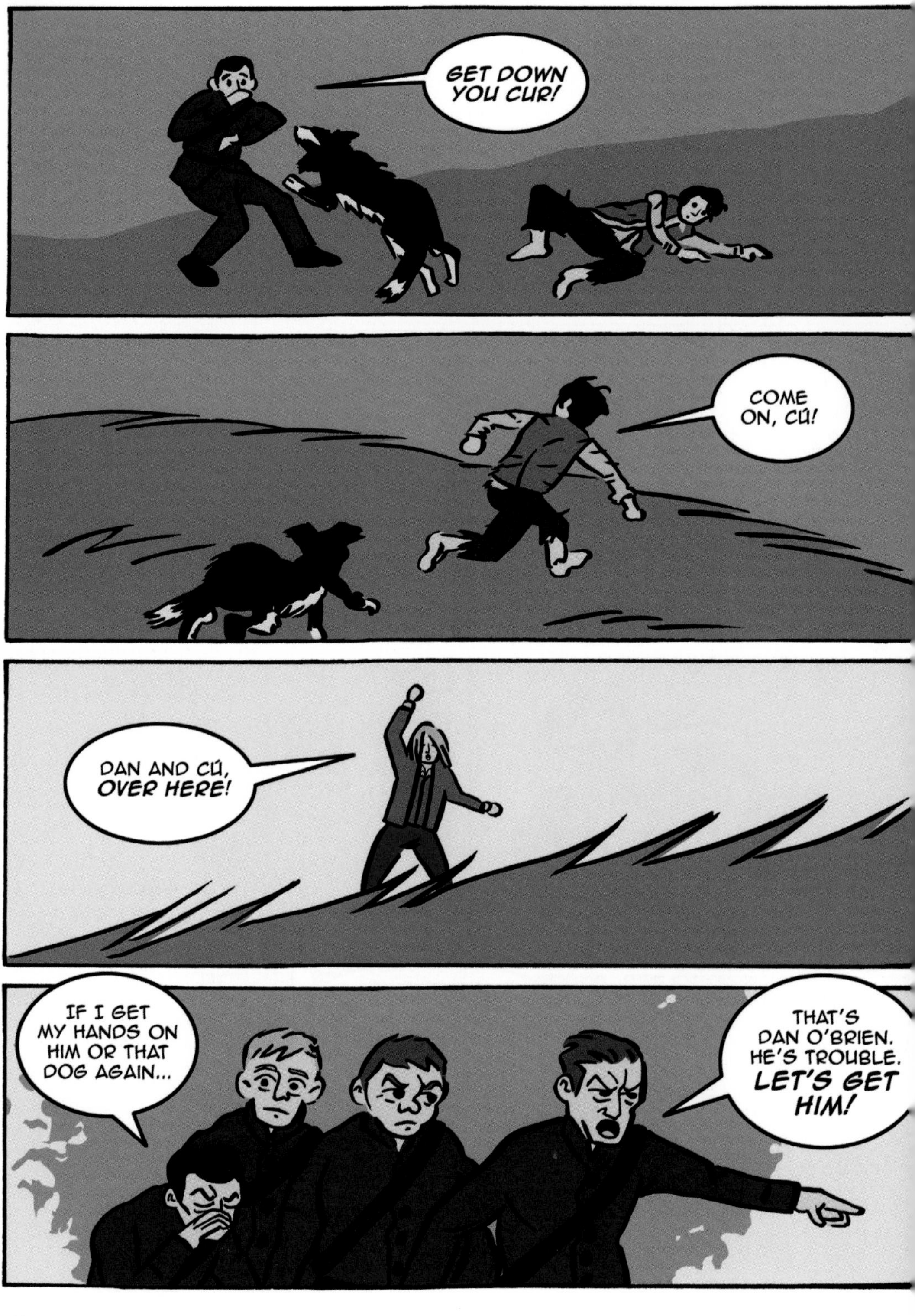
GET DOWN YOU CUR!
COME ON, CÚ!
DAN AND CÚ, OVER HERE!
IF I GET MY HANDS ON HIM OR THAT DOG AGAIN...
THAT'S DAN O'BRIEN. HE'S TROUBLE. LET'S GET HIM!

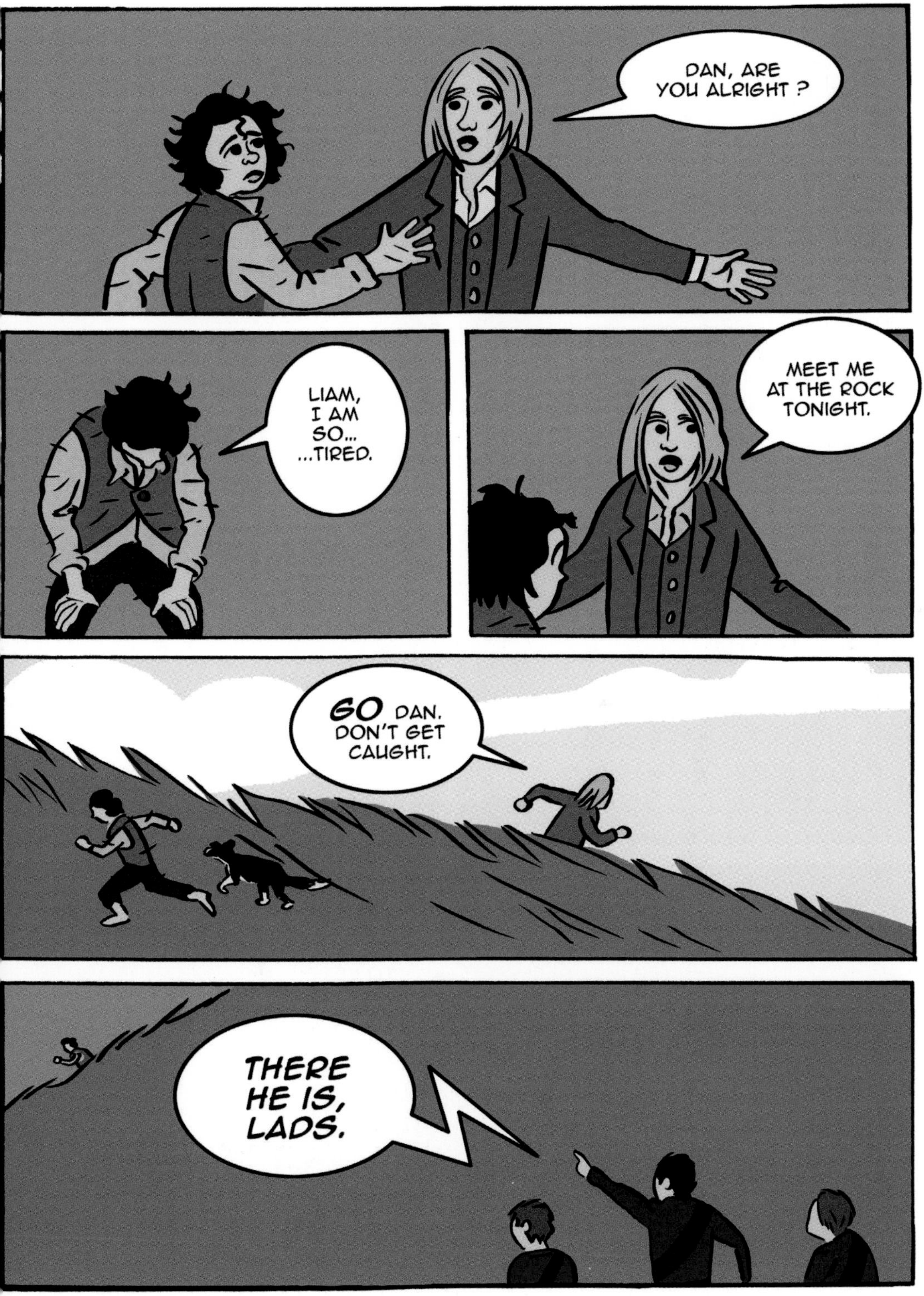
DAN, ARE YOU ALRIGHT ?
LIAM, I AM SO... ...TIRED.
MEET ME AT THE ROCK TONIGHT.
GO DAN. DON'T GET CAUGHT.
THERE HE IS, LADS.

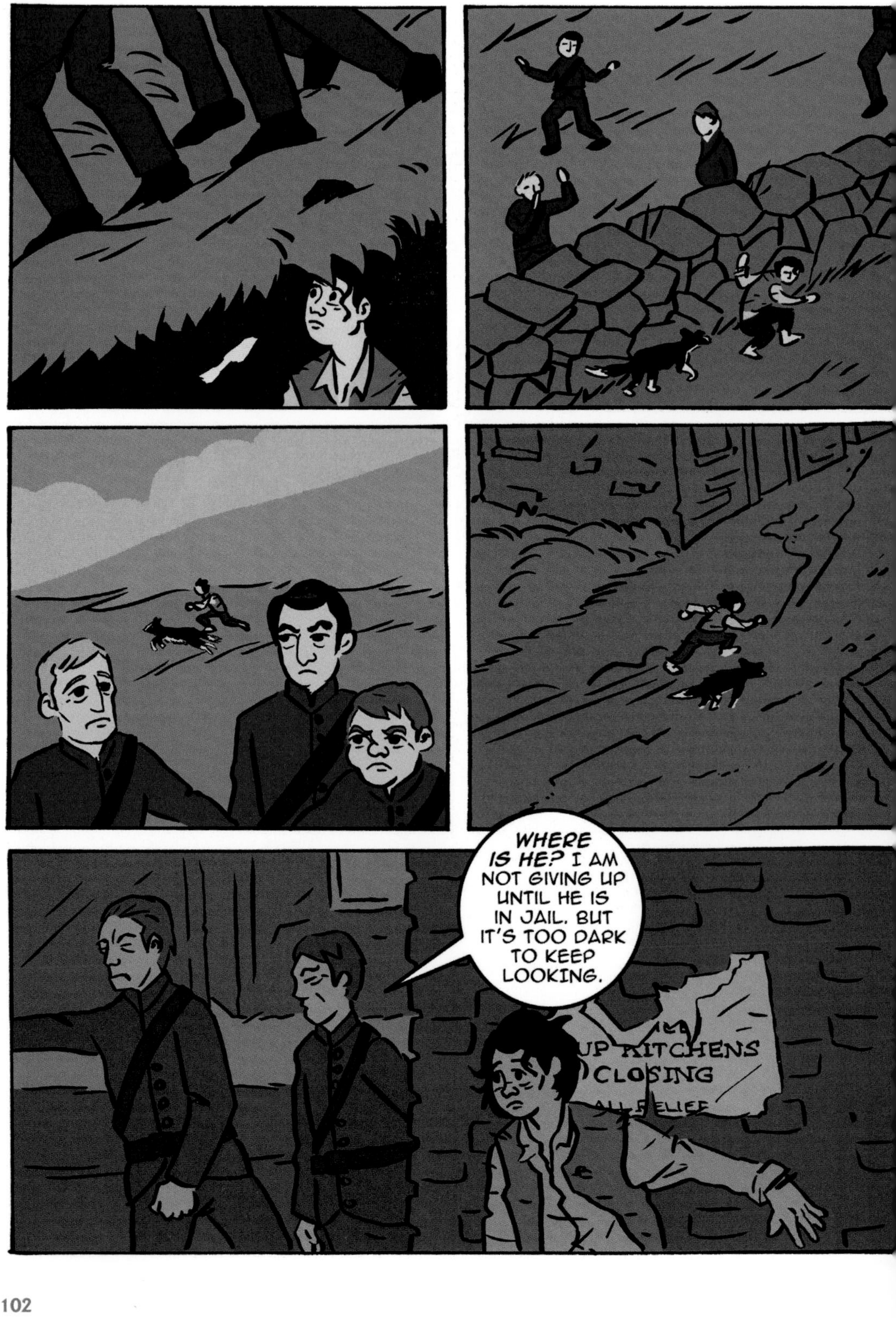
WHERE IS HE? I AM NOT GIVING UP UNTIL HE IS IN JAIL. BUT IT'S TOO DARK TO KEEP LOOKING.
UP KITCHENS
CLOSING

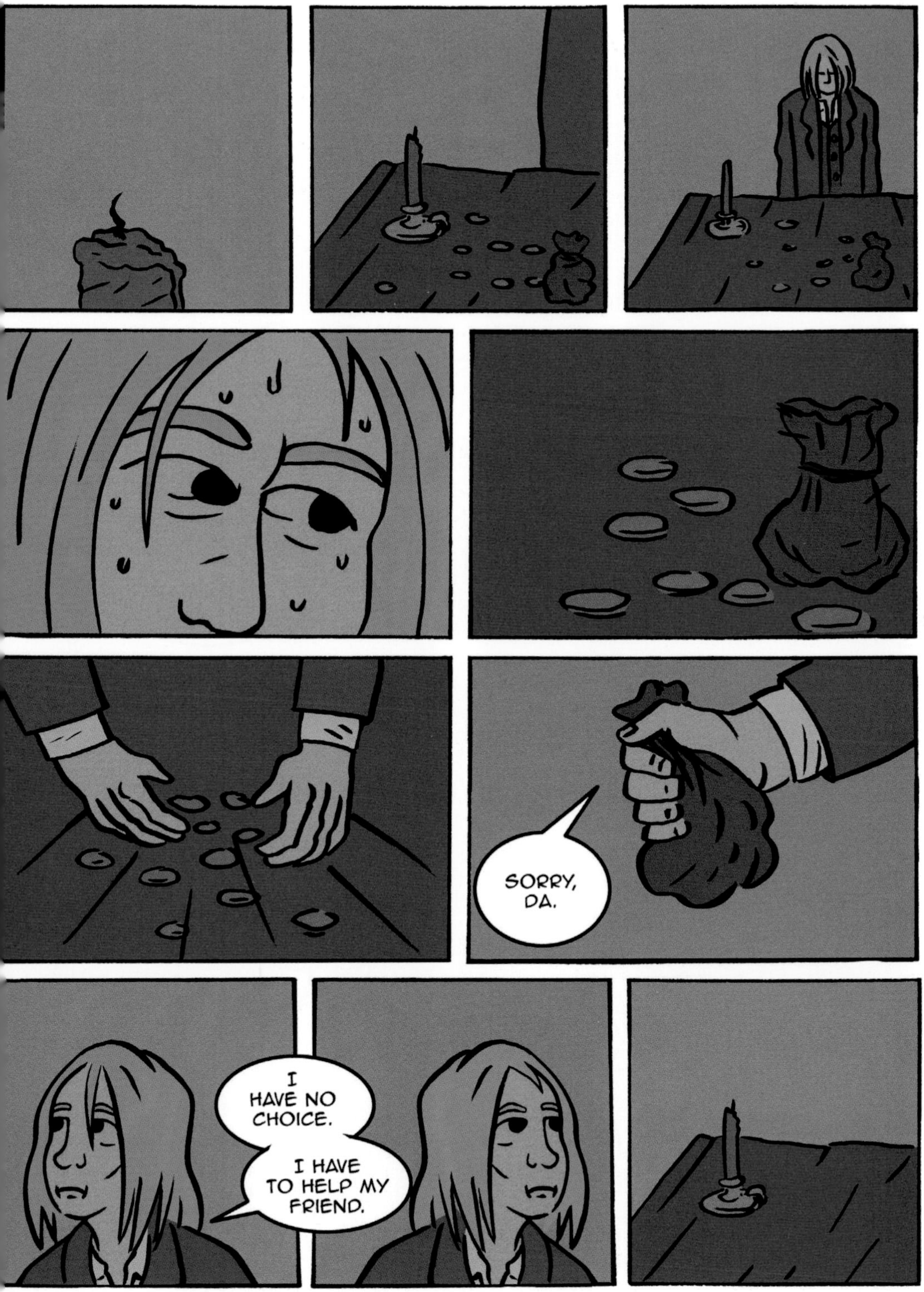
SORRY, DA.
I HAVE NO CHOICE.
I HAVE TO HELP MY FRIEND.

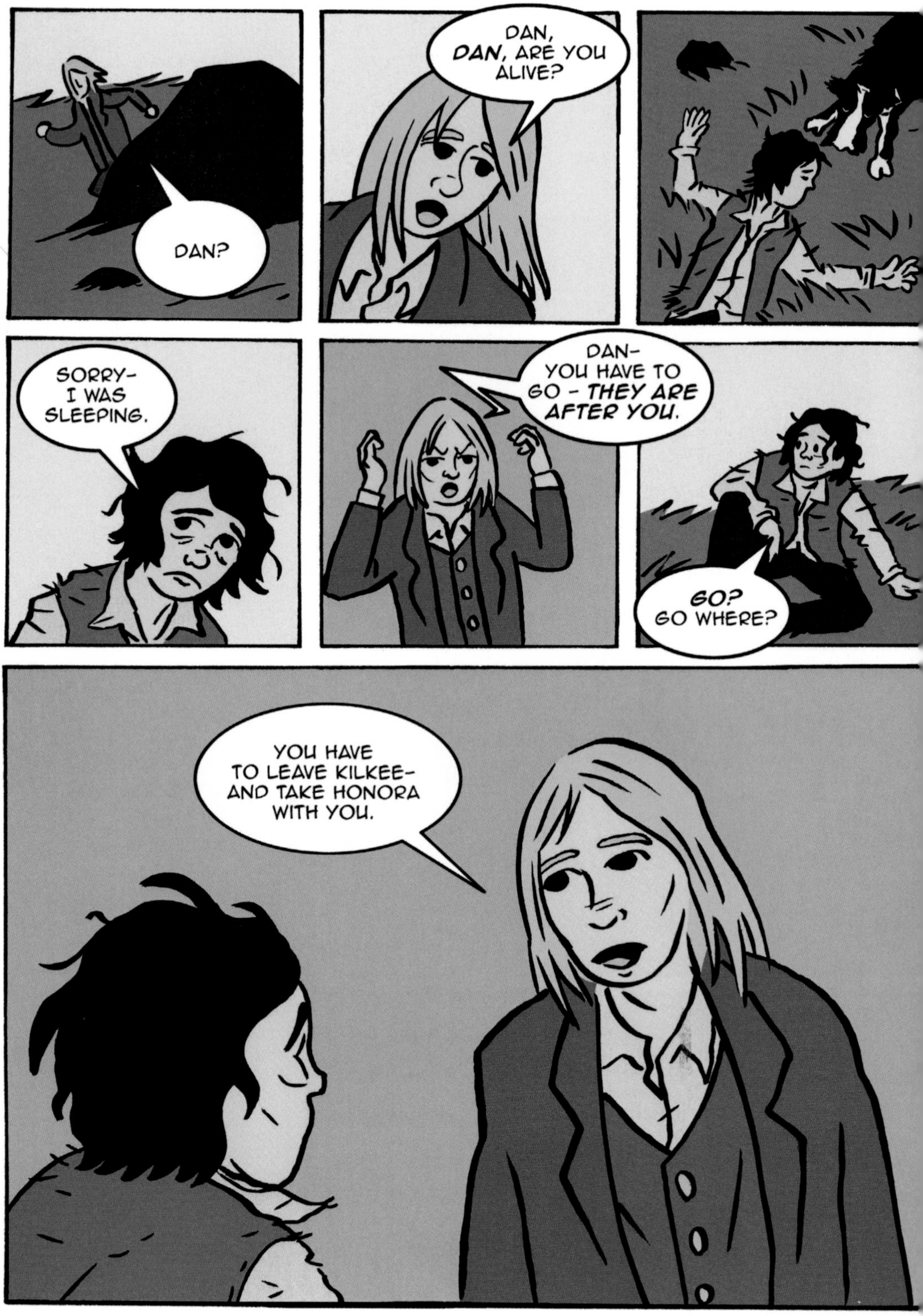

DAN?
DAN, DAN, ARE YOU ALIVE?
SORRY- I WAS SLEEPING.
DAN- YOU HAVE TO GO - THEY ARE AFTER YOU.
GO? GO WHERE?
YOU HAVE TO LEAVE KILKEE- AND TAKE HONORA WITH YOU.

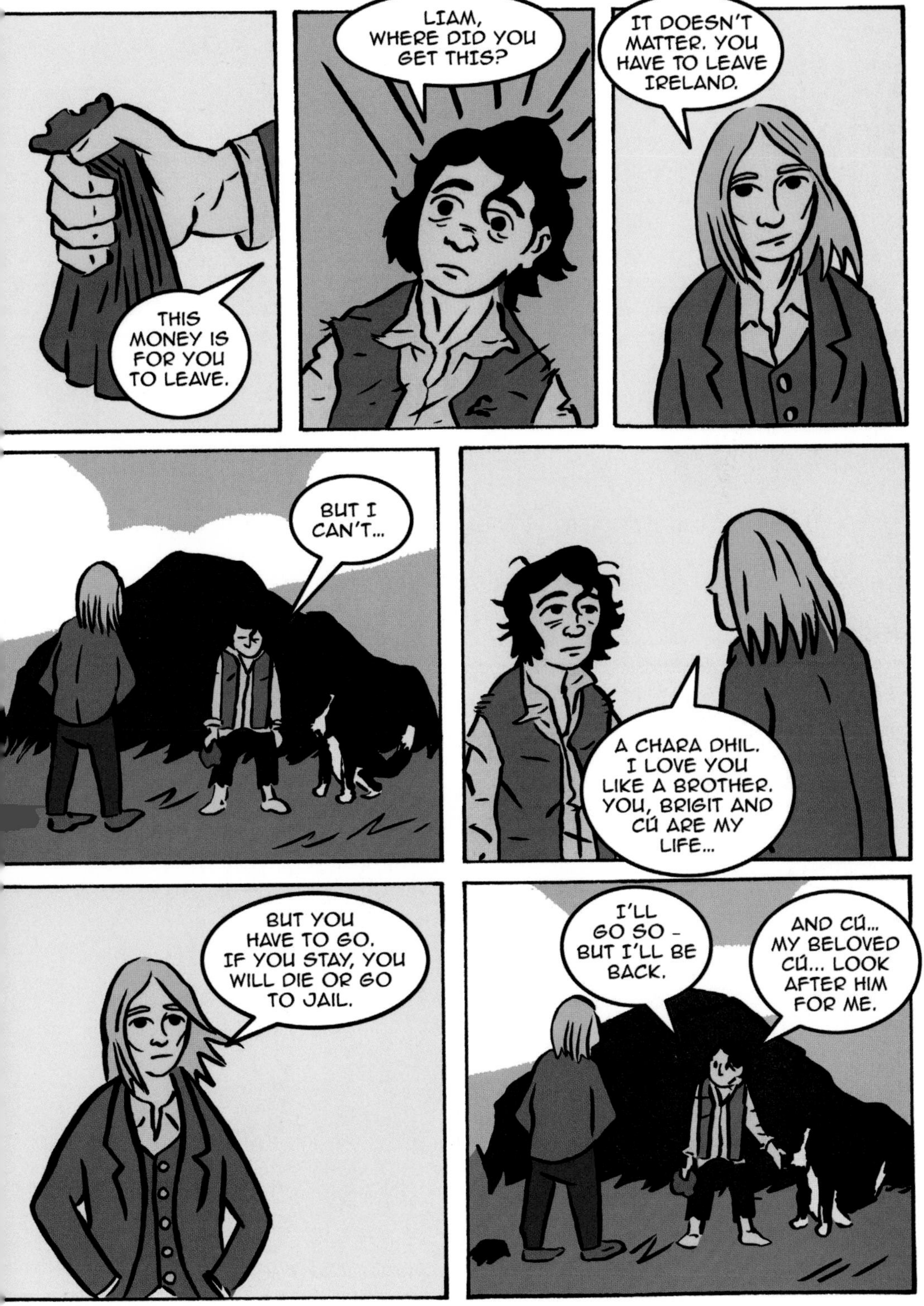

THIS MONEY IS FOR YOU TO LEAVE.
LIAM, WHERE DID YOU GET THIS?
IT DOESN'T MATTER. YOU HAVE TO LEAVE IRELAND.
BUT I CAN'T...
A CHARA DHIL. I LOVE YOU LIKE A BROTHER. YOU, BRIGIT AND CÚ ARE MY LIFE...
BUT YOU HAVE TO GO. IF YOU STAY, YOU WILL DIE OR GO TO JAIL.
I'LL GO SO - BUT I'LL BE BACK.
AND CÚ... MY BELOVED CÚ... LOOK AFTER HIM FOR ME.

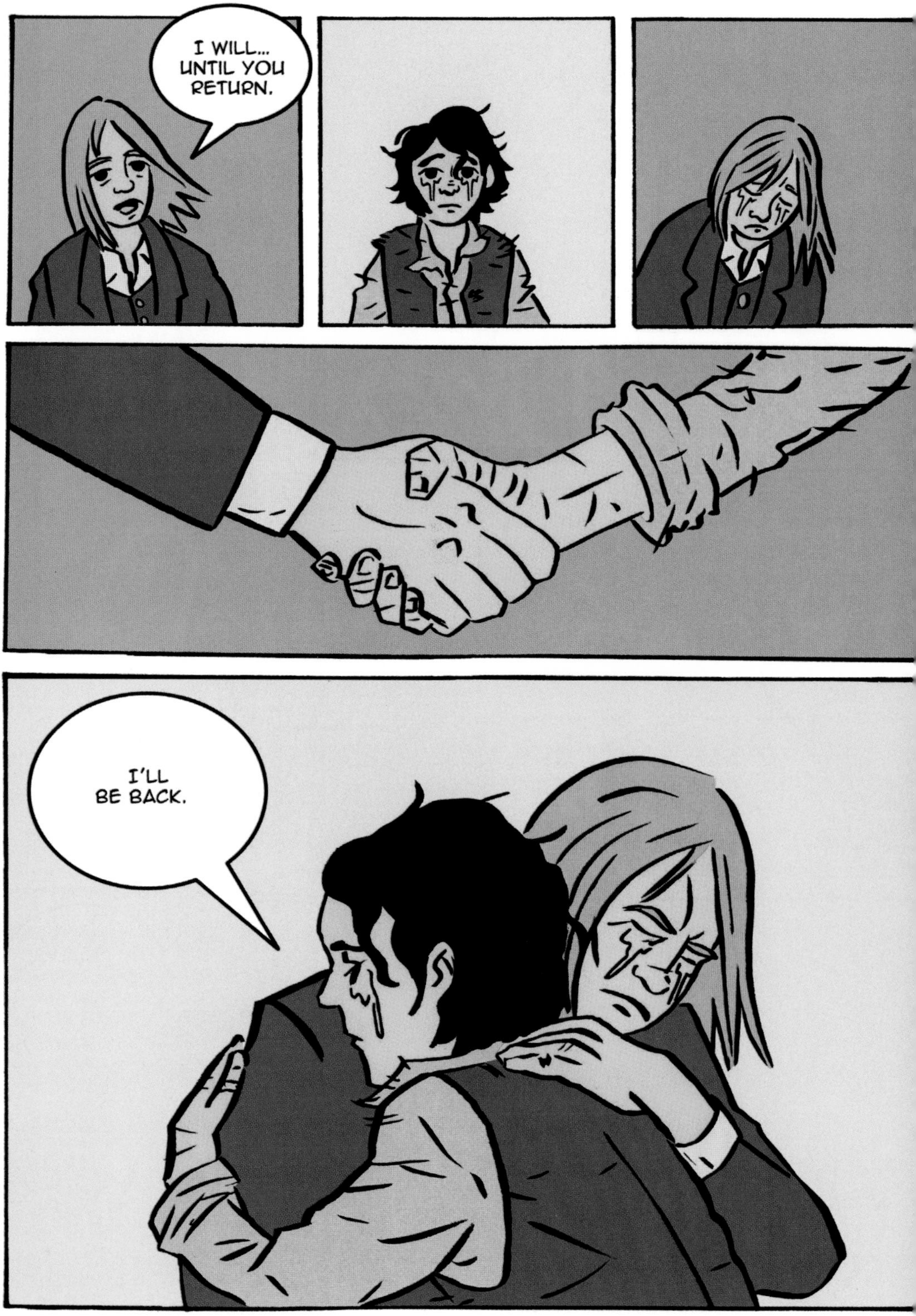
I WILL... UNTIL YOU RETURN.
I'LL BE BACK.

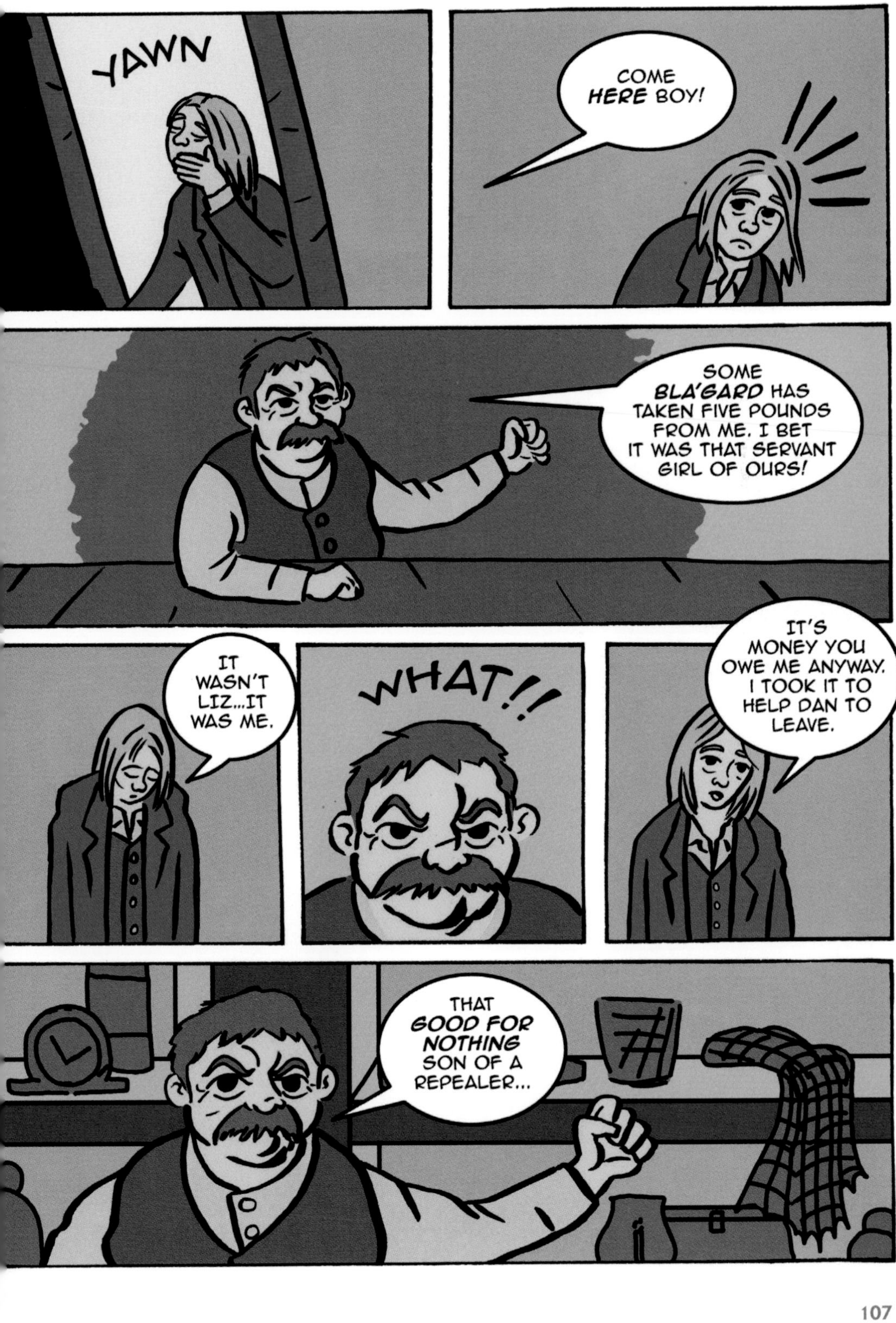
YAWN
COME *HERE* BOY!
SOME *BLA'GARD* HAS TAKEN FIVE POUNDS FROM ME. I BET IT WAS THAT SERVANT GIRL OF OURS!
IT WASN'T LIZ...IT WAS ME.
WHAT!!
IT'S MONEY YOU OWE ME ANYWAY. I TOOK IT TO HELP DAN TO LEAVE.
THAT *GOOD FOR NOTHING* SON OF A REPEALER...

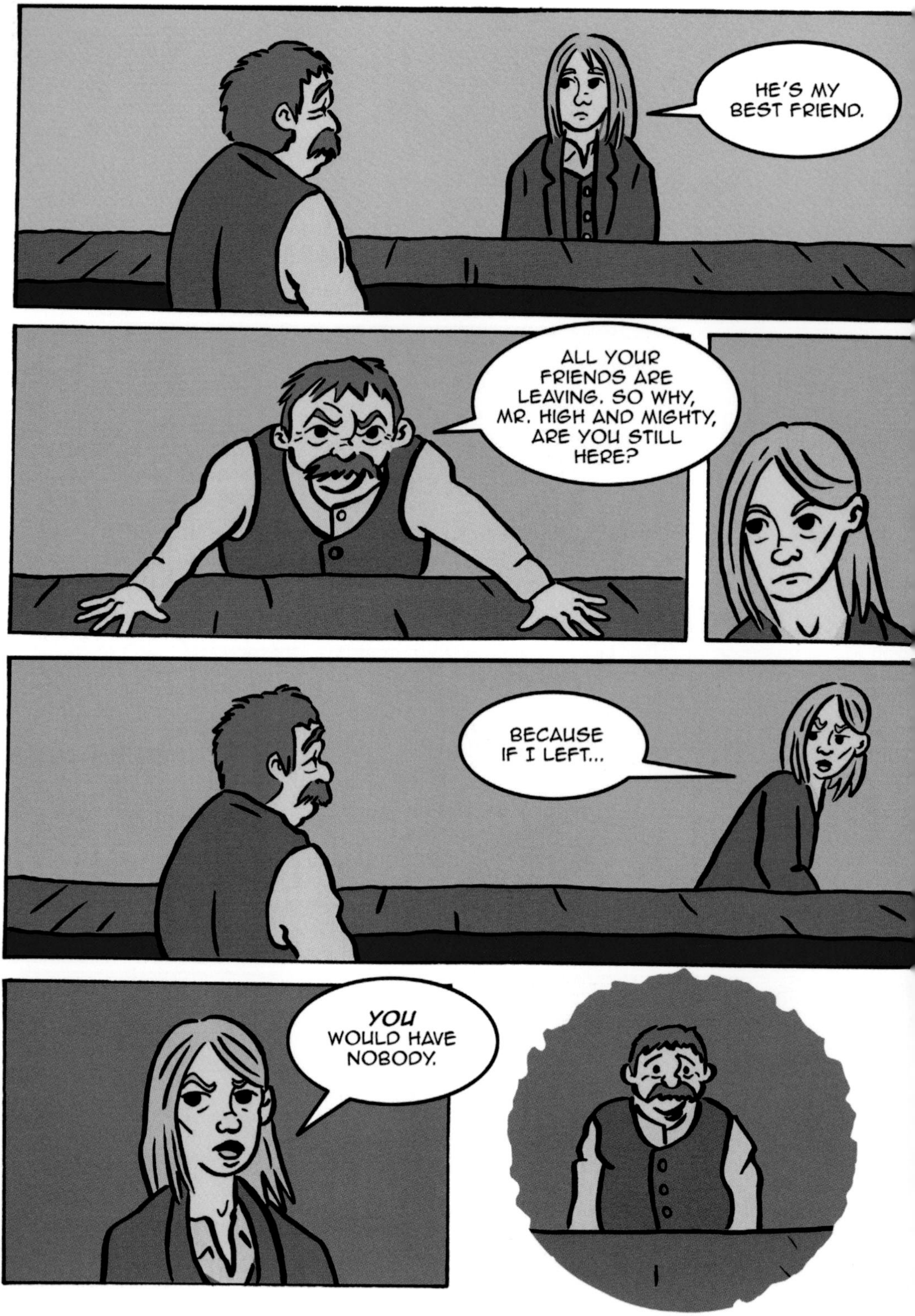
HE'S MY BEST FRIEND.
ALL YOUR FRIENDS ARE LEAVING. SO WHY, MR. HIGH AND MIGHTY, ARE YOU STILL HERE?
BECAUSE IF I LEFT...
YOU WOULD HAVE NOBODY.

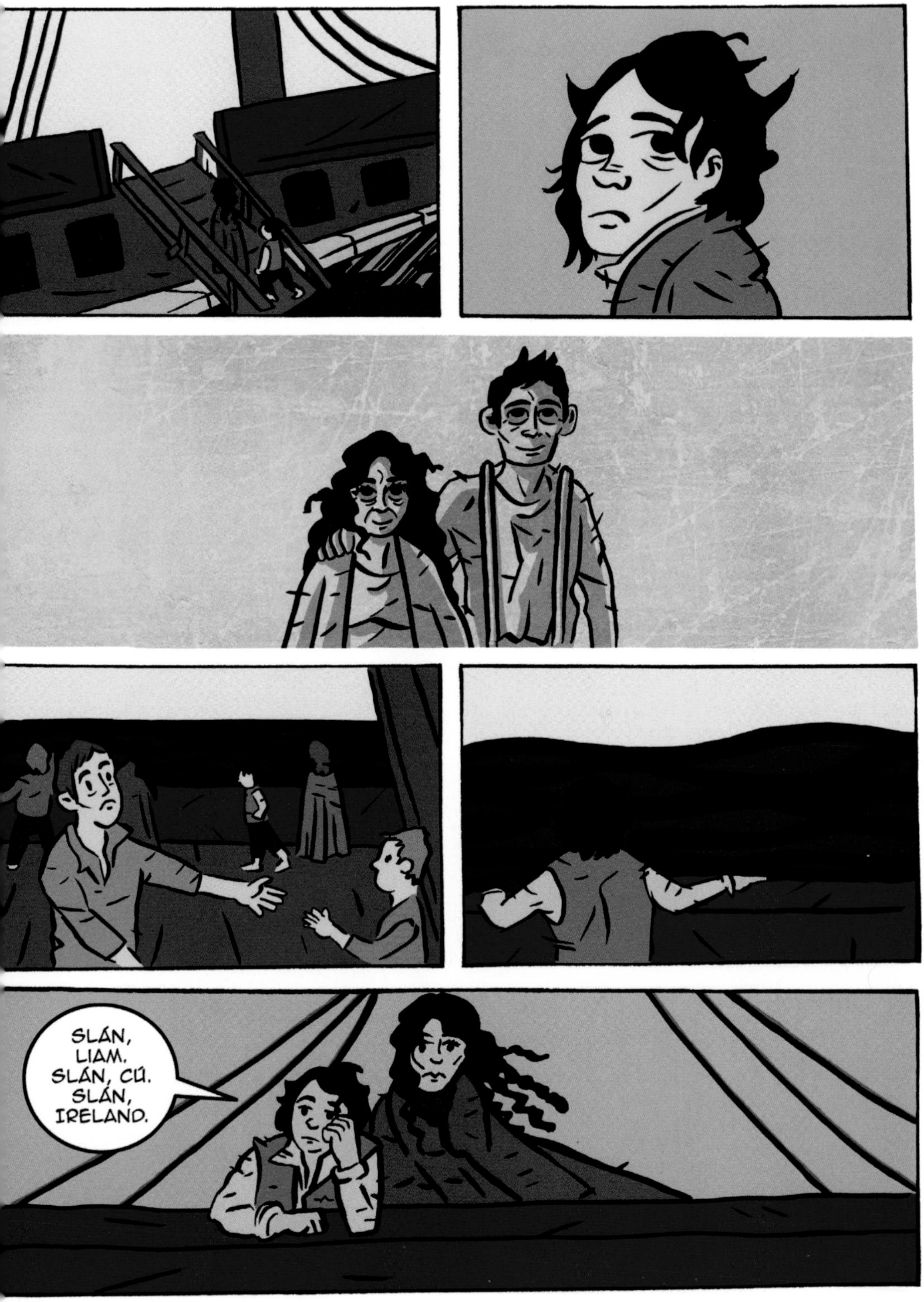
SLÁN, LIAM. SLÁN, CÚ. SLÁN, IRELAND.

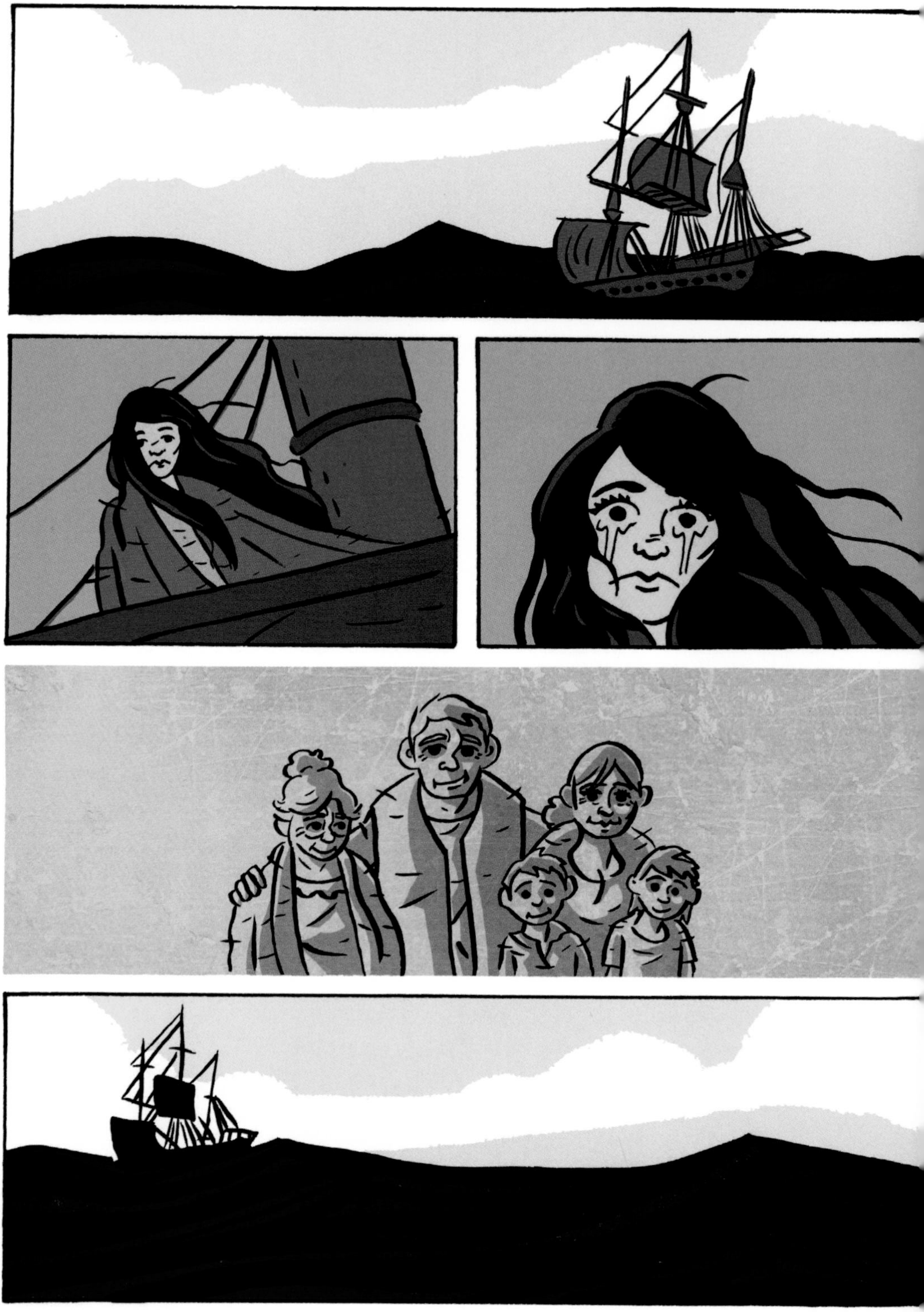

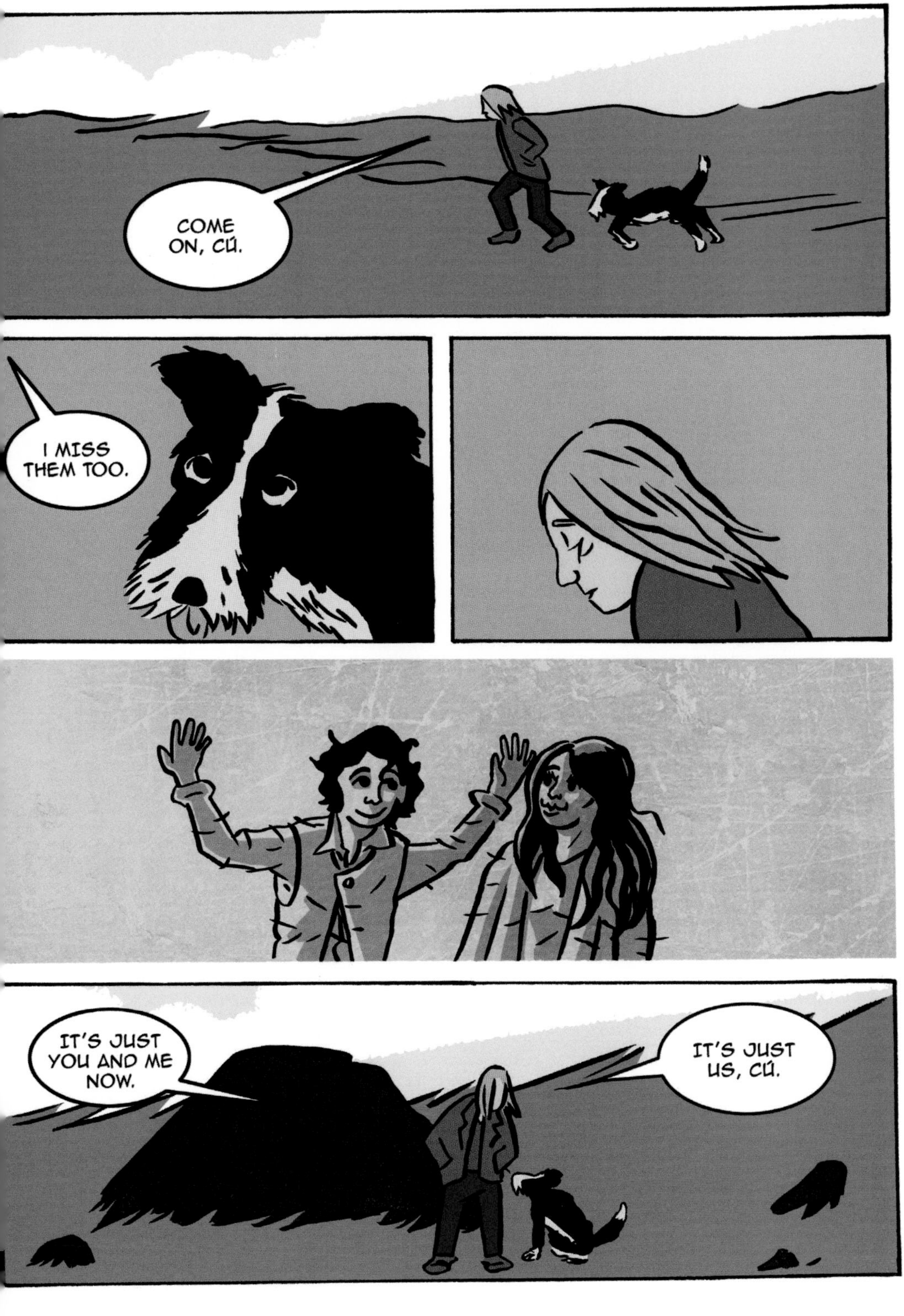
COME ON, CÚ.
I MISS THEM TOO.
IT'S JUST YOU AND ME NOW.
IT'S JUST US, CÚ.

KILKEE,
COUNTY CLARE,
SEPTEMBER, 1850.

Glossary

An Drochshaol – (an drock hale) means the bad times or the hard life, which was a traditional way of describing periods of starvation and suffering.

Ar dheis Dé go raibh a hanam – May her soul be on the right hand of God.

bia – food.

Big House a way to describe the large houses lived in by wealthy landowners.

black leg – in Irish, cos *dhubh*. Probably scurvy, caused by lack of vitamin C, which caused bleeding gums and the legs to turn black.

bla'gard – from blaggard, or blackguard – an unprincipled person, usually male.

blight – word often used to describe the disease that destroyed the potato crop.

bó – cow.

a chara dhil – my dear friend.

a chara m'anama – friend of my soul.

Cú [coo] – traditional word for dog or hound. The name of Dan's faithful dog.

da – dad or father.

Daniel O'Connell – (1775-1847), Irish nationalist leader, who promoted the rights of Irish Catholics and wanted an Irish parliament in Dublin.

Dia duit – God be with you. A traditional greeting.

Dia daoibh – God be with you all (plural).

Dia is Muire duit – God and Mary be with you. A traditional response to *Dia duit*.

Dia is Muire duit – God and Mary be with you (plural).

eejit – fool or idiot, but used affectionately.

Friends – members of the Quakers, also known as the Society of Friends.

fiabhras buidhe – also known as yellow fever, the symptoms include sickness and nausea, and in its more advanced form, bleeding of the mouth and eyes, and a yellowing of the skin.

Fiddle – violin.

fraocháin – bilberries, traditionally eaten around harvest time.

gentry – people who have social status and wealth.

gombeen man (from Irish, fear *gaimbín*) – somebody who exploits his fellow Irishmen.

Go mbeire muid beo ar an am seo arís – May we be alive at this time next year.

grá mo chroí – love of my heart.

Go raibh maith agat – thank you.

I measc laochra na nGael go raibh sé – May he be in the midst of the heroes of the Gael.

Kilkee – from the Irish *Cill Caoidhe,* meaning Caoidhe's Church, a beautiful seaside town in County Clare.

Kilrush – a market town in County Clare. Also the location of the local workhouse.

Liberator – name given to Daniel O'Connell.

Liverpool – a major port in England.

loy – from the Irish word, *láí,* a traditional Irish shovel (spade).

Lugh (loo) – god of the harvest.

Lughnasa – festival honoring the pagan god *Lugh.* It marked the start of the harvest season.

máthair chríonna – grandmother.

a mhuirnín – sweetheart or love of my heart.

ma/mam/mammy – mother.

mamó – grandmother.

mo chara – my dear friend.

mo mhuirnín – my darling.

pawn – from the Latin word, *pignus,* meaning pledge. Exchanging some item of personal property on a temporary basis in return for a loan of money.

pawnbroker – The person who negotiates and issues the loan. Liam's father was a shopkeeper and pawnbroker.

poorhouse – officially referred to as workhouse. There were 130 in Ireland and were intended for the destitute. On entering, families were split up.

praties – potatoes.

public works – relief program introduced to Ireland by the British government in 1845 and 1846, to act as a test of poverty. Those so employed worked for six days a week, usually for 12 hours a day on hard physical labor.

repealer – somebody who wanted Irish political independence and was a follower of Daniel O'Connell.

slán – good-bye.

strand – beach, seaside, shore.

take the King's Shilling – originally, to sign up for the British Army and receive a shilling (a not insignificant amount of money) in return. More generally, to work for the British government or monarch.

townland – a small area of land.

whisht –from Irish word, *fuist,* be quiet / hush.

workhouse – see, poorhouse.

Italics denotes an Irish word.

About Quinnipiac University

Quinnipiac University, located in Hamden, Connecticut, offers more than 80 programs to 6,700 undergraduate and 2,600 graduate, law and medical students through its Schools of Business and Engineering, Communications, Education, Health Sciences, Law, Nursing, the College of Arts and Sciences and the Frank H. Netter MD School of Medicine.

Quinnipiac's 250-acre Mount Carmel Campus, next to Sleeping Giant State Park, contains academic buildings and residence halls. The nearby 250-acre York Hill Campus houses the TD Bank Sports Center, residence halls for 2,000 students, the Rocky Top Student Center, a fitness facility and a 2,000-car parking garage. A third 104-acre campus in North Haven serves as home to the School of Education, School of Health Sciences, School of Law, School of Nursing, the Frank H. Netter MD School of Medicine and other graduate programs.

Quinnipiac consistently ranks among the top regional universities in the North in U.S. News & World Report's America's Best Colleges issue. The 2015 issue named Quinnipiac the top up-and-coming university in the northern region for the third consecutive year.

Ireland's Great Hunger Institute

Ireland's Great Hunger Institute is a scholarly resource for the study of the Great Hunger, which is also known as An Gorta Mór. Through a strategic program of lectures, conferences, course offerings and publications, the institute fosters a deeper understanding of this tragedy and its causes and consequences.

To encourage original scholarship and meaningful engagement, the institute develops and makes available the Great Hunger Collection, a unique array of primary, secondary and cultural sources, to students and scholars.

Ireland's Great Hunger Institute was established in September 2013 and its founding director is Professor Christine Kinealy.

Quinnipiac
University Press

Quinnipiac University Press is a service
of Quinnipiac University in Hamden
and North Haven, CT. Quinnipiac offers
undergraduate and graduate programs
to more than 8,000 students in business,
communications, education, engineering,
health sciences, nursing, medicine, law
and the arts and sciences.

www.quinnipiac.edu

The inspiration to write a graphic novel
based on the experiences of three young
adults during the Great Hunger came from
Daniel Macdonald's haunting oil painting,
'Irish Peasant Children' (c.1847). It is in
the collection of Ireland's Great Hunger
Museum at Quinnipiac University.

About the Authors

Christine Kinealy, director of Ireland's Great Hunger Institute, has been named one of the most influential *Irish Americans* by Irish *America* Magazine. Since completing her PhD at Trinity College in Ireland, Professor Kinealy has worked in educational and research institutes in Dublin, Belfast and Liverpool. Since 2007, she has been based in the United States. In 1997, Christine was asked to speak on the Great Hunger in the Palace of Westminster, the seat of the British Parliament. In the same year, she addressed an Ad Hoc Committee on Irish Affairs in the U.S. Capitol in Washington.

Christine has published extensively on modern Irish history, with a focus on the tragic period known as the Great Famine or "An Gorta Mór" (the Great Hunger). Her publications include the award winning *This Great Calamity. The Irish Famine, 1845-52* (1994 and 2007) and *Making Sense of History: Evidence in Ireland for the Young Historian* (1995). Since 2011, Christine has volunteered to teach at the annual weekend Gael Scoil (Irish school) in Lawrenceville, New Jersey, working with young people aged 4 to 17.

Christine has two children, Siobhán, who was born in Dublin, and Ciarán, who was born in Belfast.

John A. Walsh tells stories. Some are told with words; others with pictures.

John's stories are told with both.

John's passion for storytelling comes from being the youngest of five children, a lifetime of daydreams and from reading too many comic books. In order to tell stories, he has swept church floors, sold women's shoes, designed advertisements and even carried his own weight in fresh fruit. His graphic novel, "GO HOME PADDY," about 19th-century Irish immigration to America, is being serialized online. John lives in Boston with his wife and daughter.

More of his work can be discovered at www.johnawalsh.net